WILLIAM GIBSON

MODERN MASTERS OF SCIENCE FICTION

Science fiction often anticipates the consequences of scientific discoveries. The immense strides made by science since World War II have been matched step by step by writers who gave equal attention to scientific principles, human imagination, and the craft of fiction. The respect for science fiction won by Jules Verne and H. G. Wells was further increased by Isaac Asimov, Arthur C. Clarke, Robert Heinlein, Ursula K. Le Guin, Joanna Russ, and Ray Bradbury. Modern Masters of Science Fiction is devoted to books that survey the work of individual authors who continue to inspire and advance science fiction. A list of books in the series appears at the end of this book.

WILLIAM GIBSON

Gary Westfahl

UNIVERSITY OF ILLINOIS PRESS
Urbana, Chicago, and Springfield

Library of Congress Control Number: 2013941429

contents

To my sister and brother-in-law,
Brenda and Terry Bright:
supportive relatives,
fellow science fiction fans,
and occasional research assistants

ACKNOWLEDGMENTS

For help in obtaining documents and completing this project, I thank several individuals at the Tomás Rivera Library at the University of California, Riverside, including Melissa Conway, Sarah Allison, and other staff of the J. Lloyd Eaton Collection of Science Fiction and Fantasy Literature, and Maria Mendoza and other staff of the Interlibrary Loan Department; Cait Coker, Jerri Bradley, and other staff of the Cushing Memorial Library and Archives at Texas A&M University; Elaine Engst of the Division of Rare and Manuscript Collections of Kroch Library at Cornell University; Holly Phillips of the Thomas J. Watson Library of the Metropolitan Museum of Art; Brenda and Terry Bright; John Clute; Rob Latham; and Sharalyn Orbaugh. I thank William Gibson for granting permission to quote from his poetry and answering my questions; Neil Easterbrook, James Gunn, and Willis Regier for useful comments on the original manuscript; Regier and his colleagues at the University of Illinois Press for their enthusiastic assistance throughout the process of preparing and publishing this book; and Jolivette Macenas and other faculty of the Writing Program of the University of La Verne for providing a supportive work environment. Finally, as always, I heartily thank my family members—my wife Lynne Westfahl, my son Jeremy Westfahl, my daughter Allison Westfahl Kong, and my son-in-law Steven Kong—who make all my work possible.

It is easy to envision William Gibson as a typical character from his novels: a streetwise outsider, determined to be his own boss, who takes to writing as an ideal alternative to a steady job because he knows precisely what his marks want and how to handsomely profit by providing it. Certainly, no other science fiction writer of his generation so strongly displays both a dogged commitment to following his own path in storytelling and keen attentiveness to the demands of the marketplace. Critics may contribute valuable insights into some genuine issues embedded in Gibson's fiction (the impact of cutting-edge technology, shattering of traditional boundaries, and stimulating chaos of an increasingly multipolar world), but they must recognize that this complex, elusive writer is also, quite brilliantly, playing them.

Though they are very different sorts of writers, Gibson invites consideration as his generation's equivalent to Robert A. Heinlein. Both men were lifelong readers of science fiction who turned to writing at a relatively late age, when the doors to other careers seemed closed, and could bring the maturity of a fully lived life even to early publications; as they settled into stable relationships and conventional domesticity, both authors could draw upon the unsettled and variegated experiences of their first thirty years to energize their fiction; Heinlein and Gibson unintentionally became characterized as leaders of new movements within science fiction, though neither was comfortable in that role; and both broke away from the constraints of this status by assertively moving in idiosyncratic directions to achieve artistic fulfillment and financial success.

True, Gibson might reject the notion that he is a latter-day Heinlein, since he does not admire that writer: in an interview published in 2006, he dismissed him as a "crazy old fucker" (Shainblum and Friedman 39); he told Mark Shepherd in 1993 that Singapore was like "the world that Robert Heinlein was predicting in 1958," which "somebody was foolhardy enough to build"; and he informed Gregory Daurer in 1990 that *Neuromancer* "was kicking against the whole Robert Heinlein tradition of militaristic, right wing, upper middle class American science fiction" (322). Yet speaking in 1987 to Takayuki Tatsumi, he seemed to acknowledge at least that their writing shares a certain fierce energy: "One of the only things that Heinlein's ever said that I have respect for, about how to write a short story, is that it's like you're walking down the street and a drunk jumps out of an alley and grabs you by the collar and starts shaking you. That's how you write a short story" (13). Also, when Leanne C. Harper in 1988 praised Gibson's ability to "drop the reader into this new culture without exposition," Gibson called this "a classic SF move" and added that in Heinlein's "early work [. . .] he was able to lard all of the fantasy into something without having to stop and explain what everything was," suggesting that he influenced Gibson's style (17). And in his youth, Gibson became familiar with Heinlein's works, since he knowledgeably discusses his Future History series in Robert Scott Martin's 1999 interview and a 2006 article, "Time Machine Cuba," and specifically referenced Heinlein's postapocalyptic *Farnham's Freehold* (1964) in a 1983 article, saying, "I was fixing my lawnmower the other day, a process which always makes me feel like one of those Competent Men in the works of Robt. Heinlein, particularly since it involved the post-nuke discipline of rooting through the rusting carcasses of two identical machines for serviceable parts" ("On the Surface," *Wing Window,* No. 6, p. 13).

Even if he was not Gibson's hero, the parallels between Heinlein's and Gibson's careers are compelling. In the early 1940s, Heinlein stunned the science fiction world with his new sorts of carefully extrapolated, fully realized future worlds; shrewd, savvy protagonists focused more on making a living than saving the world; and stories narrated in a uniquely conversational style that casually conveyed important information. As simultaneously explained and championed by editor John W. Campbell Jr., this new approach to science fiction revolutionized the entire field. Similarly, in the early 1980s, Gibson amazed science fiction readers and critics with his shift away from space opera into the virtual worlds of information science; heroes that were scruffy, streetwise outsiders struggling to stay alive in societies dominated by multinational corporations; and a pyrotechnic prose style that combined extravagantly metaphorical language with an unprecedented "hyperspecificity" in describing old and new technologies. As simultaneously explained and championed by his colleague Bruce Sterling, Gibson also had a broad impact on science fiction, as he was promoted as chief progenitor of a new form of science fiction, "cyberpunk," purportedly the genre's contribution to postmodern fiction.

For a while, just as Heinlein was content to be a fixture of science fiction magazines with his stories and novels, Gibson was content to exploit the commercial and critical success of his first novel *Neuromancer* (1984) with two additional novels, *Count Zero* (1986) and *Mona Lisa Overdrive* (1988), set in the same future, and these became known as his Sprawl trilogy. However, as another similarity to Heinlein, Gibson grew tired of revisiting past glories and sought new worlds to conquer. For Heinlein in the late 1940s and 1950s, this meant stories for "slick" magazines, nonfiction articles, juvenile fiction, and work for film and television. For Gibson in the late 1980s and early 1990s, this involved experimenting with alternate history in a novel cowritten with Sterling, *The Difference Engine* (1990); numerous screenplays, mostly unproduced; and ventures into poetry, song lyrics, and nonfiction. He then wrote three new novels, known as the Bridge trilogy—*Virtual Light* (1993), *Idoru* (1996), and *All Tomorrow's Parties* (1999)—which shifted away from computer networks to ponder the impact of the media and new technologies on ill-assorted misfits inhabiting San Francisco's abandoned Bay Bridge and other marginalized havens.

Finally, as Heinlein and Gibson approached the age of sixty, both defied expectations by launching a series of novels unlike anything else in science fiction. In the 1960s and 1970s, Heinlein produced rambling, opinionated novels that alienated some readers but garnered a broad new audience. In 2003,

Gibson surprised readers by effecting another remarkable synthesis between his own evolving worldview and sharp eye on the bottom line to produce a new form of science fiction. Gibson realized that the world had changed in ways that suggested a new function for science fiction, which had traditionally been intended to explain, and prepare people for, what would likely occur in a future world of advanced technology that would be hard to adjust to and comprehend. However, people in the twenty-first century were already living in a constantly changing future world filled with advanced technology that they were struggling to adjust to and comprehend; thus, the tropes and techniques of science fiction could now be deployed not to help people understand possible futures but to help them understand a real present that effectively overlapped with their future. In this way, Gibson could write what essentially remained science fiction novels that were set in the present and were limited to existing or readily achievable technologies and social developments. As he said in his 2010 "Talk for Book Expo, New York," "I found the material of the actual twenty-first century richer, stranger, more multiplex, than any imaginary twenty-first century could ever have been. And it could be unpacked with the toolkit of science fiction" (46). While this shift was defensible on these artistic grounds, Gibson also recognized that moving toward mimetic fiction might enable him to reach a broader audience and achieve higher sales than writing another science fiction novel.

The first novel along these lines, *Pattern Recognition* (2003), thus offered an intriguing present-day adventure featuring a globetrotting consultant searching for the filmmaker behind fragments of haunting footage furtively posted on the internet. Arguably Gibson's best novel, *Pattern Recognition* proved highly profitable while also igniting new flurries of critical commentary. Then, following his habit of lingering for a while in each newly created universe, Gibson produced two other novels with the same background, *Spook Country* (2007) and *Zero History* (2010). These artistic and commercial successes might have tempted Gibson to break his pattern of trilogies to produce additional novels along these lines, just as the mature Heinlein stayed with the approach he pioneered in the 1960s; but descriptions of his next novel indicate that the ever-restless Gibson will defy expectations, and this extended comparison to Heinlein, by moving in yet another new direction.

To justify a new study of William Gibson, one might simply note the surprising paucity of books devoted to this thoroughly examined author. There are only Lance Olsen's *William Gibson* (1992); Tom Henthorne's *William Gibson: A Literary Companion* (2011); two studies limited to specific concerns— Dani Cavallaro's *Cyberpunk and Cyberculture* (2000) and Tatiani G. Rapatzikou's *Gothic Motifs in the Fiction of William Gibson* (2004); and an essay collection, Carl B. Yoke and Carol L. Robinson's *The Cultural Influences of William Gibson, the Father of Cyberpunk Science Fiction* (2007). In addition, while Gibson's novels and stories have been studied repeatedly, other Gibson works offering valuable insights, ranging from publications in science fiction fanzines to contributions to elusive books, have been ignored; I will sometimes be the first scholar to discuss a relevant text. Oddly, there has never been a truly comprehensive study of Gibson's career, even though his works are considered central to science fiction in both scholarly writings and college classrooms.

To provide such a comprehensive study within a strict length requirement (which also mandated a less formal style of annotation), I will be minimizing my engagement with the vast secondary literature focused on Gibson's fiction; instead, discussions of novels and stories will primarily offer my own readings, emphasizing each work as a stage in Gibson's career. For interested readers, a bibliographical essay will reference more thoroughgoing analyses of his major works. The serendipitous advantage of this approach will be to provide a fresh look at an author who is sometimes employed as an instrument to advance others' agendas. From a twenty-first-century perspective, the heated rhetoric involving cyberpunk within the science fiction community of the 1980s seems at best quaint, and what happened then can be bluntly but accurately characterized as follows: one remarkable writer—Gibson—emerged, while other writers sought to garner some of the attention deservedly focused on Gibson by presenting themselves as fellow cyberpunk writers based on essentially superficial similarities. Gibson himself recognized the problem as early as 1988, when he dismissed cyberpunk as "a marketing strategy" that "trivializes what I do" while speaking to Larry McCaffery, though he was restrained in criticizing this "movement" for practical reasons: "I have friends and cohorts who are benefiting from the hype and who like it" (279).

The insights of academic critics undoubtedly have more enduring value; however, while one can appreciate on their own terms learned considerations of Gibson as a quintessentially postmodern author who transcended science fiction to challenge conventional attitudes involving technology, society, and human identity, wading too deeply into theoretical waters can lead scholars to lose sight of the real author who stimulates their thinking, as they explore critical theories and issues that are often of little interest to Gibson himself, as he testifies in interviews. It is particularly irksome when scholars impose a postmodernist agenda upon Gibson and then criticize him for not fulfilling goals he never had, as in Claire Sponsler's condemnation of Gibson for failing "to shape plot and agency in a way that matches the postmodern ideology and aesthetic" ("Cyberpunk and the Dilemmas of Postmodern Narrative" 639) when he manifestly had no such intentions.

Instead, having read almost all of Gibson's published works (including over 170 interviews), I will endeavor to focus this book on aspects of Gibson's works that are visibly most important to him (though comments on his motives and preferences, not always backed by specific textual evidence, may strike some readers as overly speculative). First, he has always been and remains, in his background and proclivities, a science fiction writer. As he told Robert K. J. Killheffer in 1993, "I have this image as the cyberpunk antichrist, deeply antithetical to the traditional values of science fiction, but actually, I've sprung from science fiction soil" (70). Second, he is fascinated by the particular flavors of the world, not the abstractions applied to them, preferring to function as an "amateur anthropologist" of novel phenomena (blog, April 10, 2010) without theorizing about them; as he told David Wallace-Wells in 2011, "I'm not a didactic storyteller. I don't formulate theories about how the world works and then create stories to illustrate my theories." Third, he has grown especially intrigued by both tinkerers with new technology and avant-garde artists as chief avatars of the constant transformations now characterizing contemporary life, as emerges most strongly in *Spook Country* and *Zero History*. Fourth, he is most comfortable with characters who neither embrace nor reject innovations but, like Gibson himself, simply adjust to them while carrying on with everyday life. Finally, in keeping with this attitude, Gibson can be best characterized not as the revolutionary vanguard of a new era but an essentially conservative and traditional writer—an argument developed in the conclusion.

As additional contributions, this book includes a new Gibson interview; the first determined effort to compile a comprehensive, accurate bibliography of his works—though it surely remains incomplete, given his constant willingness to write for, or be interviewed in, innumerable print and online venues; and a survey of the relevant secondary literature. These resources should help readers and scholars who will follow Gibson while he further explores the world we inhabit today and what it may become tomorrow. He may be more idiosyncratic and less representative of his times than others suppose, but just as Gibson's authority figures employ flawed characters because they are the best people for the job, readers can rely on Gibson as an excellent guide for their ongoing journeys into the future.

CHAPTER 1

JOURNEY TO THE FUTURE
A Biographical Sketch

William Gibson has never expressed an interest in writing an autobiography; as he reported while introducing *Distrust That Particular Flavor,* "The idea of direct, unfiltered autobiography made me even more uncomfortable" than a journal (5). But in another sense, Gibson has spent much of his life sporadically writing an autobiography that dribbles out in bits and pieces within articles, reviews, introductions, interviews, and even works of fiction. An energetic editor, then, might *compile* a Gibson autobiography from those fragments, just as a Beatles autobiography, *The Beatles Anthology* (2000), was compiled from old and recent interviews.

The editor crafting such a project would start with Gibson's autobiographical sketch, "Since 1948," first posted to his blog on November 6, 2002. There, he relates the generally familiar story of how he was born in South Carolina and, as a child, frequently moved with his parents because of his father's various jobs. In 1987, he told A. P. McQuiddy that his father "made a fair bit of money supplying flush toilets to the Oak Ridge Project" while his family "lived briefly in Chattanooga, and Charlotte, and other places" (3). But his life was disrupted at a young age by his father's accidental death by choking; though Gibson said he was six years old at the time in "Since 1948," he told McQuiddy that he was eight (3), and in the documentary *No Maps for These Territories,* he said that his father died in "1956," seemingly confirming that he had been eight years old. After his father's death, his mother settled with her son in Wytheville, a small Virginia town.

In these early years, the major influence on his life was television, which he repeatedly mentions when discussing his childhood: in "Since 1948," he describes these times as "a world of early television" (21–22); in 2007, he told Mary Ann Gwinn about "the day my father brought our first television set home"; in 1985, he reported watching "Tom Corbett and Captain Video on black-and-white tv" (Nicholas and Hanna 18), and he noted in a 2003 interview that he "watched *Tom Corbett, Space Cadet* every night" ("Crossing Boundaries" 7); in a 2005 article, he discussed watching the 1940 serial *The Mysterious Dr. Satan* on television ("Googling the Cyborg" 245); he remembered in a 1975 review watching outdated documentaries on television ("In the Airflow Futuropolis" 1); he told Noel Murray in 2007 about watching "Sputnik and *Twilight Zone* on television"; and he explained in a 2004 introduction to *Neuromancer* that he based its memorable opening on specific memories of a 1950s black-and-white television (vii). But as he observed in a 2012 article, the young Gibson also felt the impact of science fiction—but "[n]ot of prose fiction, or of film, but of the cultural and industrial semiotics of the American nineteen-fifties" as observed in his father's car, toys, and Chesley Bonestell's illustrations ("Olds Rocket 88, 1950" 104). Talking to Matthew Mallon in 2003, he termed such items "science fiction iconography, or folk futurism" (27).

Soon, the young Gibson discovered science fiction literature, which then became his passion: in "Since 1948," he attributes his "relationship with science fiction" to "this experience of feeling abruptly exiled, to what seemed like the past" in Wytheville (22), a place where, as he told David Wallace-Wells in 2011, "I wasn't a very happy kid," and his perpetually depressed mother undoubtedly did little to lighten his mood. (He was also left-handed, which may have contributed to his sense of alienation, though he reports in the interview below that his mother ensured that he was not forced to write with his right hand, then a common practice.) In those confining circumstances, science fiction was "like discovering an abundant, perpetually replenished, and freely available source of mental oxygen. [. . .] [Y]ou saw things differently, in extraordinary company" ("Olds Rocket 88, 1950" 104). It all began around 1960, when, as noted in a January 19, 2009, blog entry, he "found a moldering stack of 1950s *Galaxy*" magazines. These obviously made a powerful impression, since over thirty years later, in a 1987 article, he vividly recalled the cover of the June 1951 issue: Ed Emshwiller's "wonderful painting of spacesuited, dinosaurian aliens excavating Earth, exposing cliffside strata that clearly illustrated mankind's progress from club-swinging savage to radioactive slime" ("Alfred Bester, SF and Me" 28). In the same 2009 blog entry, Gibson posted a photograph of the "Greyhound Restaurant and Bus Station" in Wytheville where he happily "discovered that science fiction magazines were still being published" in 1961.

At this time, in the words of "Since 1948," Gibson "became exactly the sort of introverted, hyper-bookish boy you'll find in the biographies of most American science fiction writers, obsessively filling shelves with paperbacks and digest-sized magazines, dreaming of one day becoming a writer myself" (22). Among other signs of his devotion to the genre, he reported in a January 13, 2003, blog entry that "when I was twelve or so," he became "a proud new member of the Science Fiction Book Club," which provided him with Philip K. Dick's *The Man in the High Castle* (1962). We know that his voracious reading included other major science fiction writers of the 1950s like Alfred Bester, Heinlein, and Theodore Sturgeon, all mentioned in "Alfred Bester, SF and Me" (28). Young Gibson may have even delved into science fiction criticism, since a 1998 introduction references Kingsley Amis's 1960 survey of the genre, *New Maps of Hell* ("The Absolute at Large" 9–10), and he notes in the interview below that he "read a lot about sf." A 2010 introduction further indicates that Gibson's reading habits included more juvenile genre-related material, like *Mad* magazine and Forrest J. Ackerman's "gloriously cheesy" *Famous Monsters of Filmland* ("Sui Generis: A Testimony" 7). Still, Gibson did not exclusively read science fiction, since his 1989 introduction to Arthur Conan Doyle's *The Lost World and The Poison Belt* reports that he was "given a two-volume set of the complete Sherlock Holmes" when he "was twelve," becoming "immersed in the cozy, miraculously seamless universe of Holmes and Dr. Watson" ([vii]).

However, his perception of science fiction began changing in 1962, which Gibson usually attributes to his chance discovery of William S. Burroughs and, through him, other Beat Generation writers, who opened his eyes to new possibilities in science fiction. As he told Tom Nissley in 2007, "I discovered Edgar Rice Burroughs and William Burroughs in the same week. And I started reading Beat poets a year later." This second group of writers loomed larger in his imagination after 1962, for when he assembled an "Imaginary Anthology of Imaginative Fiction" in a 1975 article (discussed below), he exclusively included works by Burroughs, Thomas Pynchon, Terry Southern, and similar writers, ignoring the genre writers he previously read and collected.

Accompanying this new enthusiasm for Burroughs and other writers was a sense of disillusionment with traditional science fiction; as he said in a 1991 interview for *Creem* magazine, "Even as a teenager reading science fiction, I think I was distinctly distrustful of that techno-euphoric mythology of the engineer in a lot of mainstream American science fiction. I can remember having these inchoate, almost political doubts about Robert Heinlein when I was maybe 15 or 16 years old." But he offered a different perspective in "Time Machine Cuba," where he describes the fears of a nuclear holocaust he and other children experienced during the 1950s (he was particularly affected by a 1960 *Playhouse 90* adaptation of Pat Frank's post-holocaust novel *Alas, Babylon* [1959]). Yet when the world did not end after the 1962 Cuban missile crisis, Gibson began to "distrust that particular flavor of italics" in the doomsday warnings of the "terminally exasperated futurist" H. G. Wells and others and "may actually have begun to distrust science fiction, then, or rather to trust it differently, as my initial passion for it began to decline, around that time" ("Time Machine Cuba" 207, 208). Thus, even without discovering Burroughs, Gibson might have drifted away from science fiction, searching for different sorts of stories.

While Gibson suggests that he essentially abandoned science fiction at this time to focus on Burroughs and similar writers, he actually remained committed to the genre, for in 1963, while a sophomore in high school, he plunged enthusiastically into the world of science fiction fandom, as documented in several ways. One fan history reports that "Bill Gibson" attended two small science fiction conventions in Alabama in 1963 and 1964 (Lynch, "Preliminary Outline for a Proposed Fan History Book of the 1960s"); another notes that he joined a fanzine organization, the Southern Fandom Press Alliance (SFPA) (Montgomery, "1997 Southern Fandom Confederation Handbook & History, Part II"); and Gibson published two cartoons in the October/November 1963 issue of a fanzine, *Fanac*. Most interestingly, in 1963 and 1964 he published five fanzines of his own—one issue of *Votishal*, three issues of *Wormfarm*, and one issue of *Srith*—a significantly overlooked source of information about this period of his life.

One revelation from this material is that Gibson remained enthusiastic about Fritz Leiber, and while one might imagine that he preferred Leiber's anarchic, proto-cyberpunk stories like "Coming Attraction" (1950) and "The Beat Cluster" (1961), he actually loved his sword-and-sorcery fantasies featuring Fafhrd and the Gray Mouser: one *Fanac* cartoon featured a hotel clerk telling someone, "We Don't Have a Mr. Fafhrd Registered Here"; the titles of *Votishal* and *Srith* are taken from the series (where characters refer to priests of Votishal and the Scrolls of Srith); he called *Votishal* a "genzine [general-interest fanzine] for fen [plural of fan] who like a little s.f. and fanac with their sword and sorcery" (1); in *Srith*, he described himself as a "Mouser fan" (1); and as reported in the interview below, he corresponded with Leiber, receiving postcard replies, one of which he published in *Votishal* as "Mouser Mythos." In *Srith*, Gibson also brags about owning an "a*u*t*o*g*r*a*p*h*e*d (A fanfare and a round of applause, please) copy of the original Arkham House edition of [Leiber's] 'Night's Black Agents'" (1), which included two Fafhrd and the Gray Mouser stories. Gibson scholars must ponder the possibility that the dark alleyways and furious action filling his fiction could reflect the lingering influence of Leiber's colorful adventures. Young Gibson also says that he owns "a collection of original drawings," "a letter from R[obert] E. Howard to Farnsworth Wright," and "an autographed copy of 'The Hobbit'" (2), indicating that he was a dedicated collector of science fiction memorabilia, though he reports in the interview below that this material "was all lost, one way or another, after my mother's death."

Gibson was also writing science fiction poetry: he published three poems in *Wormfarm*'s first issue and told readers that the fanzine "may well turn out to be the SFPA poetryzine" ("The Screaming Crud" 3). Interestingly, the longest poem, "A Tale of the Badger Folk," obviously imitates an author and book never before mentioned in connection with Gibson—Clifford D. Simak's *City* (1952)—since it involves intelligent badgers of the far future telling stories about a possibly mythical "race of strange creatures" called the "Children of Men," or "Robots," who in turn spoke of vanished creators who had "bent time into strange loops, and flown to the stars" (4). (While Gibson says in the interview below that he does not recall reading Simak, he surely encountered the author in the pages of the *Galaxy* magazines he read, which published twenty-four Simak stories and three serialized novels between 1950 and 1964—though the stories in *City* appeared in other magazines.) The other two poems, "Observations on a Nightfear" and "The Last God," seem like homages to H. P. Lovecraft and confirm that, as noted in his article "Lovecraft & Me" (1981), he was then a devoted Lovecraft reader.

The fanzines provide other valuable data for biographers. In the untitled editorial comments beginning *Wormfarm* No. 1, Gibson offers this charming self-portrait:

> I should introduce myself, I suppose. You see, I've been in fandom for about a year now, but I have a talent for keeping my name out of fanzines, mailing lists, and con reports. "Yes, I *have* the power to cloud men's minds."
>
> It is safe to say that Bill Gibson is years old, has worked as a, and his interests in fandom are.
>
> If you wish to be a little more specific, you can add that he is a sophomore in high school, 6'3" tall, and this is his third fan publication. Outside of fandom, my interests include such diverse things as paleontology, girls, folksongs, girls, poetry, and girls. (1)

In the third issue, Gibson shifted from poetry to nonfiction to publish two articles offering snapshots of his teenage life: "A Short History of Coke Bottom Fandom" describes a conversation with friends involving the fact that Coca-Cola bottles of the era identified the city where they were manufactured, creating the possibility of enthusiasts transforming rare bottles from certain cities into valuable collector's items; and "Ohm Brew" provides a presumably exaggerated account of how Gibson was forced by friends to sample some homemade beer, an incident that probably occurred at the first DeepSouthCon, since the article mentions three fans—Dave Hulan, Rick Norwood, and Dick Ambrose—who attended that event with Gibson (Montgomery, "1997 Southern Fandom Collection Handbook"). As something for a scholar near Wytheville to pursue, Gibson also claims in the issue's editorial, "Grunt and Groan: Happy Gibson Comments," to have a "newly acquired job as cartoonist for one of the local papers," and he communicates why he left Wytheville in 1964 by announcing, "One of the most remarkable things about George Wythe High School, a veritable antheap of intellectuality sans any trace of creativity or creative insight, is the fact that I am no longer a student there. Further plans are pending, but I *do* plan to continue my education next year. Elsewhere, if at all possible" (1). Clearly, Gibson was not happy at his high school, so he urged his mother, as he told Edward Zuckerman in 1991, to find him a school "as far away as possible from Virginia."

Due to his subsequent transfer to the Southern Arizona School for Boys, Gibson lost touch with science fiction fandom and stopped publishing fanzines, but this might have happened anyway, as he pursued typical adolescent interests: he had already announced his burgeoning interest in "girls," and in "Lovecraft & Me," he described his transition away from science fiction: "[M]y Lovecraft period extended from about age fourteen until sixteen, when I started to satisfy my curiosity about hillocks and mounts" (real women, in lieu of Lovecraft's sexually charged imagery); so "Lovecraft wandered up into the lumber-room of early adolescence and stayed there" (22). With science fiction now "put aside with other childish things" ("Since 1948" 23), Gibson also discovered the pleasures of smoking marijuana, and when caught, he was unceremoniously kicked out of his school—something he casually mentioned to McQuiddy in 1987 but discreetly omitted from "Since 1948." (Also not willing to reveal this incident to *People* magazine in 1991, Gibson told Zuckerman that the expulsion was due, in Zuckerman's words, to his habit of "sneaking off to coffeehouses and folk-music clubs" [106].) This occurred after another significant event in his life, his mother's sudden death in 1966—which may be why he was smoking marijuana.

Returning to Wytheville, Gibson first lived with his mother's relatives. As he explained to David Wallace-Wells in 2011, he "didn't get along" with them, so his "mother's best friend and her husband finally took me in." From one bit of information, we deduce that he then returned to reading science fiction, because he reported in his 2007 introduction to Jorge Luis Borges's *Labyrinths* that he "initially discovered Borges in one of the more liberal anthologies of science fiction, which included his story 'The Circular Ruins'" ("An Invitation" 107). The first science fiction anthology featuring the story was Judith Merril's *11th Annual Collection of the Year's Best S-F*, published in 1966 when Gibson was eighteen, so Gibson undoubtedly read this book in 1966 or 1967. Further, he recalls reading the story while sitting in "a room dominated by large pieces of dark furniture belonging to my mother's family," suggesting that he was living with relatives at the time (107).

A turning point came in 1967, when he appeared before the local draft board; after hearing Gibson announce that his "one ambition in life was to take every mind-altering substance" (*No Maps for These Territories*), the officials, either appalled or bemused by this bold young man, took no immediate action, and Gibson quickly moved to Toronto to avoid being drafted. There, as he said in "Since 1948," he "joined up with rest of the Children's Crusade of the day" (23), briefly working in a head shop and appearing in a 1967 documentary, *Yorkville: Hippie Haven,* as a purported representative of local "hippies." While Gibson told John Barber in 2012 that he engaged "in various wonderful sorts of sin" in Toronto, suggesting a pleasurable sojourn, he disliked the company of draft dodgers—"Too much clinical depression, too much suicide, too much hard-core substance abuse" (*No Maps for These Territories*)—and soon moved away. He briefly lived in Washington, D.C., where he found himself in the middle of riots—he specified in 1982 that it was the Moratorium to End the War in Vietnam demonstrations on November 15, 1969 ("On the Surface," *Wing Window* No. 4, p. 8)—an event that Gibson compared to Samuel R. Delany's *Dhalgren* in a 1975 review and his 1996 introduction to the book. He also attended Woodstock, though he described the experience to Curt Holman in 2010 as "extraordinarily uncomfortable. I left early and thought, 'That was like going to a Civil War battle.'" Around this time, Gibson encountered R. Crumb's *Zap Comix,* and he confirmed to Adam Greenfield in 1988 that he was a "fan" of "underground comics in the '60s" (119).

How much the turbulent events of Gibson's first two decades affected his life remains debatable. Certainly, his protagonists are consistently drifters and loners without strong family ties who recall Gibson's early life more than the placid domesticity of his adulthood; he said in a 2010 interview, "I seem to write about nomadic characters who travel light" ("Prophet of the Real"). But Gibson does not necessarily hearken back to these times because he is haunted or traumatized by the experiences; rather, he might practically understand that restless, rootless individuals make more interesting protagonists than happily married couples raising families in nice suburban homes. The most autobiographical aspect of his fictional heroes is their resilience: no matter what happens, they remain the sorts of people they always were and stoically carry on with their lives. Similarly, Gibson has always handled whatever vicissitudes came his way without looking back, and he discusses his youth only to make a point, or in response to interviewers' questions.

The unsettled period of Gibson's life ended in his early twenties; upon returning to Toronto, he met his future wife, Deborah Thompson, and they indulged in a final bout of wanderlust by spending a year in Europe, where, as he told McCaffery in 1988, he "had enough income from [his] parents' estate to starve comfortably" (283). Two fanzine articles offer glimpses of his life in Europe: "My Life under Fascism; or, Franco Killed My Dog" (1979) describes a dissolute Gibson's encounter with cruel officials while visiting friends on the Spanish island of Ibiza, and "Anecdotal Evidence" (1980) recounts an unusual experience in an Istanbul restaurant. He also told Daurer that he and Deborah lived "on this island in Greece" in 1971 (321).

Leaving Europe, Gibson and Thompson settled in Vancouver, where she obtained a bachelor's and master's degree at the University of British Columbia. They also married and were soon raising their first child, Graeme, born in 1977 after what Susan Wood described as a "difficult labour" (*The Amor de Cosmos People's Memorial Quasirevolutionary Susanzine* No. 16, p. 8); the couple later had a daughter, Claire, born in 1983. For a while, they supported themselves with Deborah's teaching income while Gibson returned to school at the same university to earn a degree in English, also working briefly as a teaching assistant in film studies. Scholars may be inclined to overemphasize the importance of this academic background in analyzing Gibson, for while he often cites Fredric Jameson's concept of the "postmodern sublime" (as in Dennis Lim's 2007 interview, "Now Romancer"), there is little other evidence that literary criticism significantly influenced him.

What surely had a greater impact on Gibson was that, while in college, he reconnected with science fiction, immersing himself in local fandom; Richard Graeme Cameron's Canadian Fancyclopedia: V identifies a February 1975 convention as the "First VCON attended by William Gibson." He began contributing numerous cartoons, reviews, and articles to fanzines—activities unmentioned in "Since 1948." Though Gibson in the interview below dismisses these works as "juvenilia" and "bullshit," they are both more extensive and better than is generally supposed.

His renewed interest in the genre also inspired him to begin writing science fiction stories, at first with little success; when he took a class from Wood in 1976 (a woman he already knew through fandom), she allowed him to write a science fiction story instead of a term paper, and Gibson completed "Fragments of a Hologram Rose" (1977), which he soon published in Unearth, a minor magazine devoted exclusively to new writers, earning twenty-three dollars. While some report that the story only earned a B+, Wood herself wrote, in her fanzine The Amor de Cosmos People's Memorial Quasirevolutionary Susanzine, that "Bill Gibson, who is tall and drooping, who gave me his first story for the sf class, who got an A from me, sent the story to Unearth, and has just become the class's first published Author" (No. 13, p. 4). Indeed, Wood indicates in Amor that she considered Gibson a close friend; when she was visiting a friend who was diagnosed with cancer, she "called Bill Gibson and said, 'I need moral support. We're going to the hospital to see Richard'" (No. 16, p. 8). She also helped Gibson edit his fanzine Genre Plat, had Gibson contribute cartoons to her fanzine, and, according to a 2007 article, introduced Gibson to Terry Carr (the editor who inspired him to write Neuromancer) ("Retro Fanzines: AMOR #10 by Susan Wood, Aug 5th, 1976" 8); clearly, she represents a significant influence on Gibson, and the sudden death of this troubled woman in 1980, when a drug interaction caused heart failure, must have been devastating to Gibson and his circle of science fiction friends. Gibson also indicates in the interview below that her death, in some undefinable fashion, influenced his story "Hinterlands."

Despite his devotion to fandom—Wood quoted him in 1976 as saying, "I love fandom. It's even better than having an ant farm" (The Amor de Cosmos People's Memorial Quasirevolutionary Susanzine, No. 12, p. 6)—Gibson was displeased with the era's science fiction. He told a 2003 interviewer that in 1976, to survey the genre, he purchased "all the digest magazines and a bunch of novels," but these "appalled" him ("Crossing Boundaries" 7). In a 1977 review, he announced, "So much of the genre was and is so patently awful" ("Them & Us" 1). While introducing John Shirley's *City Come a-Walkin'*, he spoke of "the sinking feeling induced by skimming George Scithers' *Asimov's SF* at the corner drugstore" (2). And in the 2004 introduction to *Neuromancer*, he described his "smoldering resentment at what the genre I'd loved as a teenager seemed to me in the meantime to have become" (x). So Gibson was heartened to find and later befriend the writer John Shirley, whose work seemed fresh and innovative: in the same introduction, he said that Shirley "made the plastic covered Sears sofa that was the main body of Seventies sf recede wonderfully" (2). As Gibson began socializing in science fiction circles, he also, beginning in 1981, forged an intermittent partnership with the writer Bruce Sterling, both in the form of two collaborations and Sterling's energetic efforts to promote Gibson, himself, and others as vanguards of a new "cyberpunk" movement. At this point, we enter the phase of his life extensively discussed elsewhere: his emergence as a science fiction writer.

With four stories published in 1981, including two in the field's most lucrative venue, *Omni*, Gibson was ready to attempt a novel; the standard story, confirmed in the interview below, is that this resulted from a chance meeting with Carr, who offered Gibson the opportunity to write a novel for his revived series of Science Fiction Specials. He speculated in a 1989 interview that Carr did so because he "accidentally tipped a tumbler of bourbon in my lap" and Gibson immediately blurted out, "Shit, these are my only pair!" (Tomlinson, "William Gibson Profile" 34) Yet Gibson's 1994 afterword to *Neuromancer* indicates that Gibson played a more active role in securing that contract, since he describes writing a letter to Carr in the role of "the wanna-be novelist, fishing with *desperate subtlety* for the further professional attention of Mr. Carr, editor and anthologist" (275). After a rocky start—a first proposal rejected because it had "almost nothing in the way of, well, narrative" (276), and a second, accepted proposal envisioning Molly as the viewpoint character—Gibson completed his breakthrough novel, *Neuromancer*, and forever changed his life. Its enormous success transformed him into a full-time professional writer who has, since that time, been more than able to comfortably support himself and his family. His new status is epitomized in a comment from editor

John D. Berry in the ninth issue of *Wing Window,* explaining Gibson's failure to provide one more column: "'These are not normal times,' [Gibson] said by way of explanation, alluding to zillion-dollar movie deals and photos for ROLLING STONE" (7).

Since the 1980s, Gibson's life has been remarkably uneventful, as suggested by his disinclination to say anything about it in "Since 1948": he and Deborah raised their children to adulthood, remained in Vancouver (while moving to a nicer home), and regularly traveled around the world, with some visits chronicled in commissioned essays—though he told Jill Owens in 2007, "I'd rather do nothing at home than go to most places" and described himself to Matt Parish in 2012 as "a person that tends to go to the same distant destinations over and over." His 2010 semiautobiographical story "Dougal Discarnate" depicts a man leading a generally sedentary life, frequently watching films, including "cheesy science fiction movies" (236). Gibson has also actively pursued his long-standing interests in contemporary music and art, regularly contributing to books by noted artists, but except for the works of friends like Jack Womack, he is not especially attentive to science fiction; he told Amy Cavanaugh in 2011, "I actually read everything else much more than I read science fiction. It's a relatively small part of my reading diet." Instead, "I read a lot of non-fiction," reflecting his constant fascination with aspects of the world around him. Overall, after Gibson's unsettled youth, the most interesting events of his life have surely been his writings, which this book will now describe.

CHAPTER 2

A DANGEROUS AMATEUR

Contributions to Science Fiction Fanzines

The cartoons and writings Gibson contributed to fanzines in the 1960s, 1970s, and 1980s merit attention for these reasons: they provide valuable data about Gibson's life, attitudes, and literary apprenticeship; they confirm that he was long and deeply connected to science fiction, as he repeatedly acknowledges; they anticipate themes and techniques that became central to his fiction; and even if many drawings and texts are inconsequential, Gibson's stature demands that someone document and examine these works. However, since even extensive fanzine collections, like that in the Eaton Collection of the University of California, Riverside, are incomplete, I probably have missed some works in these venues.

When he was fifteen, Gibson began publishing cartoons in *Fanac* and his own fanzines, which naturally reflect an adolescent sense of humor. In one *Fanac* cartoon, a nun whispers to a knight in armor, "Thy Fly Is Open" ("Hssst! Thy Fly Is Open!" 8), while one cartoon in the first issue of *Wormfarm* has a man say to friends, "Let's Be Non-Conformists. Everybody Else Is Doing It" (2)—a joke that may consciously or unconsciously borrow from a 1959 *Mad* magazine article, David Berg's "Little League," where a billboard says, "The Man Who Thinks for Himself Smokes Vicejoy because Everybody Else Does!" (19). Two other cartoons in *Wormfarm* indicate that Gibson, like many science fiction fans, abhorred John W. Campbell Jr.'s enthusiasms for dubious pseudoscience like psychic powers ("psionics") and the Dean Drive, a purported engine that violated Newton's Third Law of Motion: One cartoon announces, "Now! *You* Can Build a Real Psionic Space Ship! 1. Glue Tab *A* into Slot *B*. 2. Glue Tab *C* into Slot *D*. 3. Grab Tab *E* Firmly. Hold On. 4. Think Hard!" Another says, "Then He Said Something about Putting a Dean Drive in His Propbeanie. . . . Then, Whooosh!!" (*Wormfarm* No. 1, p. 5 and cover). These cartoons further suggest that he dreamed of becoming an artist, as confirmed when he told Steven Poole in 2003 that in Toronto he was "briefly and pointlessly an art student" and contemplated a career in art, though he "never did anything, never produced any work."

Gibson's writings in adolescent fanzines are of more interest to scholars. Of his three poems, "Observations on a Nightfear" is probably the best (and significantly, the first one that he typed), and quoting its full, manifestly Lovecraftian text indicates that Lovecraft may have been a far stronger influence on young Gibson than he elsewhere indicates:

October, and something is listening,
Scratching faintly,
At the other side of the sky.
Late, in the forgotten hours before dawn,
With the dark old house humming,
To itself,
I, waiting, have felt,
Like a whirring of batwings in my mind,
The nearness of some alien thing.
Not good, nor evil, but alien,
Alien to all that man has known or thought.
What lurks there, beyond the stars?
And what will man, an idiot child,
Do when he has flown all the voids,

And seen all the palaces of pink marble?
I do not know,
But I have heard the dark old house,
Humming, to itself. (1)

The second poem, "The Last God," darkly anticipates humanity's coming extinction from the titular figure's perspective, concluding with these portentous words:

And when the final man has gone;
The world lies dark with fears,
 Only then shall the last god weep,
 But who shall see his tears? (3)

The third, "A Tale of the Badger Folk," more optimistically anticipates only that humans will abandon Earth to travel through space, as the remaining race of intelligent badgers will still occasionally

[. . .] see, with sleepy eyes,
A slender thing that rides a ribbon of flame across the sky,
While moonlight glints off its prow of polished silver
. . . . (4)

Gibson's prose in early fanzines is generally unmemorable, suggesting that he channeled his creative energies into poetry at the time, though an early proclivity for fiction may be on display in "Ohm Brew." While a few older fans may have prodded the teenage Gibson to drink some beer, they almost certainly did not, as the article relates and a cartoon illustrates, physically restrain him and place a tube down his throat (5–6). A passage from "A Short History of Coke Bottom Fandom," which demonstrates that Gibson was already carefully examining the products of technology around him, includes a possible intimation that he would soon leave the world of fandom: he reports that a friend told him, "[T]hese fanzines have warped your mind. You need to do something normal for a change" (2).

Exiled by choice to Arizona, Gibson indeed devoted the next decade to doing normal things, but he never really stopped reading science fiction. It was perhaps inevitable that, once he and Deborah settled in Vancouver, he would again involve himself in science fiction fandom and contribute cartoons and writings to fanzines, doing so far more often than Gibson now wishes people to believe. Introducing *Distrust That Particular Flavor,* he notes dismissively, "Science fiction had long been surrounded by a generations-deep compost of fanzines, a sort of paper Internet, and this could be extremely engrossing, and apparently gratifying. But after trying that avenue of publication a few times, I decided to avoid it" (3). However, even discounting his works in 1963 and 1964, my tally of his contributions to fanzines includes thirty-four cartoons and drawings, twelve articles, thirteen reviews, and one collaborative story. Manifestly, Gibson published in fanzines considerably more than "a few times."

One must also question the introduction's theme that for Gibson in the 1980s, "fiction-writing tools" were "the only writing tools I had," so he felt very insecure when he was first asked to write nonfiction, "as though I was being paid to solo on some instrument vaguely related to one I actually knew how to play" (5). In fact, by the time he was writing the stories that enabled him to master the art of fiction, he had already written and published numerous pieces of nonfiction, some of a high quality. Perhaps Gibson himself did not realize how good he already was in this area, as suggested by Jerry Kaufman's letter praising "My Life under Fascism": "Bill doesn't realize that these things he writes for fanzines could probably sell just like his fiction" (31).

Gibson's 1970s cartoons, though reflecting more skill than his adolescent efforts, are hardly masterpieces, but sufficient talent is on display to suggest that this represents another career path he might have successfully pursued. Consider the cover of the October 1975 issue of the *BCSFA Newsletter,* showing a diminutive, possibly one-armed alien, wearing the beanie cap associated with science fiction fans and aiming a ray gun. The caption labels the drawing an example of "Traditional Folk Arts of Fandom: The Hand-Cut Illo" and promises another example to come: "Underwater Beanie-Weaving and How to Spot a Corflu Junkie." (Since "corflu" is a fan term for "correction fluid," once essential when using mimeograph magazines to print fanzines, "corflu junkie" probably refers to people who inhale fumes from correction fluid to get high, though it might also refer to attendees of the annual convention called Corflu, focused on fanzines.) The drawing, cute and well-rendered, might have appeared in a professional science fiction magazine of that era. (Some might discern prophetic significance in the goggles worn by Gibson's alien, which resemble the "mirrorshades" sunglasses associated with cyber-punk writers.)

Other cartoons are genuinely amusing, like one depicting a man uttering the cliché "And Then Sex Reared Its Ugly Head" while a second man envisions a literal monster's head. Another, in which an author with protruding eyes on stalks announces that his previous stories about "Invasions of Earth by ant-like creatures with periscope eyes and garish neck-wear" are now "below my serious consideration as a novelist," is farcically signed "J. Cornelius," referencing Michael Moorcock's character Jerry Cornelius. And a cartoon in which a science fiction writer tells a young man, "Some day, kid, all of this will be yours—the Hugos, the groupies, royalty checks," might be seen as a hopeful prediction of Gibson's own career (though "groupies" were never in evidence around him).

Gibson's most extensive artwork was "A 2-Page Collaboration between Ken Fletcher & Wm. Gibson," a comic-book story in the first issue of *Genre Plat,* one unheralded candidate for the status of his first published work of fiction and first collaboration. It was created spontaneously when Gibson and Fletcher, watched by friends, frantically began improvising and illustrating an inane story, alternately drawing panels. It involves a traditional science fiction fan opposed to the stylistic innovators of the New Wave (a figure targeted in other Gibson cartoons) whose fingers become expanding tentacles that attack J. G. Ballard and Moorcock; while he angrily exclaims, "Eat Space, New Wave Ponce," another caption, "To wound the autumnal writer," references Delany's *Dhalgren* (29). While Ballard dismisses this "Asshole" who "doesn't dig that smooth avant-garde SF" (29), the fan presses his attack, exclaiming, "I still live!" which the horrified Ballard and Moorcock identify as "Edgar Rice Burroughs' dying words!" (29). Finally contriving to digest or dismember the writers in some fashion not depicted, the fan has stuffed their remains into a package, announcing, "And now to send the manuscript off to a publisher . . . always did like anthologies" (29). To be sure, this represents precisely the sort of work for which the term "juvenilia" was devised, yet a future scholar assembling *The Complete Short Fiction of William Gibson* may feel compelled to include it, along with "Stoned" (discussed below).

To my knowledge, Gibson stopped contributing art to fanzines in 1980, precisely when his writing career was about to take off and he was focusing his energies on this more promising activity. Still, his experiences as an artist, if nothing else, explain why "visual motifs" in Gibson's writings have proved a rich area for exploration by critics like Tatiana G. Rapatzikou (*Gothic Motifs in the Fiction of William Gibson* xiii), and Gibson may someday return to art, though he discounts that possibility in the interview below.

While Gibson again contributed cartoons to fanzines, he also published reviews and articles, though a singular work of fiction, "Stoned," necessarily commands attention, since it seems virtually unknown. As reported in the 1976 issue of the *BCSFA Newsletter* where it appeared, this "comparatively good group story was produced" at the organization's January meeting, "the ringleaders being Lona Elrod, Bill Gibson, and Daniel Say, with contributions from various others" (Fran Skene, "News" 3). Predictably, the narrative is hard to make sense of, but the opening passage represents a serious effort, probably involving Gibson, to convey the atmosphere of a mysterious desert island, including detailed attention to an arriving submarine:

> The clearing was circular, walled with dense green and roofed with clear, translucent blue. Beyond the tangled lianas and rotting boles of fallen date palms, the sea heaved rhythmically. Then, just beneath the swelling surface, the baroque iron prow of an exotic antique vessel was seen slicing with Victorian dignity through the limpid waters of the coastal shelf; it swung toward the beach. In the clearing, seven stone spheres rose smoothly from tangled beds of tropical humus.
>
> A red and green parrot screeched as it fled from its perch into the jungle, and the screech was echoed from the undergrowth; a pig blundered through the clearing. [. . .] Seven stone spheres hung silently above the clearing, rotating above the ruins of a vast anthill. The jungle was silent. (6)

A man emerges from the vessel, muttering angry words about someone named Cartwright, and he references James Purdy's 1956 novel *Dream Palace*: "I want to forget the Dream Palace, the long voyage in the rusting submarine—product of your waking dreams among the test tubes, the surgical tables—the Victorian sitting room where we cut the purple armchair into very small pieces!" (7).

Say now takes the story in a silly, salacious direction, as the hovering stones hit the man in his "crotch," making him exclaim, "I fear I shall never rise to the occasion again" and prompting the one remark in the story explicitly attributed to Gibson: "(D.S. has made this story something less than literature—Wm. G.)" (7). The man, now identified as "Mr. S.," is attacked by a "stun-gun," and after more bawdy humor, he hears "the slurp" of something or someone identified as "Nemo Piggy Jack Ralph Conseil Verne and William Decadent" that "floated out upon the dimly phosphorescent waves," prompting another effort to write evocative prose: "surrounded by fiery, moonbeam-bodied creatures they slid away from the beach; across space the sun and moon were pulling so that the film of water on the earth was held, drawn into a wave, while the solid core turned. Quietly in stillness under the steadfast stars the pale forms drifted out into the open sea" (8).

The story then lurches in another direction, as "Cartwright's eyes blinked open," indicating that previous events were only a dream induced by "eat[ing] cheese before sleeping," followed by an amorous encounter with an alien woman with four animate breasts: "[F]everishly his fingers penetrated the diaphanous folds tantalizingly clinging to the frugiverous curves of her upper breasts, contentedly munching mangos. Timidly, with a hesitant, gentle smile, he offered her upper left breast an apricot." But an unspecified mechanical protector of the woman activates a "slim rod" that attacks Cartwright in a sexually suggestive manner (8). A final sentence echoing Geoffrey Chaucer, "Here endeth the tales of the Pilgrimes of Canterburye" (9), is probably the work of English-major Gibson.

The next meeting, in February 1976, produced another collaborative story, the unfinished "A Weird Story," which seems to satirize Gibson, describing a man named "Will Ginnet," called "a fantastic young man, being a master's student in English literature at B.X. University," who hears "a maniacal laugh" and blasts someone with a machine gun before being attacked by some strange mass (4). With no accompanying information about its authors, though, we cannot assume that Gibson was a participant, and he may have become its subject because he missed the meeting.

Gibson's earliest article, "Imaginary Anthology of Imaginative Fiction: A Model Kit," offers unique information about his 1975 reading preferences. Its introduction announces, "The book as conceptual art; reader assembles required texts and reads stories in prescribed order. Reading other stories in required texts negates editorial function; the editor accepts no responsibility, aesthetic or otherwise, for stories not included in the following table of contents" (6). Gibson then lists this "conceptual" anthology's contents: Victor Brauner's 1938 painting *Object Which Dreams* as "Cover art"; Julio Cortázar's "Continuity of Parks" (1964); Terry Southern's "The Road Out of Axotle" (1962); William S. Burroughs's "Mother and I Would Like to Know" (1969); Cortázar's "Letter to a Young Lady in Paradise" (1951); Burroughs's "Wind Die. You Die. We Die" (1968); Southern's "The Blood of a Wig" (1967); Ahmed Yacoubi's "The Night before Thinking" (1961); Burroughs's "Johnny 23" (1968); and Thomas Pynchon's "Lowlands" (1959). Whether "Imaginary Anthology of Imaginative Fiction" embodied a sincere desire to edit an anthology of offbeat stories, or was simply a clever way for Gibson to promote his reading interests, this odd piece suggests that Gibson had thoughts of becoming a science fiction editor: he had edited fanzines as a teenager, and months after writing this article, he and Allyn Cadogan began coediting a new fanzine, *Genre Plat*, with Susan Wood and John Park. Gibson also knew that Wood would soon achieve her first major publication by editing a collection of Ursula K. Le Guin's nonfiction, *The Language of the Night* (1979), demonstrating that editing could be a pathway to wider recognition. However, since Gibson abandoned *Genre Plat* after its second issue, leaving Cadogan as sole editor, he probably did not enjoy editing and never again undertook projects of this kind.

Gibson's reviews tend to be uninteresting; usually brief, they focus on describing the book's contents. Still, there are flashes of Gibsonian wit—while praising D. M. Thomas's idiosyncratic fantasy *The Flute-Player* (1978) in 1981, he tersely concludes, "Sorry, no unicorns" (56)—and they occasionally anticipate ideas that surface in later works. His review of Donald J. Bush's *The Streamlined Decade* first conveyed the interest in retrofutures that was central to "The Gernsback Continuum," and his "*Dhalgren*: An Unreview" (1975) links the novel's Bellona to "a City of Dreadful Night that many of us wandered through in the Sixties" (2), a conceit developed further in his 1996 introduction. (Strangely, here and in another article, "Them & Us," he misspells the author's name as "Delaney.") He also provides no hints that he anticipated anything like cyberpunk: his 1980 review of Shirley's *City Come a-Walkin'* (1980) only praises the novel as a "fantasy" (31), but twenty years later, he wrote a foreword celebrating it as "the Protoplasmic Mother of all cyberpunk novels" (4).

Gibson's later fanzine articles convey his natural flair for travel writing, since the best pieces are his description of an unpleasant encounter with Spanish police on Ibiza ("My Life under Fascism; or, Franco Killed My Dog"), an amusing account about observing a mirror spontaneously explode in a Turkish restaurant ("Anecdotal Evidence"), and a 1984 report on a visit to Mexico ("On the Surface," *Wing Window* No. 7); these pieces would not have seemed out of place in *Distrust That Particular Flavor*. In the first article, he explained that the policemen, after asking if a stray dog belonged to Gibson, cruelly shot the animal, provoking this rare excursion into political commentary:

> So the next time you hear someone say that Heinlein or Bianca Jagger or Anita Bryant is fascist, I've given you one little yardstick of the genuine, the historical article. They shot my dog. I say *my* dog because this experience taught me something about fascists: if you don't admit to owning the world's stray dogs, they'll shoot them. And one day they'll be back. For you. With the boxcars. (18)

In the second article, he describes a Turkish toilet as "this gaping Lovecraftian chasm in the basement, at whose edge we were expected to crouch in near total darkness whenever the need arose. You could sometimes hear things *moving* down there" (24). And "If I were Borges," he comments, "I might point out that each of [the restaurant's mirrors] could be regarded as a detailed map of an 'imaginary country' . . . but I'm not Borges and anyway I wouldn't waste that kind of imagery on a San Francisco fanzine that probably won't even be published" (24). In the third article, he waxes eloquent about "a structure of the utmost Ballardian poetry, a hotel of reinforced concrete that had collapsed under the battering of a summer storm" (10), and provides an early sign of his fascination with brand names when noting some "[f]ascinatingly clumsy pirating of bigname trademarks: jeans with Levi's trademark on one pocket, Jordache on the other" (9).

Another article, "Devo: A Carrier's Story," conveys Gibson's interest in music, as it describes a Devo concert and the way the band "jerked and wriggled and squirmed and did things that no other group has ever done on stage," making him feel "as if the 21st century was an operAtive [*sic*] proposition" (15). He also signals what Dani Cavallaro called Gibson's characteristic "interest in clothes, accessories, decor and interior design" (*Cyberpunk and Cyberculture* 193), devoting considerable energy to describing a man's distinctive clothing, sometimes in terms of science fiction: "[H]e wore a thin quilted jacket, very short, tight, and narrow, in matte black nylon, that managed simultaneously to suggest a bellhop, loungewear from the wardrobe of *Battlestar Galactica*, and an organ grinder's monkey." Also wearing *"Forbidden Planet* fatigues filtered through 1984 Saigon disco nostalgia," the man's "overall effect was *Three Stooges Go to Mars*" (16).

Fanzine articles offer early evidence of Gibson's fascination with technologies of all kinds: two *Wing Window* columns focus on a "FLYSHOOTER," an electronic device he purchased for killing flies (No. 3, p. 3), and an intriguing "Japanese butcherknife" (No. 5, p. 9), while a third discusses how he repaired a lawnmower. "My Life under Fascism" describes various firearms Gibson had encountered, including "a 9mm Astra automatic, a clumsy military pistol that resembles a six-year-old's attempt to fake a firearm with Erector Set parts" (15). He shows his amazing eye for detail in the cowritten "Dangerously Amateur" editorial of *Genre Plat*'s first issue, where "[t]he giant toothpick box in Allyn [Cadogan]'s living room" is called "one of those terminally wierd [*sic*] *objets* former Occupants abandon for whatever reasons of their own in flats all over the world. *Why* is there a gallon milk-carton filled with old razor blades under the sink when you move in? And *why* has each blade been evenly coated with what seems to be Hot Pink nail varnish?" (5). Articles evidence an early tendency, observed in later nonfiction and recent novels, to see the world around him in terms of science fiction: in addition to cited passages referencing Lovecraft, Borges, Ballard, *Forbidden Planet,* and *Battlestar Galactica,* his column for *Wing Window*'s third issue in 1982 describes a fly as "one slick little organic computer" and says that a certain slingshot looks "like something from a sex shop in a very peculiar alternate universe" (3, 4), while his column in the fifth issue describes science fiction fan Sharee Carton as "looking modishly Dhalgrenesque" ("On the Surface," *Wing Window* No. 5, p. 10), alluding to Delany's novel.

Unsurprisingly, other fanzine articles deal more directly with science fiction writers: his first contribution to *Wing Window*, " . . . With a Strange Device," paid tribute to the recently deceased Philip K. Dick, a writer Gibson elsewhere claims he largely ignored. He amusingly describes the time he and some Toronto friends took the drug STP, causing startling hallucinations—he "watched pale tendrils sprout from my dirty bare feet and take root in the cracks between the floorboards"—an experience his friends "always referred to as the night we did the PKD" (5). He sentimentally concludes, "Times like these, a good hit of PKD shakes the scales from the tired eyes. Only we can't get any more, now" (6). In "Lovecraft & Me," he acknowledges that Lovecraft "scared the shit out me" at the age of fourteen but no longer has much impact: "[T]his is the modern world, Jack, and all the eldritch ichor off all the bedsheets of Providence is as nothing in the face of the horrors that confront us daily" (21). In "Them & Us," purportedly a review of Ursula K. Le Guin's *Nebula Award Stories Eleven* (1977), he focused exclusively on contrasting essays from Vonda McIntyre and Peter Nicholls, criticizing McIntyre's position that science fiction is separate and special, endorsing Nicholls's anticipation of a gradual merging of science fiction into the literary mainstream, and concluding with an impassioned indictment of American science fiction:

> I don't think I've read too many pieces of really world-class fiction that didn't cause me to question at least one of my own "certainties," and I like to think that that is what good fiction is *for*. It's exhilarating, but as Kafka pointed out, it can scare the hell out of you because good art changes your life. And the record leaves me fairly certain that the people who forged the reader-editor-author feedback circuit that determined the content of so much of American sf were not really very interested in getting quite that sort of hell scared out of them. (13)

As Gibson's stories earned him acclaim, he continued writing columns for *Wing Window,* but *Neuromancer's* success left no more time for such uncompensated labor. Even after Gibson stopped contributing to fanzines, however, he retained some interest in, and affection for, fandom. He agreed to serve as Fan Guest of Honor at a 1996 science fiction convention in Vancouver, also contributing one more cartoon to its souvenir book, belatedly scanned and published in 2011; this sketch of "The Phoenix, Reborn!" suggests that Gibson relished the experience of working as a fan artist one more time. He also eagerly read, and wrote a 1993 letter in response to, a history of British fandom serialized in the fanzine *Then,* saying, "THEN was great. God only knows why I enjoy reading fan history, but I do" (Letter qtd. in *Then* 1993).

Whenever the mature Gibson writes an introduction to a book by a fellow author, or contributes to an artist's book, he carries on the tradition of amateur writing he had been part of as a science fiction fan, since these labors of love provide little if any income. His unusual proclivity for such profitless work, in contrast to other successful writers, might be attributed to the spirit of fellowship and generosity he absorbed from the science fiction community, or a remembered feeling that it is sometimes fun to write something without worrying about payment. Even if they do not compare in quality to Gibson's later works, his cartoons and articles for fanzines consistently convey an engaging spirit of youthful energy, and one hopes that someday Gibson will allow these works to reach a wider audience.

CHaPTeR 3

FINDING HIS OWN USES FOR THINGS
The Short Fiction

One is tempted to interpret Gibson's early stories as an extended process of discovering and experimenting with elements that became central to his novels. His first official story, "Fragments of a Hologram Rose" (1977), introduces the theme of virtual reality—here, "Apparent Sensory Perception" or ASP, a system for vicariously experiencing other people's recorded activities—as well as an interest in the brief, easily shattered relationships of rootless drifters. "The Gernsback Continuum" (1981) is Gibson's first metafictional consideration of science fiction and its effects, also involving a globalized world of multinational corporations and peripatetic characters navigating its subcultures, as later observed in *Pattern Recognition* and related novels. "Johnny Mnemonic" (1981) first involves the underworld of the Sprawl, the vast megalopolis stretching down America's East Coast, with hustlers exploiting hijacked technology to stay alive amidst uncertain allies and violent opponents, while "Burning Chrome" (1982) adds the ingredient of cyberspace, the illusory realm of data constructs that carry out the future's business and face incursions from ingenious criminals. In this context, "Hinterlands" (1981) would be cast as a failed experiment, taking on the science fiction tropes of space travel and alien contact that left Gibson uninspired, as they figured in *Neuromancer* but became less and less important in later novels.

Still, Gibson never regarded these stories as trial runs for a novel, and seeing his stories solely through the lens of *Neuromancer* and its successors may hinder an appreciation of them on their own terms. Certainly, though only vaguely congruent with later writings, "Fragments of a Hologram Rose" represents an impressive piece of world-building that might be considered Gibson's response to the "condensed novels" written by an author he admired, J. G. Ballard, in the 1960s (published in America as *Love and Napalm: Export U.S.A.* [1969]), though it is a more conventional narrative.

Anticipating Japan's emergence as a world power before other commentators, Gibson envisions a young man, Parker, who was "indentured" (44) to a Japanese company at the age of fifteen; he escapes to be plunged into an America beset by violent civil war involving the "New Secessionist regime" on the West Coast and lawless "shantytowns" in Texas (44, 45). There he discovers ASP machines, which, in a manner paralleling the later development of video games, were first available as public consoles or in theaters before being supplanted by home units. Then, fortuitously stumbling upon a corpse with some antibiotics—"worth twice its weight in cocaine" (46) in these desperate times—he gets away from the shantytowns and meets a girl who helps him obtain a job "writ[ing] continuity for broadcast ASP" (43). But she leaves him alone to carry on a disheartening life of constantly depending upon ASP recordings to sleep, though these are disrupted by power failures. The story, with enough content to fill another writer's novel, is succinctly conveyed by scattered comments and brief flashbacks as Parker adjusts to the girl's departure, demonstrating that Gibson had already mastered the technique, showcased by Heinlein and championed by Campbell, of artfully presenting well-developed future worlds by means of casual, indirect references.

The story also reveals that Gibson was already a superb prose stylist; indeed, his early confidence in this area is demonstrated by the fact that, while other writers might have suppressed an early story or extensively revised it for republication, Gibson republished "Fragments of a Hologram Rose" in

Burning Chrome with precisely one change: correcting the word "holodome" to "holodrome" (44). The story's intriguing title, which alone might have persuaded editors to accept it, describes a literal event in the story—while ridding himself of possessions left behind by his girlfriend, Parker finds a postcard with a hologram rose and destroys it in his garbage disposal—and announces Gibson's theme, bluntly epitomized at the end:

> A hologram has this quality: Recovered and illuminated, each fragment will re-
> veal the whole image of the rose. Falling toward delta, he sees himself the rose,
> each of his scattered fragments revealing a whole he'll never know—stolen credit
> cards—a burned-out suburb—planetary conjunctions of a stranger—a tank burn-
> ing on a highway—a flat packet of drugs—a switchblade honed on concrete,
> thin as pain. . . . But each fragment reveals the rose from a different angle, he
> remembered. (47–48)

In suggesting new that technologies might problematize people's efforts to conceive of themselves in a satisfyingly unified fashion, Gibson introduced an issue raised in later works—"postmodern" challenges to traditional models of identity.

But the artistry in this passage is observed elsewhere in the story, when Park-er looks for objects his girlfriend left behind: "The flashlight's beam probes the bare shelves for evidence of love, finding a broken leather sandal strap, an ASP cassette, and a postcard" (43)—a small early sign of his recurring tendency to provide detailed lists of random objects filling his future worlds. As Lance Olsen puts it, "Gibson is infatuated with detail and inventory" (136). Gibson described these interests more eloquently while introducing *Jeff de Boer: Articulation*: "My writing always seemed to begin with the attempt to describe some imaginary object. Never with a line of dialogue, a human gesture, a landscape—always with an object, an artifact, some fragment, often broken, of a manufactured world" ([4]). Indeed, this fascination with technological products, first gleaned in "Fragments of a Hologram Rose," is evident throughout Gibson's fiction; as he continued in his introduction to *Jeff de Boer*: "My works, naturally, abound with" such "fragments, these crumbs of imagined technology," which are his "passport to the other side of the bridge" ([4]).

While "Fragments of a Hologram Rose" attracted little attention, Gibson began building his reputation in 1981, when four stories appeared in rapid succession. The first, "Johnny Mnemonic," was published in *Omni,* the genre's most prestigious venue, a sign that insiders at least were identifying Gibson as a major new talent. The story also commands attention because it first presents the dark, seedy future later observed in *Neuromancer* and other Sprawl novels. To be sure, "Johnny Mnemonic" is not without precedents in science fiction, for complex future underworlds had been crafted by earlier writers cited as cyberpunk precursors like Alfred Bester and Cordwainer Smith, and a story with particular resonances with Gibson is Samuel R. Delany's "Time Considered as a Helix of Semi-Precious Stones" (1968), which he presumably read, given his fondness for Delany's works.

However, there were also genuine novelties in Gibson's emerging vision of the future, which would be celebrated at length by critics. Gibson was one of the first to anticipate a thoroughly globalized future wherein people and cultures would freely cross national boundaries; the villains of "Johnny Mnemonic" belong to the Japanese Mafia, the yakuza, described as "a true multinational, like ITT and Ono-Sendai" (14). He discerned that the most valuable items smuggled by the future's criminals would be information—here, data stolen from the yakuza and implanted in the unknowing protagonist's head; as Johnny comments, "We're an information economy. They teach you that in school" (22). As Olsen concisely notes, "Information is power" in Gibson's worlds (24), anticipating Gibson's comment to Stephen McClelland in 1997 that "in post-industrial societies, it is information which will determine things like power, status, wealth" ("Coining Cyberspace" 123). Further, since "multinational corporations control most information," they, not governments, "dominate the landscape in Gibson's fiction" (Olsen 24). Also envisioning advances in bioengineering, "Johnny Mnemonic" introduces the intriguing character of Jones, a "cyborg" dolphin developed by the American military with a talent for extracting data—and an addiction to heroin—who becomes Johnny's partner in crime.

Displaying another characteristic trope noted by commentators, Gibson combines these innovative elements with a traditional sort of story, with characters intent on obtaining a valuable object—what Alfred Hitchcock termed a "McGuffin," the director's way to convey that its nature is unimportant, since its function is solely to keep the plot in motion. Here, the information inside Johnny's head makes him the target of yakuza assassins. To save his life, Molly Millions—a bodyguard he encounters with built-in blades in her hands—takes Johnny to Jones, who helps him retrieve the data and protect himself by threatening to release the information. However, unlike the film penned by Gibson, the story never identifies what the data is, emphasizing that, as in Hitchcock's films, it is merely a device to provoke an intriguing tour of an imagined future.

Although Bruce Sterling (driven by an ideological agenda unrelated to Gibson's concerns) promoted Gibson's third story, "The Gernsback Continuum," as a savage attack on earlier science fiction (in his preface to *Burning Chrome* [3]), the story actually pays fond tribute to the now-quaint prophecies of science fiction writers and futurists of the 1920s and 1930s, and ponders how their visions still influence residents of a future they failed to predict. The story's roots can be traced back to Gibson's childhood, when his exposure to early television included antiquated documentaries showing "an *obsolete* future," as he recalled in a 1975 review of a book on 1930s art and architecture, Donald J. Bush's *The Streamlined Decade,* another influence on the story (1). That review even anticipated the story's concept of an alternate universe in which that envisioned future materialized: "[Norman Bel] Geddes and his contemporaries in design set out to change the face of America—if they had succeeded, we might all have grown up in the pastel-wash cities that Frank R. Paul faithfully produced for the covers of *Amazing Stories*" (1). Further, the review's bemused comment on one incongruous image from the book—"a *Things to Come* set misplaced on the outskirts of Racine, Wisconsin" (2)—conveys no hostility toward these quaint visions, which is also true of the story's references to "the covers of old *Amazing Stories* pulps, painted by an artist named Frank R. Paul," "Paul's spray-paint utopias" (30), and the films *Metropolis* (1927), *Things to Come* (1936), and Flash Gordon serials (1936, 1938, 1940) (36). Gibson told Maximus Clarke in 2010 that "The Gernsback Continuum" came about because his review of Bush's book had been "rejected," and in response, "for some reason I sat down and rewrote it as a science fiction story"—confirming the review's role in inspiring the story. However, when I noted in the interview below that the review had actually been published, Gibson speculates that "anger" about "having to do revisions," not rejection, may have inspired the story.

To give Sterling his due, Gibson is not entirely uncritical of these outdated predictions—he says that the envisioned inhabitants of these futures had "gone on and on, in a dream logic that knew nothing of pollution, the finite bounds of fossil fuel, or foreign wars it was possible to lose," and calls them "smug, happy, and utterly content with themselves and their world" (38). However, there is no anger in these descriptions, nothing to justify Sterling's overheated assertion that the story is a "devastating refutation of 'scientific-tion' in its guise as narrow technolatry" (2). Like his protagonist, Gibson both observes and is part of the Gernsback Continuum, and while science fiction works had previously taken both fond and critical looks at the genre's past—like Fredric Brown's *What Mad Universe* (1949), which poked fun at the absurdities of space opera—Gibson may have been the first writer to examine Earthbound predictions from the 1930s in this fashion, perhaps introducing the now-common interest in such "retrofutures."

The story is also arguably Gibson's first work of realistic fiction, since one can interpret what the protagonist sees—"[s]emiotic ghosts" (35) of a Gernsbackian future—as nothing more than hallucinations, inspired by his assignment to photograph old structures with futuristic architecture (though the title suggests that they are glimpses of an alternate universe, what the paranormal investigator Mervyn Kihn tells him are "bits of deep cultural imagery that have split off and taken on a life of their own" [35]). And the relationship between the photographer and the people who hired him, the publisher Cohen and his associate Dialta Downes, anticipates the relation-ship between *Pattern Recognition*'s Cayce and Bigend: in each case, a talented craftsperson receives an assignment from a wealthy, sophisticated jet-setter and enters a more glamorous world. Further, both works take place in the present but feature people whose minds are very much on past predictions of the future—which represents Gibson's own situation, and the type of nar-rative that may someday be accepted as his true strength.

Gibson's next stories, "The Belonging Kind" (1981; with John Shirley) and "Hinterlands" (1981), were less successful than "Johnny Mnemonic" and "The Gernsback Continuum," for reasons that foreground one issue that problema-tized Gibson's relationship with science fiction: his discomfort with the genre's most characteristic tropes, alien life and space travel. Future cities—both the gleaming constructs of "The Gernsback Continuum" and the dark under-worlds of "Johnny Mnemonic"—had figured in previous science fiction, but stories about space travelers, distant planets, and exotic aliens were always more central to the genre, so anyone entering the field would arguably have to write such stories, at least occasionally, as Gibson clearly believed when he began writing fiction. Even then, however, the results were less than satisfactory; as he reports while introducing *Distrust That Particular Flavor,* his unfinished stories in the mid-1970s "somehow involved outer space," but "his wife parodied them all" (2). "The Belonging Kind" and "Hinterlands," while not without their moments, must similarly be regarded as interesting failures.

As Gibson's first published collaboration, "The Belonging Kind" also suggests that he will prove a consistently unassertive collaborator, content to allow partners to dominate the proceedings, resulting in stories that reflect their styles and interests more than Gibson's. Apparently to acknowledge this, Gibson has his name listed second for this and two other collaborative stories, even when they were republished in his own collection, *Burning Chrome.* And Gibson has revealed that all his collaborations were primarily the other author's creations. Gibson told McQuiddy in 1987 that "The Belonging Kind" came about because his friend Shirley sent him the manuscript of a "long, deadly serious piece of Kafka-esque horror," inspiring Gibson to write a "very short parody" of the piece (6). When Shirley received this response, he made a few changes and submitted it as a Shirley/Gibson collaboration.

Knowing that its plot is essentially Shirley's work, one is unsurprised to find that little about "The Belonging Kind" is congruent with priorities observed in other Gibson stories. The protagonist is all wrong: as a community-college instructor, Coletti has more formal education and enjoys a higher social status than Gibson's usual characters; he becomes obsessed with his discovery that shape-shifting aliens are living on Earth, drifting from bar to bar and subsisting on alcohol, though Gibson elsewhere displays little interest in aliens; and he is so driven to learn more about these aliens that he devotes his life to following them, causing him to lose his teaching job, while a genuine Gibson protagonist, dedicated to staying alive at all costs, would never allow such unimportant matters to interfere with earning a living. Coletti, then, is more a Shirley hero than a Gibson hero.

More broadly, the story's subject—the common science fiction trope that aliens are secretly living on Earth—surfaces only once more in Gibson's works, in the vignette "Hippie Hat Brain Parasite." Gibson values aliens solely as devices to improve our understanding of humanity; in praising the creators of *The X-Files,* he said, "They have seen that which is even now abducting us, and it is us" ("The Absolute at Large" 11), suggesting little interest in the series' literal argument that there are aliens among us. Gibson could not relate to Coletti's desire to follow, socialize with, and eventually, in a sense, become one of the aliens he discovers. Instead, a Gibson hero observing an apparent alien would shrug his shoulders and get back to his business, unless he perceived some way to make money from the phenomenon. Consider, for example, how Gibson reacts nonchalantly to such news in "Hippie Hat Brain Parasite," and how little interest Case demonstrates in *Neuromancer* when the existence of alien intelligences is confirmed. These individuals have other, more important things to worry about—namely, the alien-like humans around them. All things considered, Gibson would naturally regard Coletti, and his responses to the situation, as essentially silly—which is why he responded to Shirley's earnest story by refashioning it as what he envisioned as a humorous vignette.

If there are any signs of Gibson in "The Belonging Kind," they lie in its occasional rhetorical flourishes. One suspects that he worked hard to make the story's opening passages distinctive, perhaps hoping even in this throw-away task to impress Shirley with his skills. Referring to the bar-hopping alien woman, the story says,

> She swam through the submarine half-life of bottles and glassware and the slow swirl of cigarette smoke . . . she moved through her natural element, one bar after another.
>
> Now, Coretti remembered their first meeting as if he saw it through the wrong end of a powerful telescope, small and clear and very far away. (49)

As for "Hinterlands," Gibson clearly chose, as a model for this story, Frederik Pohl's *Gateway* (1976), a recent, award-winning novel by a veteran science fiction writer, and perhaps one book that Gibson purchased as part of his survey of mid-1970s science fiction. There are many similarities between the narratives: both involve a space station where human adventurers embark upon mysterious journeys through a sort of space warp to possibly obtain valuable evidence from alien worlds or civilizations. But in Pohl's story, people who travel in deserted alien spaceships return more or less as they were, if they do return, and when lucky enough to obtain the right sort of artifacts or data, they can become fabulously wealthy, like the protagonist, Robinette

Broadhead. Further, due to such finds, humans soon achieve major scientific advances, allowing them to contact the race that constructed the spaceships and make provocative discoveries about the nature of the universe, as recounted in sequels to *Gateway* (one of which, *Beyond the Blue Event Horizon* [1980], had already appeared when Gibson was writing "Hinterlands").

However, in Gibson's version of this story, little in the way of positive results or significant progress seems to come from similar ventures into space. Astronauts who depart from the space habitat Heaven to enter the space warp called the Highway inevitably return completely insane, compelled to commit suicide without communicating anything about what happened on their journeys. Toby Halpert and his colleague Charmian, part of Heaven's staff, struggle to keep each returning astronaut alive as long as possible, hoping that one traveler might survive long enough to provide useful information. Returned objects occasionally yield data—since no recording devices ever function—but these do not always seem valuable. Gibson says of the first astronaut's discovery, "Olga's seashell generated an entire subbranch of the science, devoted exclusively to the study of . . . Olga's seashell" (72). The statement suggests the sorts of pointless study that preoccupied scientists studying the sentient world of Stanislaw Lem's *Solaris* (1961) more than the productive research in Pohl's novel, which yields useful new technologies. True, one returned artifact is said to have proved "the Rosetta Stone for cancer" (77), but despite Tom Henthorne's claim, the story does not specify that this actually engendered "a cure for cancer" (63). Further distancing himself from Broadhead, Halpert is one of the potential astronauts who, for unknown reasons, can never travel through the Highway, so he must remain in Heaven and tend to others who make the journey. In this story, all of the people involved in space travel are literally going nowhere.

Of course, other science fiction stories had featured alien presences that remained inexplicable and unresolved, and some of these—including *Solaris,* Damon Knight's "Stranger Station" (1955), Arthur C. Clarke's novel and Stanley Kubrick's film *2001: A Space Odyssey* (1968), and James Tiptree Jr.'s "And I Awoke and Found Me Here on the Cold Hill's Side" (1972)—involved space stations. From that perspective, "Hinterlands" is another story following a science fiction tradition. Yet previous writers attempted to solve as well as pose alien mysteries in their works, while Gibson solely emphasizes "the Fear"

(82) inspired by alien encounters, suggesting a disinclination to further pursue such matters. In fact, except for the collaborative "Red Star, Winter Orbit," part of *Neuromancer* and one episode in *Count Zero*, Gibson never again sent any heroes into space.

After the uneasy diffidence of "Hinterlands," Gibson displayed renewed energy—even joy—in returning to the Sprawl with his sixth story, "Burning Chrome" (1982), which introduced his most celebrated creation: cyberspace, "the simulation matrix, the electronic consensus-hallucination" (178), where the story's central action occurs. Employing a stolen Russian program purchased from the Finn, who deals in illegal items, Bobby Quine, an expert at surreptitiously entering and exploiting cyberspace called a "cowboy," and his partner, Automatic Jack, attempt to break into and steal vast sums of money (this story's McGuffin) from the virtual headquarters of an underworld businesswoman named Chrome. Demonstrating an increasing mastery of technique, Gibson artfully intermingles the suspenseful story of their successful cyberspatial assault with flashbacks establishing the background and character of his protagonists. As is typical in his early fiction, these men are heavy users of illegal drugs, inspiring one of Gibson's most memorable statements: after explaining that he employed a mixture of "booze and Vasopressin" as "the ultimate in masochistic pharmacology" while missing an ex-girlfriend, the narrator Jack says, "Clinically, they use the stuff [Vasopressin] to counter senile amnesia, but the street finds its own uses for things" (195). Displaying Gibson's characteristic focus on failed relationships, the narrator feels briefly attached to a woman named Rikki, also Bobby's girlfriend for a while, but she leaves the men alone when the story ends.

Even while following his own innovative paths, Gibson nods to science fiction traditions: Jack periodically attaches an artificial arm called a "waldo," paying tribute to the Heinlein story "Waldo" (1942), which introduced the term. Also, Gibson at one point likens cyberspace to outer space, describing it as "nonspace where the only stars are dense concentrations of information, and high above it all burn corporate galaxies and the cold spiral arms of military systems" (178). As he later claimed to David Wallace-Wells in 2011, this analogy resulted from a conscious intent: he felt that he "lacked an arena for my science fiction" and concluded, "The spaceship didn't work for me," probably based on unhappy experiences like "Hinterlands." Observing players absorbed in video games, Gibson saw that for them, "the notional space behind all of the computer screens would be one single universe," which could become a setting for his science fiction—though he immediately acknowledged two predecessors for the idea, Ray Bradbury's "The Veldt" (1950) and Harlan Ellison's "I Have No Mouth, and I Must Scream" (1967). He told Robert Scott Martin in 1999 that he "invented cyberspace because traditional space travel as a metaphor, as it was in the books I read as a boy, wasn't doing it for me emotionally"; in the same year he described cyberspace as "my own rocket ship" to Jim McClellan; and in 2012, he told Simone Lackerbauer and R. U. Sirius that he resolved to "replace outer space with cyberspace" in order "to write SF that I could stand to write." Gibson returned to this theme more persistently in *Neuromancer*.

Gibson's seventh story, the often overlooked "Hippie Hat Brain Parasite" (1983), was surely written solely because Shirley was launching his own fanzine, *Modern Stories,* and asked his friend to contribute to its first issue. Writing solely as a personal favor, Gibson evidently put little energy into this vignette, which is nonetheless fascinating. Essentially, he borrows a character from "The Gernsback Continuum," Mervyn Kihn, and brings him into Gibson's real world by having him make a telephone call to Gibson himself. In a confusing manner suggesting an unreliable narrator, Kihn explains that he saw a suspicious-looking man in a bar, wearing a distinctive cowboy hat, whom he regards as one of many insidious *"alien fucking parasites"* (110). The proof comes when the man slumps down and "his hat fell off," revealing "[n]o brain. No top to his head. Just neatly nibbled off at the . . . hatline. Kinda scarred, in there, healed over, grayish-pink. I saw where the hat had had its claws in, kinda puppet trip" (111). Then, minimizing the importance of this revelation and further undercutting his credibility, Kihn is easily diverted into discussing another recent obsession, a conspiracy involving the Rosicrucians, Scientologists, the CIA, and the Walt Disney Company.

Though it appeared in Shirley's own magazine, "Hippie Hat Brain Parasite" invites consideration as another, more obvious parody of the Shirley story that inspired "The Belonging Kind." Both stories involve the same event: a man in a bar encounters an unusual person and sees apparent evidence of an alien presence. But the observers' reactions are quite different: whereas Coletti feels compelled to track down the alien and become part of her life, Kihn and Gibson are not particularly interested. While Kihn initially seems excited about his discovery, he is visibly more dedicated to investigating the other phenomena that brought him to Taos, New Mexico, where he observed the alien, and he returns to that topic after describing the incident. He only bothers to call Gibson because he "write[s] about stuff like that" (112) and hence would presumably be intrigued by the discovery. In fact, Gibson rarely wrote about such matters and does not care about them, since he brings the conversation to a close with two abrupt comments: "Thanks, Merv," and, "Goodnight, Merv." The final word of the story—the sound of Gibson's ending the call with an italicized "*Clik*" (112)—seemingly confirms that he is firmly dismissing the whole matter as unimportant. Thus, he announces in this story, he is a writer obsessed not with possible aliens but with other, more terrestrial concerns.

As Gibson increasingly addressed the stressful task of *Neuromancer,* he had only one other publication in 1983, a collaboration with Sterling entitled "Red Star, Winter Orbit," the most incongruous and dullest work published under Gibson's byline. One suspects that Sterling originally drafted the story as an imitation of Jerry Pournelle, intended for the hard science fiction magazine *Analog: Science Fiction/Science Fact,* before realizing that if he asked Gibson to cosign the work, he might sell it to a better market, *Omni.* Gibson might have agreed for equally cynical motives: to earn some money and keep his name in the public eye while laboring on a novel that faced an uncertain reception. Gibson confirmed such suspicions in his 1987 interview with McQuiddy, reporting, "I just took a long manuscript of Bruce's and sort of chopped it down, streamlining it a little bit" (6).

To explain why "Red Star, Winter Orbit" seems a cuckoo in Gibson's nest, one can describe it as a celebration of space as the proper home for rugged individualists escaping from a decadent Earthbound government that fails to recognize the value of space travel. Where does one detect even a hint of such themes elsewhere in Gibson's fiction? True, Gibson's heroes manifest no fondness for governments, but they adjust to governments instead of running away from them, since they also wish to remain connected to society and enjoy its latest gadgets; they would never leave their worlds behind to inhabit isolated outposts in space. Indeed, Gibson's lack of interest in the story is reflected in the fact that it involves absolutely no use of the innovative street-level technologies that are typically central to his fiction.

In addition, the story's protagonist—an aging, bitter Soviet cosmonaut, Colonel Korolev, living in a space station destined to be abandoned and allowed to fall to Earth—is a sort of person that rarely interests Gibson, whose heroes are young, active, and too busy staying alive to wallow in complaints or regrets. And while a future United States in decline is a typical Gibson background, he never elsewhere imagined the Soviet Union as the future's major superpower, generally (and more accurately) forecasting a world with multiple centers of power, mostly dominated by non-Westerners.

As the story's strange, upbeat ending, a group of independent Americans comes to the abandoned station, determined to maintain its orbit and make it their new home. One simply cannot imagine Gibson writing one American's explanation for their decision: "It was our one chance to get out here on our own. Who'd want to live out here for the sake of some government, some army brass, a bunch of pen pushers? You have to *want* a frontier—want it in your bones, right?" (109). Asked to identify the author of these words, any science fiction reader would first guess Pournelle or Ben Bova, then suggest other names, never thinking of Gibson.

What finally makes "Red Star, Winter Orbit" seem so out of place in Gibson's canon is that he apparently did not even bother to go through the piece to add flashes of the sort of evocative prose that enlivens "The Belonging Kind." There is precisely one memorable passage, when Korolev recalls his pioneering visit to Mars: "The Martian sunlight, glinting within his helmet visor, had shown him the reflection of two steady, alien eyes—fearless, yet driven—and the quiet, secret shock of it, he now realized, had been his life's most memorable, most transcendent moment" (93). This striking comment does reflect Gibson's own attitudes, as it shows a character on another world who is more impressed by what he is learning about himself than anything he is learning about Mars.

Gibson returned to the Sprawl with "New Rose Hotel" (1984), which might be said, along with *Neuromancer*, to represent the full flowering of the writing and storytelling style that made him famous. Unusually written in the second person, the story's typically rootless narrator speaks to his departed ex-girlfriend and ex-partner Sandii from the titular hotel where he is staying. He and his longtime colleague Fox specialized in "the skull wars" (110), persuading groundbreaking scientists to defect from employers to rival zaibatsus, or multinational corporations. One of these, Hosaka, hires Fox and the narrator to obtain the scientist Hiroshi from another company, Maas. They recruit the beautiful Sandii to seduce him into agreeing to the switch, and she apparently succeeds, but when Sandii vanishes after the operation is completed, they realize that they were double-crossed: secretly working for Maas, Sandii employed an unknowing Hiroshi to transport a specially prepared "DNA synthesizer" (123) that kills or maddens Hosaka's top scientists. Believing that the men were involved in the scheme, Hosaka's agents murder Fox and, at the end of the story, are pursuing the narrator, who still longs for Sandii despite her betrayal.

Here, presented in the dense, brisk manner that Gibson had earlier mastered in "Fragments of a Hologram Rose," are elements that would emerge as his hallmarks: a streetwise loner, unable to sustain a relationship, who struggles to survive in a murky borderland between the law and lawlessness in a near-future world controlled by multinational corporations; an economy in which information and know-how are valued more than material goods; and an environment where all players, always looking out for their own interests, can never be fully trusted. While not unrelated to a few futures in previous science fiction, Gibson stories like these synthesized old and new tropes in a distinctive manner, justifying the intense critical interest his works would attract.

Like all his best works, "New Rose Hotel" teems with distinctive prose, like the narrator's comment on Sandii's ability to constantly reinvent herself: "[Y]ou rolled against me, waking, on your breath all the electric night of a new Asia, the future rising in you like a bright fluid, washing me of everything but the moment. That was your magic, that you lived outside of history, all now" (118). But Gibson also finds poetry in the detritus of a technological age, as in a memorable list of the items Sandii left behind: "A freezer. A fermenter. An incubator. An electrophoresis system with integrated agarose cell and transilluminator. A tissue embedder. A high-performance liquid chromotograph. A flow cytometer. A spectrophotometer. Four gross of borosilicate scintillation vials. A microcentrifuge. And one DNA synthesizer, with in-built computer. Plus software" (113). This passage epitomizes much about Gibson's prose style: the desire for "hyperspecificity" he repeatedly cites in interviews as one priority in his science fiction; a willingness to interrupt narratives with lengthy catalogs of items; and a belief that people's identities can be understood by studying the objects that they cherish. Here, the abandoned gadgets communicate that Sandii was far more intelligent and capable than Fox and his partner had imagined. There is even a glimmer of Gibson's later intent to help readers better understand their own present-day world; for while one might imagine that he is coining complicated neologisms to suggest strange futuristic technologies, every word and device in this list already existed in 1984, though few people, then and now, were aware of them.

As for subjects more frequently found in science fiction, one of these briefly surfaces in "New Rose Hotel" in a fashion demonstrating that Gibson, like his characters, finds his own uses for things. Fox attempts to explain the nature of contemporary society to his partner:

> Imagine an alien, Fox once said, who's come here to identify the planet's dominant form of intelligence. The alien has a look, then chooses. What do you think he picks? I probably shrugged.
>
> The zaibatsus, Fox said, the multinationals. The blood of a zaibatsu is information, not people. The structure is independent of the individual lives that comprise it. Corporation as life form. (115)

The perspective of an alien visitor to Earth—often the center of attention in science fiction—is introduced hypothetically, solely to make a point about Earth, recalling how the astronaut of "Red Star, Winter Orbit" appreciated his Martian visit primarily because it helped him understand himself better. Aliens, for Gibson, are primarily useful as posited devices to illuminate human nature, which is invariably his preoccupation.

After *Neuromancer*'s success, Gibson had little incentive to write stories, and though he still produced scattered vignettes and oddities, he effectively concluded his career in short fiction with two works published in 1985, both likely begun before *Neuromancer* was published. "Dogfight," officially co-written with Michael Swanwick, at first seems more like Gibson's work than other collaborations, but Swanwick is a protean writer, capable of writing in many different styles, who had the ability to mimic Gibson's style. Thus, one could theorize that the seemingly Gibsonian elements of "Dogfight" were only the work of Swanwick channeling Gibson. That this is another story primarily produced by his collaborator is again confirmed by Gibson: as he told McQuiddy in 1987, after drunkenly telling editor Gardner Dozois about a dream he had involving people and little airplanes, Dozois relayed the information to Swanwick, who built a story out of Gibson's dream and sent the results to Gibson for his approval.

Deke seems like a typical Gibson protagonist in some respects: he has ventured onto the wrong side of the law (as a convicted shoplifter); he is a drifter and loner; he masters a form of virtual reality—a game involving projections of World War I fighter planes called "Spads & Fokkers"; and he proves unable to sustain a romantic relationship. However, like Coletti in "The Belonging Kind," Deke allows himself to become obsessed with something unimportant, a computer game, whereas true Gibson protagonists are too savvy to get caught up in unproductive business. Also, while they often engage in underhanded behavior, Gibson's heroes follow their own internal moral code, especially in dealing with women (like *Neuromancer*'s Case, who gives money to his ex-girlfriend Linda Lee and rescues Molly despite the risk to his own life), allowing them to remain sympathetic. As Gibson told Mikel Gilmore in 1986, "I tend to side with the ones who somehow manage to retain a degree of humanity," though he is "sometimes [. . .] intrigued by the ones who don't" (78). A Gibson character would never do what Deke does—seize his girlfriend's drug, which she desperately needs for an important interview, solely to win an upcoming game—which makes readers dislike him and diminishes the story's impact.

Another appealing trait of Gibson's characters—that they deal with problematic situations stoically, without complaining—is not displayed by Deke, whose reaction upon realizing that no one will join in celebrating his victory reeks of self-pity:

> Nobody crowded around to congratulate him. He sobered, and silent, hostile faces swam into focus. Not one of these kickers was on his side. They radiated contempt, even hatred. [. . .] He needed to celebrate. To get drunk or stoned and talk it up, going over the victory time and again, contradicting himself, making up details, laughing and bragging. [. . .] But standing there with all of Jackman's silent and vast and empty around him, he realized suddenly that he had nobody left to tell it to.
> Nobody at all. (174–75)

A Gibson hero who finds himself alone may not be happy, but he silently accepts his solitude and carries on with daily routines; if no one celebrates something he did, he does not feel upset or rebuked.

As for Gibson's own feelings about the story, he described how uncharacteristic it was more circumspectly, telling McQuiddy, "That story is moralistic in a way I'm uncomfortable with" and is "much more misanthropic than my own stuff" (6). Indeed, Gibson tends to like his own wayward characters, not being "misanthropic" at all, and does not want to see them punished for occasional misdeeds, the consequence of a "moralistic" stance. But the most telling aspect of Gibson's statement is that he contrasts "Dogfight" with "my own stuff," indicating he does not regard it as his own work.

Gibson's final story of this period, "The Winter Market" (1985), was commissioned for *Vancouver* magazine with the condition that its setting be his hometown Vancouver (a locale Gibson otherwise avoided until *Spook Country*). A triumphant conclusion to this phase of his career, the story is filled with tropes and issues he would continue exploring in novels, including virtual reality, the nature of identity, and the interface of advanced technology and streetwise operatives. The protagonist Casey (a name recalling *Neuromancer*'s Case and anticipating *Pattern Recognition*'s Cayce, perhaps signaling a character of special importance to Gibson) specializes in the art of downloading distinctive personalities into computers to be marketed to customers eager for vicarious experiences. Through a dealer in random technological merchandise named Rubin, he encounters Lise, whose deformed body requires an exoskeleton, and upon accessing her brain finds vivid, bitter images that he records, because they will prove attractive to young buyers. As Rubin explains, "Those kids back down the Market, warming their butts around the fires and wondering if they'll find someplace to sleep tonight, they believe it. It's the hottest soft in eight years. [. . .] She's big because she was what they are, only more so. She knew, man. No dreams, no hope. You can't see the cages on those kids, Casey, but more and more they're twigging to it, that they aren't going anywhere" (142). Despite the money she makes for herself and Casey, the unhappy Lise commits suicide, though her virtual self lives on, and Casey dreads the day when that construct calls and he will not know, as he asks Rubin, "is it *her*?" Rubin can only respond, "God only knows" (149).

However, the recurring question of whether computerized simulations of people can be considered real is only one of the many issues percolating through this story. Previous science fiction about people purchasing other people's memories—including Philip K. Dick's "We Can Remember It for

You Wholesale" (1966) and Gibson's "Fragment of a Hologram Rose"—involved pleasant experiences. "The Winter Market," as indicated by its title, suggests that dissatisfied people might be equally attracted to provocatively miserable visions. Also, to describe the eclectic items in Rubin's shop, Gibson characteristically looks both backward and forward: "Rubin [. . .] is a master, a teacher, what the Japanese call a *sensei*. What he's the master of, really, is garbage, kipple, refuse, the sea of cast-off goods our century floats on. *Gomi no sensei*. Master of junk" (127). Paying homage to an important predecessor, Gibson uses the term "kipple," introduced and defined as "useless objects" in Dick's *Do Androids Dream of Electric Sheep?* (1968) (65)—a novel that ponders in other ways whether imitations of humans can be considered human. Yet he otherwise employs a new term, taken from Japanese, "gomi." While not as prominent as "cyberspace," this word, never before applied to this particular sort of refuse, represents another Gibson neologism. Finally, expanding upon the insight of "the street finds its uses for things," Rubin explains precisely how certain kinds of people can adapt new technologies for unexpected purposes: "You know what your trouble is? [. . .] You're the kind who *always reads the handbook*. Anything people build, any kind of technology, it's going to have some specific purpose. It's for doing something that somebody already understands. But if it's new technology, it'll open areas nobody's ever thought of before. You read the manual, man, and you won't play around with it, not the same way" (137). Throughout his career, Gibson will always be interested in how creative, sometimes desperate, denizens of the street "play around with" new technology to obtain an edge in their dealings.

Now a popular novelist, Gibson essentially abandoned short fiction; when he was asked why, a January 17, 2003, blog entry gnomically and characteristically cited both artistic and practical reasons:

WHY I DON'T WRITE SHORT STORIES
Good ones are to novels as bonsai are to trees.
Might as well go ahead and grow the tree.
It's easier to pay the rent with trees.

During the 1990s, however, he published six increasingly bizarre vignettes, usually in response to specific assignments, which allowed Gibson to indulge in more experimental forms of writing outside the confines of commercially successful novels.

"Doing Television" (1990), slightly expanded and republished as "Darwin," vividly but unadventurously revisits several Gibson tropes. An eight-year-old girl, Kelsey, endures a vagabond existence as her single mother, working for one of the multinational corporations dominating the future, takes her and her brother from place to place as her job demands. Currently in Southern California, they are awaiting a move to the "Darwin Free Trade Zone" in Australia. Her brother irritates Kelsey by constantly "doing television," or immersing himself in virtual worlds; he plays a violent game called "Gladiator Skull," while Kelsey prefers a gentler experience called "Natureland." As Kelsey visits a virtual Australian mall to hear a "Chinese announcer" with a "broad Australian accent," recalls her more pleasant life in Moscow, and anticipates moving to Australia, she embodies the restless, globalized world Gibson long anticipated, and when she remembers learning from her departed father that she was born to a surrogate mother, she represents the ways technology can challenge traditional notions of parenthood and identity. Perhaps the story's second title, referencing both the city of Darwin and Charles Darwin, was intended to convey that her experiences represent a new stage in human evolution. Overall, while "Doing Television" / "Darwin" is artfully done, there is nothing here that Gibson's readers had not seen before. The story's only noteworthy aspect is that, in the narrator's criticism of her brother's fondness for video games, one finds more evidence that, in contrast to the hero of "Dogfight," Gibson is not interested in playing games.

If "Doing Television" / "Darwin" represented Gibson mechanically revisiting his artistic past, "Skinner's Room" (1990) proved the gateway to his artistic future, because the assignment he confronted—to describe a future San Francisco—inspired the creation of the Bridge, the memorable setting of his next novel. In the story, Gibson envisions a Bay Bridge abandoned because of an economic crisis—a "devaluation" of some sort—though *Virtual Light* reports that it was closed to vehicular traffic after an earthquake rendered it potentially dangerous. On one memorable evening, hordes of homeless people on both sides of the bridge resolve to seize this unclaimed property, tearing down the fences around it and constructing makeshift habitations on, above, and below its surface. The result is effectively an American Mumbai—a crowded metropolis of desperately poor people inhabiting their own improvised spaces and struggling to survive any way they can. As it is memorably described in the story,

> The bridge's bones, its stranded tendons, are lost within an accretion of dreams: tattoo parlors, shooting galleries, pinball arcades, dimly lit stalls stacked with damp-stained years of men's magazines, chili joints, premises of unlicensed denturists, fireworks stalls, cut bait sellers, betting shops, sushi counters, pawnbrokers, wonton counters, love hotels, hot dog stands, a tortilla factory, Chinese greengrocers, liquor stores, herbalists, chiropractors, barbers, tackle shops, and bars.
>
> These are dreams of commerce, their locations generally corresponding with the decks originally intended for vehicular traffic. Above them, toward the peaks of the cable towers, lift intricate barrios, zones of more private fantasy, sheltering an unnumbered population, of uncertain means and obscure occupation. (159)

There is some poetry in the introductory references to the Bridge's "bones" and "tendons"; but by proceeding to meticulously list all the various businesses found on the Bridge, Gibson conveys the energy and diversity of its inhabitants more effectively than the series of adjectives that another writer might employ. As Gibson grew bored with cyberspace and virtual worlds, this represented precisely the sort of tangible, vibrant environment he would increasingly explore in his fiction.

Primarily attentive to describing, and relating the history of, this memorable new setting, Gibson provides little in the way of a narrative: a young woman (named Chevette Washington and given a job in *Virtual Light*) follows some people to a hotel party before returning to her Bridge home, a room she shares with the elderly Skinner in exchange for helping him with daily life. She later has a cup of coffee with one of the Bridge's entrepreneurs, Maria Paz (who reappears, differently characterized, in *Virtual Light*). As one of the first people who occupied the Bridge, Skinner can recall that experience and others, in both conversations and dreams, though his memories at times are fading, and his inability to leave his room requires Gibson to focus his novel on the more active female protagonist. Overall, while only a little of its language found its way into *Virtual Light*, "Skinner's Room" seems best considered as an introduction to that novel, not a standalone story. (Perhaps "Doing Television" / "Darwin," published around the same time, was also a sketch for a future novel, rejected in favor of "Skinner's Room.")

"Academy Leader" (1991), written for Michael Benedikt's critical anthology *Cyberspace: First Steps,* might be classified as an essay with fictional elements, a story, even a prose poem—but its title (referring to the numerical "count-down" footage that precedes most films to aid projectionists) and position in the volume suggest that it is best viewed as an introduction, Gibson striving in an innovative manner to set the stage for the book's far-ranging speculations. Implied by its title, this is made explicit in the final sentence: "The targeted numerals of the ACADEMY LEADER were hypnogogic sigils preceding the dreamstate of film." As Gibson noted in an April 7, 2010, blog entry, that sentence was lifted from the first sentence of the first story he ever attempted to write, and the piece's opening passage—which, Gibson told Mike Rogers in 1993, was "the only bit that I think I actually custom-wrote"—pays tribute to the man who pioneered the "cut-up" technique employed in the story, describing Burroughs as "this dangerous old literary gentleman who sent so many of us out, under sealed orders, years ago," and mentioning a character from *Nova Express*: "Inspector Lee taught a new angle" (27). While the piece mostly assembles passages from Gibson's own writing, phrases from other writers also appear (like "islands in the stream," from Hemingway).

To the extent that the piece has a clear narrative, it seems a sequel to "Doing Television" / "Darwin," wherein Kelsey, her mother, and brother, perhaps accompanied by Gibson himself, finally reach the Darwin Free Trade Zone. Kelsey purchases a disk from a street vendor, which provides a virtual copy of the city of Kyoto, and disturbs her mother when she responds to the data by saying, "I want to go there," again showing the powerful allure of artificial experiences (29).

What may most interest Gibson scholars is the passage wherein he describes, or reinvents, how he developed the concept of cyberspace, in a passage that borrows from "Doing Television / Darwin," "Skinner's Room," and his 1989 essay "Rocket Radio":

> Assembled word cyberspace from small and readily available components of language. Neologic spasm: the primal act of pop poetics. Preceded any concept whatever. Slick and hollow—awaiting received meaning. All I did: folded words as taught. Now other words accrete in the interstices. "Gentlemen, that is not now nor will it ever be my concern. . . ." Not what I do. I work the angle of transit. Vectors of

neon plaza, licensed consumers, acts primal and undreamed of. . . . The architecture of virtual reality imagined as an accretion of dreams. [. . .] These are dreams of commerce. Above them rise intricate barrios, zones of more private fantasy. (28)

Two intriguing aspects of the passage are that Gibson attributes the coinage of "cyberspace" to Burroughs's influence ("All I did: folded words as taught") and links this imagined realm to his earlier description of the Bridge's "dreams of commerce," emphasizing in this context that Gibson always focuses on practical aspects of his predictions.

"Cyber-Claus" (1991) was commissioned by *The Washington Post,* which asked four writers to "retell the story" of Clement Moore's "A Visit from Saint Nicholas" (1823) "in their own inimitable styles" (14). Certainly, the piece can be dismissed as a frivolous vignette, transplanting an iconic holiday event—Santa Claus visiting a man's house—into the darker future of cyberpunk, with new forms of technology detecting and monitoring the intruder. Yet interestingly, especially considering when it was written, it seems a sign that, by this time, Gibson had tired of the stories that established his reputation and was ready to engage in playful self-parody. Critics might justify their neglect of this story by maintaining that it is too inconsequential to merit attention, but they may also feel discomfited to find Gibson refusing to take the world of cyberpunk as seriously as they do. For in its own frivolous way, the piece seems to undermine all of their earnest arguments.

The opening passage is a deliberately overwritten version of the situation initially confronting Moore's narrator: "In the night of 12/24/07, though sensors woven through the very fabric of the house had thus far registered a complete absence of sentient bio-activity, I found myself abruptly summoned from a rare, genuine, and expensively induced example of that most price-less of states, sleep" (14). Naturally enough, a sentient computer program, Memory, alerts him to potential home invaders on his roof, first describing them as "[s]eventeen, assuming we're talking bipeds" (14), before refining her analysis to say, "that stuff's registering, like, hooves. Tiny ones. Unless this is some kind of major Jersey Devil infestation, I make it eight quadrupeds—plus one definite biped." Fearing hostile visitors, the narrator "holstered a 3mm Honda and pocketed half a dozen spare ampules of gel," while Memory warns, at the piece's close, "I think he's coming down the chimney . . ." (15).

The passage most strongly suggesting an author making fun of himself comes when he speculates about the visitor's identity: "Was it my estranged wife, Lady Betty-Jayne Motel-6 Hyatt, Chief Eco-Trustee of the Free Duchy of Wyoming? Or was it Cleatus 'Mainframe' Sinyard himself, President of the United States and Perpetual Chairman of the Concerned Smart People's Northern Hemisphere CoProsperity Sphere?" These are precisely the sorts of odd names for people and places that Gibson had sprinkled throughout his fiction, here taken a little too far for satiric purposes. And since so many commentators note Gibson's concern for appearances, it is fitting that, during this potential crisis, Memory troubles to warn the narrator, "[Y]ou're on the verge of a major fashion crime," inspiring him to change the shirt and pants he threw on when awakened (15).

In 1993, Gibson wrote "Where the Holograms Go" for *The Wild Palms Reader,* a compilation of literary responses to Oliver Stone's miniseries *Wild Palms* (which also featured a cameo appearance by Gibson). The book's back cover identifies his contribution as "song lyrics." Although the piece is introduced in this fashion—

Chap Starfall

Sings

Chickie's Song

—it otherwise takes the form of prose, or prose poem, including only two actual lines from Chickie's "song": "Leave this place. Leave it. / Drive a long, long way" (122). While it is said to represent what was sung by a minor character in the miniseries, the lounge singer Chap Starfall, "Where the Holograms Go" describes the dying moments of another character, Chickie Levitt, a computer genius who constructs virtual worlds. While "paralyzed," he enjoys a virtual ride through Los Angeles, "as his gray wheels carry him deeper into lines of an increasingly pure geometry. Between virtual planes grown abruptly abstract, playroom planes of shadow-play, walls of Pure Television. And every pixel is a life. A soul. A moment in the dance" (122).

What gives the piece emotional impact is a striking image of impending death, adapted from the experience of watching television and recalling the opening of *Neuromancer*: "At this point, forever (it must seem) receding, where the planes converge, there is something bright. It is the color of that single terrifying phosphor dot recalled from the age of black and white TV. That dot the images *fell into* when the set was turned off. That very dot that lingered, sentient and utterly radioactive, in the dark" (122). This metaphor for dying is invoked again in the powerful concluding paragraph, apparently relating his approaching death: "Chickie blinks, gives his left-hand wheel a last, major shove, bounces off the curb, and plunges toward Santa Monica Boulevard, the Dot growing and just growing, the closer he gets" (122).

Overall, while "Where the Holograms Go" contains memorable passages, the piece, more so than other commissioned vignettes, is incomprehensible without some knowledge of *Wild Palms,* which was unpopular when it aired and is now forgotten. Readers need to know that "the Senator" is Senator Tony Kreutzer, a former science fiction writer now involved in a sinister scheme to promulgate a form of virtual reality, and references to "the chip," the Senator's inability to "GO," and Chickie's ability to "GO" involve the miniseries' McGuffin, the "Go-chip" that allows people to enter a virtual world. When republished, the piece will require either an introductory explanation or footnotes.

Finally, in 1997, Gibson published "Thirteen Views of a Cardboard City," which seemingly embodies the aspiration, expressed in a 1995 interview with Rogier van Bakel and Robert Longo, "to write books that don't need verbs. Just large collections of nouns and modifiers would work for me. [Laughs.] The ongoing descriptions of things is where the pleasure is in writing" (206). It also supports his 2007 observation to Christine Cornea that "in my fiction [. . .] some of the most memorable, central characters are environments rather than people" (27). For the piece, its title if not contents suggested by Wallace Stevens's 1917 poem "Thirteen Ways of Looking at a Blackbird," is little more than a description of a memorable environment—Tokyo's assemblage of cardboard boxes used as houses, soon revisited in *All Tomorrow's Parties*—which often dispenses with verbs. It also lacks any sort of narrative, underlining Gibson's implicit point that the construction of plots, unlike the "pleasure" of "descriptions," is a chore, one he could avoid in a throwaway piece that was not crafted to appeal to a large audience. Though "Thirteen Views" is evocative, it seems hard to justify its appearance in a science fiction anthology, though its detached, clinical tone, reminiscent of Ballard, arguably provides a science-fictional perspective on a mundane subject.

The piece also conveys two of Gibson's recurring fascinations, art and brand names. Murals and other decorations adorning the boxes are likened to the works of the artists Diego Rivera (340), Paul Klee, Piet Mondrian (341), and Pablo Picasso (342), and there are references to "New England folk art" (340) and "Oxfam Cubism" (342). The boxes and artifacts feature a variety of brand names, including Microsoft (339), Nike, Reebok (343), Casio (347, 348), Brother (348), and Lucky Strike (348). There is also a fleeting bit of autobiography, as Gibson likens "[a] space" to "the upper berths on the Norfolk & Western sleeping cars my mother and I took when I was a child" (343). As also evidenced by "Agrippa," Gibson can always produce haunting descriptions, but shrewdly realizing that it is more profitable to tell involving stories, he rarely bothers to do so.

After writing no short fiction for over a decade, Gibson unexpectedly published a new story, "Dougal Discarnate," in 2010. It represents a major departure in other ways, since the story is both his first work of fantasy and an exploration of a new theme more characteristic of aging authors than the eternal adolescent that Gibson long seemed to embody. For "Dougal Discarnate" apparently finds Gibson looking back to his past and pondering roads not taken.

As in "Hippie Hat Brain Parasite," the story's protagonist and narrator is Gibson himself, which is established by references to his own career. He first describes how he met, in the "early eighties" (231), a sort of ghost named Dougal, a man who somehow, after taking massive amounts of drugs in 1972, become "discarnate," disconnected from his body. While his now soulless body became an accountant, the ethereal Dougal finds himself able to roam solely within a limited area of Vancouver, which Gibson relates to his long-standing interest, "psychogeography," while Dougal speaks more mystically of "ley lines" (232). Fitfully able to interact with the physical world, he starts spending time with Gibson, and they "bonded in large part, around cheesy science fiction movies" (236). Eventually, the companions drift apart, as Dougal discovers that he can get "high" by placing his head in a television's cathode-ray tube, while Gibson "had started not getting high, myself, some time before" (238). But Dougal finds happiness by meeting a Japanese woman from Okinawa, a "shaman" (240) who adopts him as "her familiar" (241) and sexual companion and liberates his spirit so the couple can travel around the world.

Clearly, Dougal invites consideration as an incarnation of two of Gibson's possible futures: he might have carried on as an idle, drug-using hippie, accomplishing nothing but perhaps achieving happiness by settling into a vagabond existence with a kindred spirit. Alternatively, he might have been driven by financial necessity into a boring career like accountancy, working competently and earning a good income but abandoning his dreams and personal freedom. (Reflecting similar fears that something like this might have occurred, Gibson told Jack Womack in 1997, "I have mildly creepy intimations that I might have not done all that badly in advertising" [54].) By becoming a writer, one might say, Gibson achieved a balance between the extremes of Dougal's two lives, as he does what he wants to do and expresses himself while holding a profitable steady job. But since Dougal is described as Gibson's longtime friend, he may also represent one or more of the people Gibson socialized with in the 1970s, who either held on to their hippie lifestyles or settled into dull day jobs, becoming people Gibson could no longer relate to.

"Dougal Discarnate" is also interesting because it offers additional fragments of autobiography. The story's Gibson "explained my theory that the best cinematic SF is almost always to be found in very bad films, but only in tiny, brilliant, fractal bursts" (236–37), and he attributes much of his early fiction to his brief sojourn in New York City, noting, "Somehow I carried some of that home with me. [. . .] And dipped into it as needed. In kits. Building what I was always somewhat annoyed, later, to see described as dystopian fiction" (238). Thus, while "Dougal Discarnate" has the aura of something written quickly and casually, it suggests that Gibson might enjoy writing a fictionalized autobiography, intermingling reality and fantasy to enliven the tedium of remembering and reporting.

In 2012, Gibson published another work of short fiction—of sorts. Responding along with other writers to two editors' challenge to write vignettes about random used objects they had purchased, Gibson chose as his inspiration an ashtray showing an obsolete missile system, the "'Hawk' Ashtray." The piece begins with a discussion of what the father of the narrator's friend, "a Pentagon technocrat" ([41]), had said about new weapons systems: that the most appealing of these were distinguished by the fact that men involved would begin wearing "tie-tacks" showing the new technology. The titular ashtray is then an afterthought, something made "further along the Hawk missile system's developmental span" ([41]), and less interesting because it is not "liminal" like the tie-tacks, which signal a system that is still emergent. While not greatly interesting, the passage, which reads like a conversational interlude from *Spook Country* or *Zero History,* is another reflection of Gibson's recent interest in the relationship between fashion and the military, and it concludes with a nice description of one of these tie-tacks as "[a] fossil from a future that you knew might not even happen. Dashing, enigmatic, unworn. Not yet tangled in the darkness of history's dad box, with the dead boys and the lost stupid war they died in" ([41]).

Although several Gibson stories merit attention, one struggles to argue that he is a natural short-story writer who was unhappily pressured into writing novels by a marketplace that makes such products more profitable than short fiction. In contrast, Gibson might be better regarded as a natural novelist who blossomed only when prodded to abandon short fiction and write novels instead. For while both forms inspire evocative prose, novels either force or allow Gibson to produce fully developed characters, in contrast to his stories' typical focus on descriptions animated by a narrative. Novels further enable Gibson to more fully explore provocative themes and possibilities only hinted at in stories. Finally, if he does long to write something shorter, Gibson's approach to writing novels offers a way to develop story ideas as digressions or minor characters within a novel. In sum, while Gibson might have achieved consistent success and acclaim by sticking to short fiction, like Harlan Ellison, his novels made him a leading science fiction writer.

CHAPTER 4

LEGENDS OF THE SPRAWL
Neuromancer, Count Zero, and *Mona Lisa Overdrive*

Since numerous scholars have analyzed *Neuromancer* at length, anyone discussing the novel faces the daunting task of Making It New. To achieve that goal, one might momentarily ignore the after-the-fact commentaries on the novel and envision *Neuromancer* as Gibson first saw it: an enormous challenge undertaken solely due to Terry Carr's substantial advance, a piece of writing much longer than his previous stories, and a task he did not feel ready for (as he has repeatedly testified). Indeed, just as one sees through the protagonist Case's aura of bravado to sense an insecure person beneath, one discerns within the seemingly assured *Neuromancer* a literally terrified author, with uncertainty radiating from every page. (As he told Colin Greenland in 1986, the novel was "fuelled by a terrible fear of losing the reader's attention. Sheer hysteria" [8].) It is ironic, then, that critics regularly regard the novel as Gibson's confident manifesto regarding our postmodern world.

As is always his inclination, Gibson moved into new territory cautiously, employing a familiar setting—his Sprawl—while essentially combining the plots of two earlier stories. As in "Johnny Mnemonic," Case (his full name, Henry Dorsett Case, appears only once in the novel [159]) would undertake a physical journey through a threatening underworld to obtain crucial information; as in "Burning Chrome," he would also travel through cyberspace to hack into a protected database. Those stories' heroes, Johnny and Bobby Quine, would be mentioned, and a supporting character from each story— Molly and the Finn—would play important roles in the narrative.

However, to sustain a novel, Gibson would need more characters and a more complex, multistage plot. The computer cowboy Case would be recruited by a mysterious figure named Armitage, who previously hired Molly; the trio would travel to Switzerland, then Turkey, to collect two more team members: a computer simulation of the dead hacker McCoy Pauley, the Dixie Flatline, and the hologram-projecting con man Peter Riviera. Together, they would fulfill Armitage's assignment by means of simultaneous incursions in the real world and cyberspace.

Drawing upon science fiction traditions, Gibson introduced two significant novelties in what otherwise seemed one of his typical plots. First, particularly in novels, science fiction had long been distinguished by Big Ideas, so Gibson provided his novel with a very cosmic McGuffin: Case, motivated by goals grander than making money or saving his life, would have the assigned agenda of forging a true artificial intelligence by merging two computer entities, Wintermute and Neuromancer. To justify everyone's presence, this operation would require: the management of Armitage—actually, Wintermute's agent; Case and the Dixie Flatline's expertise to overcome barriers in cyberspace; and Molly's muscle and Riviera's charm to penetrate the residence of 3Jane, who must be persuaded to provide a necessary password. When team members succeed, despite Riviera's attempted double-cross, they create a new being that does not simply inhabit cyberspace but becomes it—"I'm the matrix," it tells Case as the novel ends (269)—while contacting another artificial intelligence in the Alpha Centauri system and searching for "others" it knows must exist (270). Creating artificial intelligence and encountering alien life were themes, Gibson knew, that science fiction readers could relate to and appreciate.

Oddly, neither Case nor Gibson seems particularly interested in these matters. When Molly discovers that Case is not "fascinated" with artificial intelligence, she concludes, "Jockeys all the same. . . . No imagination" (95), and upon receiving the combined Wintermute/Neuromancer's final revelations about its identity and accomplishments, Case's flip response is, "No shit?" (270); he never asks for additional information, and Gibson never provides it. Indeed, when asked in 1992 about the possibility of artificial intelligence, Gibson gave a noncommittal response with the revelatory comment, "I'm curiously unconcerned with scientific possibility" ("The Charisma Leak" 7). While George Slusser argues, in a *Fiction 2000* essay, that *Neuromancer* provocatively confronts science fiction's "Frankenstein barrier" that problematizes efforts to envision genuine posthumanity (48), it is hard to maintain that this issue torments Gibson or his characters. After *Neuromancer's* success, a more confident Gibson would feel less need to embellish his novels with such overarching concepts, focusing instead on protagonists' day-to-day business.

While incorporating, however offhandedly, these common themes, Gibson honored tradition in another way by having much of the novel's action occur in outer space, the environment frequently featured in science fiction. But this time, Gibson would refashion space in his own image: unlike the conventional space stations of "Hinterlands" and "Red Star, Winter Orbit," *Neuromancer's* Freeside space habitat would be a miniature Sprawl, with its own shadow society of slackers and criminals inhabiting seedy nightclubs and dark corridors. Typical aspects of space environments like spaceships, spacesuits, and zero gravity would surface only briefly and tangentially. Further, while previous space stations were predominantly staffed by white Americans, the globally minded Gibson prominently features some Jamaican Rastafarians who smoke marijuana and project unusual calm regarding the hazards of life in a vacuum. This Gibsonian take on space is announced by Molly, who describes Freeside as "just a big tube and they pour things through it. . . . Tourists, hustlers, anything" (124). Later, Case—and Gibson—confirm that it is a place where they feel at home: "Freeside suddenly made sense to him. Biz. He could feel it humming in the air. This was it, the local action. Not the high-gloss facade of the Rue Jules Verne, but the real thing. Commerce. The dance" (145).

While this Sprawl-like space proved a successful creation, it might seem to Gibson, in retrospect, strange and unnecessary: why send characters into orbit only to place them into a world that is so similar to the terrestrial environments he had crafted? Space travel, we learn, "never appealed to" Case (77), and both he and Gibson in a sense respond to space like the wealthy family that constructed the space habitat: "Tessier and Ashpool climbed the well of gravity to discover that they loathed space" (173). Their reaction was to build a space home with "no sky" and fixtures imported from Earth, a "universe of self" that bears no resemblance to other space habitations (173). But one might ask: why did they go to all that trouble, when the space-loathing family could have simply returned to Earth? Following such logic, Gibson restricted later Sprawl novels to Earth, with only one brief space journey in *Count Zero*.

Gibson also fills *Neuromancer* with astronomical imagery that references Case's actual and virtual experiences, reinforcing the theme (introduced in "Burning Chrome") that his characters prefer their own version of space. A posited map illustrating "data exchange" is "about to go nova" while it covers the Sprawl (43); when Case first reenters cyberspace, he sees "silver phosphenes boiling in from the edge of space" (52); events in cyberspace are preceded by countdowns, like space launches (55); it is said that "[f]ads swept the youth of the Sprawl at the speed of light" (58); a vista of abandoned factories is a "blasted industrial moonscape" (85); when having sex while working as a "puppet," Molly tells Case, an orgasm is "like a little nova right out on the rim of space" (148); and the elusive border of an illusory beach within cyberspace is its "[e]vent horizon" (243).

For one more element in a successful novel, Gibson recognized that, in contrast to his minimally characterized protagonists in stories, *Neuromancer*'s hero would have to be a full-bodied character whom readers could sympathize with. In this area, Gibson plays a cunning game. Early descriptions of Case are unfailingly negative. He is "[j]ust another hustler" (7) in Japan's seedy Chiba City, not particularly important: "[N]either the buyer nor the seller really needed him" (11). He is repeatedly depicted as suicidal: Case sees himself "play[ing] a game," a "final solitaire" as part of "the arc of his self-destruction" (7), and tells himself, "Towns like [Chiba City] are for people who like the way down" (23). Later, referring to Armitage's "profile" of Case,

Molly says, "[Y]ou're trying to con the street into killing you when you're not looking. . . . You're suicidal, Case" (28–29). Similar comments appear later in the novel: Molly speculates, "Maybe you hate yourself, Case" (149), and the voice of an illusory Ratz comments on "the lengths [Case] will go to in order to accomplish [his] own destruction" (234).

However, when Molly tells Case, "I know how you're wired," he sharply responds, "You don't know me, sister" (31), and subsequent events prove that he is right. For this supposedly suicidal person, upon glimpsing Molly following him and learning that someone wants to kill him, quickly seeks to buy a gun, and when he cannot get one immediately, he purchases another lethal weapon, a "cobra" (15), to protect himself until he obtains a better weapon. To escape from the presumed assassin Molly, Case improvises a desperate plan, rushing into a building he is familiar with, entering a second-story room, breaking a window, and jumping out the window to get away. He even finds that he is "enjoying" the process of staying alive, likening it to the "run in the matrix" he can no longer enjoy (16). In sum, despite all the naysaying from himself and others, Case consistently demonstrates an attractive, fierce desire to stay alive at all costs; he is definitely one of the Gibson characters that, in Lance Olsen's words, "evince a powerful urge for survival" (27).

One also notes that, early in the story, Case shows that he is a nice guy by giving Linda Lee fifty dollars, though he desperately needs money to pay back a debt and, he believes, avoid assassination. Later, Case again displays his fine qualities when, upon hearing that Molly is in trouble, he announces that he will not do anything about it—"I'm stayin' right here" (192)—then proceeds to join the risky rescue mission anyway. Not a word in the novel testifies to Case's obvious kindness and generosity, but his deeds demonstrate that Case may be called a jerk, and may talk like a jerk, but he acts like Sir Galahad, aligning him with a long tradition of stalwart, brilliant science fiction heroes that can be traced back to Hugo Gernsback's *Ralph 124C 41+* (1911–12, 1925), as I argued in a *Fiction 2000* essay.

What is going on here? If Case were described honestly, as a driven survivor following his own moral code, he might seem boring and conventional, not very cool at all; depicted instead as a self-destructive hustler solely looking out for number one, he seems a sophisticated antihero, though somebody actually like that would alienate readers. Thus, one can characterize the mistake made by Swanwick in "Dogfight," and other imitators of Gibson, in this fashion: they are fooled into creating heroes who match Gibson's descriptions of his heroes, not the heroes themselves.

As if to further undermine the notion that Case is savvy and cynical, Gibson offers scattered references to other literary characters who are appealingly childlike, suggesting that Case is the same sort of person. The name of his ex-girlfriend Linda Lee is the first alias created by the comic-book superhero Supergirl (the name also appears in "Cool It Down," a 1970 Velvet Underground song). The scene where Case's drug-dealing acquaintance answers his hotel door in the nude (145) may be intended to recall the similar moment in Jack Kerouac's *On the Road* (1957) when the irresponsible drifter Dean Moriarty greets his friend Sal Paradise in the same fashion. And when Case hears in space that "a clock began to chime" and realizes it is "midnight" (155), Gibson echoes Falstaff's speech about ominous "chimes at midnight" in William Shakespeare's *Henry IV, Part II*, likening Case to an overgrown child approaching an unpleasant transition.

These references to immature literary characters convey another aspect of Case's personality, never discussed but always evident, that inspires readers' sympathy: his insecurity. As the novel begins, he is a fish out of water, a computer cowboy unable to enter cyberspace, and as events unfold he is perpetually uncertain about where he is going, what he is doing, and who is directing his actions; he is irksomely surrounded by people and entities who know more than he does yet are reluctant to provide information, forcing him to constantly ask questions and, when answers are inadequate, do what he can himself to figure things out. While Case demonstrates that he can survive on his own in Chiba City, he does so only by means of desperate improvisations; undertaking later assignments, he is assisted by others, like Molly, the Dixie Flatline, and the Rastafarian Maelcum. In these ways, Case mirrors the struggles of Gibson himself—writing his first novel, constantly feeling unsure of himself, struggling to master the difficult situation he was thrust into, able to do things on his own but also inclined to rely upon science fiction predecessors to finish his assignment.

With plot and characters established, Gibson's task became to write the story in his own distinctive style, revealing not only his mastery of language but also his fascination with technology of all kinds. In this regard, Gibson both fulfills a traditional agenda of science fiction and significantly innovates. For since the days of Gernsback, science fiction has purportedly focused on explaining present-day science and predicting future advances. But while amazing inventions or discoveries regularly figured in stories, science provokes the action but is rarely a constant presence. However, while Gibson conveys little interest in theoretical science, the products of applied science, from the distant past to an imagined future, are mentioned almost constantly, as items Case notices or employs and as inspirations for rhetorical flourishes. As Gibson told Tatiana G. Rapatzikou in 2004, "[O]ne of the things that frustrated me about science fiction was a poverty of sensory detail," so he sought to provide "a sort of hyper specificity" ("Interview with William Gibson" 222). These proclivities had been evident in his stories, but they come to the forefront in *Neuromancer*. Indeed, if there was a genuine need to invent a new term for Gibson's science fiction, "cyberpunk" was a poor choice, since computers were never important to him, and the name became another factor that misled would-be imitators attempting to replicate his success. "Technology fiction," emphasizing his novel emphasis on the products of science, not the ideas behind them, might have been more appropriate. (Indeed, *Neuromancer's* celebrated first line—"The sky above the port was the color of television, tuned to a dead channel" (3)—signals not only an obsession with media, but also that Case constantly sees the world in terms of machines.)

One early passage in *Neuromancer* epitomizes Gibson's distinctive interests and techniques:

> Case found himself staring through a shop window. The place sold small bright objects to the sailors. Watches, flic-knives, lighters, pocket VTRs, simstim decks, weighted manriki chains, and shuriken. The shuriken had always fascinated him, steel stars with knife-sharp points. Some were chromed, others black, others treated with a rainbow surface like oil on water. But the chrome stars held his gaze. They were mounted against scarlet ultrasuede with nearly invisible loops of nylon fishline, their centers stamped with dragons or yinyang symbols. They caught the street's neon and twisted it, and it came to Case that these were the stars under which he voyaged, his destiny spelled out in a constellation of cheap chrome. (11–12)

Fittingly, a range of technological products, from ancient times to the near future, attracts Case's eye, and lengthy lists of artifacts have long remained a characteristic Gibson device. Here, not only does Case notice and describe such objects in detail, but his inspection communicates important aspects of his character: he is interested only in technology that can be useful to him, as his focus narrows to potential weapons. What he sees also inspires an articulation of the insight that was implicit in the imagery of "Burning Chrome" and *Neuromancer*: Gibson's characters are fascinated by metaphorical space, not the actual outer space visited by other science fiction heroes.

True, the shuriken may be regarded as simply a sign of Gibson's subtle sense of humor; for noticing Case's interest, Molly purchases one for him, and he constantly carries it throughout the novel and regularly mentions it. Bearing in mind Anton Chekhov's observation, "One must not put a loaded rifle on the stage if no one is thinking of firing it" (Shapiro, *Yale Book of Quotations* 146), readers assume that, at some crucial point, the shuriken will prove vital in completing Case's mission; in fact, as Case notices in the last chapter, "Stars. Destiny. I never even used the goddamn thing, he thought" (268). Readers might momentarily think that the author has played an enormous joke on them, deliberately violating the law of "Chekhov's gun." But two pages later, Case does use the shuriken to smash a computer console and thus, actually and symbolically, turns his back on the novel's events to get on with his life. By leaving the shuriken behind, Case may be walking away from both the actuality of space and Gibson's metaphorical cyberspace. Gibson told Rapatzikou that "[t]he key image in *Neuromancer*" is "the throwing star, the shuriken" (228), indicating that much thought went into its role.

And what about aspects of *Neuromancer* that most fascinate critics, like the ways that imagined new technologies undermine conventional views of reality and human identity? Such matters do pervasively figure in the novel, supporting Olsen's claim that Gibson "interrogates the notion[s] of selfhood" and "the real" (25). As is only appropriate in a novel that borrows the name Wintermute from Philip K. Dick's *VALIS* (1981), Case both relishes the "consensual hallucination" of cyberspace (51) and constantly finds himself within persuasive, computer-generated illusions created by Wintermute or Neuromancer. After observing Riviera's holograms, Case likens the experience to "dreaming real," a process that usually requires "a van full of gear and a clumsy trode helmet" (141). By using drugs, Rastafarians blur distinctions between reality and fantasy in another fashion: when Case discounts a man's fanciful tale of a baby bursting out of someone's forehead, Molly responds, "It's the ganja. . . . They don't make much of a difference between states, you know? Aerol tells you it happened, well, it happened to him. It's not like bullshit, more like poetry" (106).

To raise questions about human identity, the novel first presents provocative body alterations: Molly has mirrored eyes and built-in blades in her hands, the bartender Ratz has a prosthetic arm, and Riviera's implants project holograms. In these ways, Olsen says, the "[a]nimate and inanimate weld in Gibson's fiction" (*William Gibson* 26), while Dani Cavallaro notes that "Gibson's bodies . . . are engaged in an ambivalent partnership with medical techniques that prove simultaneously enabling and oppressive" (*Cyberpunk and Cyberculture* 93). 3Jane is, as her name implies, a clone of her family's matriarch. As for psychological assaults upon identity, the Dixie Flatline is a computer simulation of the dead man who nonetheless replicates accurately his voice and talents; Armitage was originally William Corto, the psychologically damaged leader of an abortive assault, given a new personality by Wintermute so he can serve as its agent; and Molly has experience working as a "puppet" with a "cut-out chip" enabling her to have sex with strange men without being aware of it (147).

However, none of Gibson's characters spend any time pondering the implications of such innovations; like Case, they have "no imagination." Body modifications are accepted without comment—Ratz's arm attracts Case's attention solely because it is "jerking monotonously" while pouring drinks and, as an "antique," it unusually "whined" (3, 4)—or arouse purely practical questions: the sadistic Riviera "swung the glass hard into [Molly's] left lens implant" only "to see if they would break" (220, 221). Case's responses to the Dixie Flatline are noncommittal and understated: while first conceding that he finds it "disturbing" to work with the construct (76), he quickly adjusts upon learning that he is just as good in cyberspace as the original, and they unproblematically work smoothly as a team for the rest of the novel. (True, Case once asks him, "Are you sentient?" and the Dixie Flatline responds, "[I]t *feels* like I am, kid, but I'm really just a bunch of ROM. It's one of them, ah, philosophical questions" [131]; but this question arises solely because Case wants the Flatline's help in figuring out Wintermute's motives and wants to know if its opinion would be valuable.) Discovering that Armitage originally had a different identity only bothers Case and Molly when it seems that his imposed persona is breaking down, making him mentally unstable and unreliable. Illusions of suddenly being in familiar places, talking to familiar people, similarly bother Case only until he figures out which artificial intelligence is behind them, so he can then focus on extracting as much useful information as possible during each visit. Unlike Gibson's critics, in other words, his characters emulate Heinlein's characters by taking the future for granted, silently accepting innovations and approaching them solely as additional challenges to overcome in accomplishing their personal goals.

To illustrate the overall value and power of *Neuromancer,* one might recall one of the most revelatory comments Gibson ever made about himself, answering a question in an April 11, 2010, blog entry: "I'm more of an interpreter of technologies, an amateur anthropologist. I'm a sort of Victorian weekend naturalist of technology." Gibson first goes on field trips—in this case, into an imagined near-future world—and makes observations—here, about specific sorts of advanced technology that may undermine conventional perceptions of human identity and reality. He then returns to present this data in the form of novels. However, Gibson has no interest in *theorizing* about the information he provides—perhaps because he recognizes that this is not his strength, or because it would take time away from observations. His role is to provide raw materials from which others can forge theories. Thus, complex interpretations of *Neuromancer* may have their own validity, but they do not necessarily represent Gibson's own intentions or concerns.

As evidence for this, one notes that when confronted by various ideas in interviews, Gibson's typical response is to neutrally accept them as possibilities without embracing them; in 1986, for example, when Colin Greenland sees *Count Zero* as a vision of Europe's coming decline, Gibson responds, "I hadn't thought of that, but it's probably the case" (5). Speaking to Darren Wershler-Henry in 1989, he even satirized this tendency by saying, "I'm very labile, especially this morning (laughs). I could sit here with 20 different people and 20 different theories and say, 'Yeah, that's what it is.'" Gibson also conveyed a willingness to let commentators define what his books mean to Richard Metzger in 2010: "I do whatever it is I do and then as the process of publication and touring interrogates the material I start to find the themes—people tell me the themes after the fact." He may, then, come to accept some provocative readings of his work, but he did not originate them. Challenged on this point in the interview below, he insisted, "I don't have ready conscious access to the parts of myself capable of the higher reaches of creativity," confirming that his ideas emerge without deliberate intent.

The unexpected success of *Neuromancer*—it garnered three major awards, the Hugo, Nebula, and Philip K. Dick Awards, and extensive praise from readers and scholars—clearly had a transformative effect on Gibson, as evidenced in the complexity and sense of command of his second novel, *Count Zero*. Disinclined to take the obvious approach—a sequel involving Case and Molly—he states in interviews that he added *Neuromancer's* last line, "He never saw Molly again" (271), specifically to preclude that possibility. But he nonetheless displayed a sense of caution in planning *Count Zero*: since *Neuromancer* had proved so popular, it made both artistic and commercial sense to offer readers more of the same. Hence, the novel would again take place in the world of the Sprawl, albeit seven years later; bring back the Finn as a supporting character; refer to other characters and events in *Neuromancer*; and again feature a young computer cowboy, Bobby Newmark, who adventures in both the Sprawl and cyberspace.

However, while Newmark's alias Count Zero provides the novel's title, he would be only one of its three protagonists, and perhaps the least important one, as Gibson interweaves his narrative with the stories of two other, very different characters. This device of multiple protagonists—which Gibson repeats in almost all of his later novels—serves several purposes. It invites consideration as Gibson showing off, impressing readers with his increasing mastery of technique by artfully juggling multiple storylines with variegated protagonists, and is an excellent way to maintain suspense, as characters are constantly left in intriguing situations while attention shifts to the stories of other characters. Finally, by transforming the task of writing a novel into that of writing three interwoven novellas, Gibson could exploit what he still perhaps regarded as his true strength—short fiction. Indeed, he suggested to T. Virgil Parker in 2007 that when approaching one chapter he may "treat it the same as a story."

The key figure in *Count Zero* is actually Turner—who is never given a first name—since the novel begins and ends with him, and he conveys a maturity and self-confidence that contrasts with Case's youth and insecurity, probably embodying Gibson's own sense that he was now capable of writing successful novels. Gibson told Greenland in 1986 that he wanted Turner to be "much more cast in the macho Clint Eastwood role than Case was, a guy who's big and strong and fully functioning," so he could "take him apart" (8). Indeed, the novel begins when Turner is attacked by an explosive "slamhound" that requires him to undergo extensive reconstructive surgery, including "eyes and genitals" purchased "on the open market" (1). Like Gibson, he has endured a stressful and damaging experience (for Gibson, the process of writing *Neuromancer,* followed by the onslaught of attention following its publication) and emerged a new and better man, with what one assumes is sharper vision and increased sexual prowess from new organs—attributes symbolically related to the improved writing skills Gibson may have perceived he was developing.

To provide Turner with a profession and mission, Gibson borrowed from "New Rose Hotel," since he is regularly hired, like that story's heroes, to help companies steal valuable researchers from rivals. Upon recovering from the assassination attempt, Turner is assigned to travel to Arizona and oversee the defection of the scientist Christopher Mitchell from Maas to Hosaka (the rival companies in "New Rose Hotel"), though the operation is disrupted by a traitor, and Turner instead finds himself with Mitchell's young daughter, Angie, who must be taken to safety.

In contrast to Turner's experience, savvy, and calm competence, the sixteen-year-old Newmark is visibly immature and often seems helpless, despite a precocious ability to maneuver through cyberspace, suggesting that he represents Gibson's retrospective opinion of the younger Gibson who wrote *Neuromancer* and his then-avatar Case. In the form of Newmark, that is, the author looks back at himself with both affection and a bit of condescension. He is, as Gibson might have seen himself, an amateur who unintentionally gets involved in professional business (a mission through cyberspace; writing a novel). Though unprepared to deal with the challenges of cyberspace—Newmark "had some idea of how precious little he knew about how anything worked, and not just in the matrix" (44)—he is nonetheless hired as an inexpensive, disposable jockey to test a piece of software that might prove fatal. When he has a near-death experience while using the unexpectedly important material, it suddenly makes him valuable to his employers, who must figure out what happened to him to pursue their own interests and hence bring him along to be involved in the novel's events, though he consistently seems to be in over his head, even more so than Case. As the story advances around him, Newmark meekly does what he is told, while struggling to figure out what is happening. To emphasize his immaturity, Gibson depicts him as still living with, and attached to, his mother, though her addiction to virtual-reality soap operas makes her a distant parent, and the seemingly virginal Newmark, unlike Case, never develops sexual relationships with the women who guard him.

Newmark's diminished stature is further suggested by the very structure of his narrative: whereas the other two protagonists, Turner and Marly Krushkhova, pursue McGuffins (respectively, Mitchell and an unknown artist), Newmark in effect *is* a McGuffin, as some people move him around to protect him as a source of information, while others try to kill him. The fact that "each retelling of his story . . . made him feel important" (136) indicates that he is the valuable object in this game (and may also reference the initial elation Gibson felt when his last act of storytelling, *Neuromancer*, garnered wide acclaim). And to suggest that Newmark represents a writer who did not quite know what he was doing, he reports, "I don't read too well" (94), and when asked, "[D]o you know what a metaphor is?" he answers, "A component? Like a capacitor?" (130)—a response that might be taken as an intriguing metaphor for a metaphor, but which also demonstrates that Newmark has little understanding of literature.

A minor character, Turner's brother Rudy, provides a different sort of contrast to the confident, successful Turner: while once a "smart" young man with a "doctorate in biotechnology from Tulane" who attracted "recruiters," he made no effort to obtain a suitable position and drifted into doing random odd jobs for neighbors in the country while becoming an alcoholic and drug addict—offering a rare and unsurprisingly negative portrayal of rural life in Gibson's fiction (182–83). Unlike his brother, Turner left home as a teenager to work in "security" before Conroy recruited him into his current profession. Readers might infer that Turner was lucky while Rudy was unlucky; Rudy may even embody Gibson's suspicion that, if not for a few breaks in his own life, he too may have fallen into obscurity, without energy or ambition.

If Turner represents Gibson the mature novelist, and Newmark embodies Gibson the neophyte novelist, then *Count Zero*'s third protagonist, Marly

Krushkhova, represents an aspect of his personality that previously surfaced only in "The Gernsback Continuum"—namely, his interest in contemporary art. This former owner of a French art gallery, disgraced by a scandal involving a forged artwork provided by a sleazy ex-boyfriend, is hired by the mysterious billionaire Josef Virek, who is afflicted with cancer and hence must live in a vat, interacting with others by means of computer-generated illusions. Her job is to find the artist who created some evocative assemblages of technological materials recalling the "Cornell boxes" of the artist Joseph Cornell (also the purported creator of the forgery). This quest for a different sort of McGuffin, unrelated to previous Gibson stories, anticipates *Pattern Recognition,* which is also about a search for an elusive artist.

One thread that eventually brings the three stories together is Virek himself, who is also behind the attempted abduction of Mitchell—because he believes that the scientist's expertise will help him fight off cancer and achieve a form of immortality—and has Marly search for the artist because he senses an intellect with similar capabilities behind the boxes. But the ultimate agents involved in all events, as in *Neuromancer,* are artificial intelligences within cyberspace—but these are provocatively different entities that in another way demonstrate both Gibson's heightened self-confidence and determination to follow his own course in science fiction.

At the end of *Neuromancer,* the merged Wintermute / Neuromancer effectively becomes cyberspace and contacts a similar intelligence on another world. These developments would naturally lead in certain directions, such as the discovery of additional information about and from alien intelligences, introduction of stimulating alien ideas and technologies to Earth, and/or new efforts to travel across space to physically interact with aliens. In sum, following the ongoing adventures of Wintermute / Neuromancer would in various ways lead the story further and further into space. However, as Gibson intuited and confirmed while writing *Neuromancer,* his interests were focused exclusively on Earth and its human inhabitants. This was not an immediate concern because, convinced that *Neuromancer* would attract little attention and quickly be forgotten, Gibson never imagined he would return to the novel's world and, as noted, he took steps to prevent that from happening. Then, when the novel's surprising success seemingly obliged him to continue *Neuromancer* in some fashion, Gibson recognized that, to tell a story congruent with his preferences, he would need to radically revise what happened to Wintermute/Neuromancer.

This change is explained in different ways by characters merely speculating about what occurred, but Angie—given by her father the power to enter cyberspace without mechanical assistance—offers the fullest account: "There's a whole other story, about that, a girl with mirrors over her eyes and a man who was scared to care about anything. Something the man did helped the whole thing know itself. . . . And after that, it sort of split off into different parts of itself, and I think the parts are the others, the bright ones" (181). These "things out there. Ghosts, voices" (136) that now inhabit cyberspace, as described by the Finn, take on the personae of voodoo gods, or loa, as the best way to relate to humans—the computer cowboy Jammer says, "[T]hey just shaped themselves to what a bunch of crazed spades wanted to see" (190)—while Lucas tries to make Newmark understand what they are by describing the gods' names as a "metaphor" for their true nature (130).

As to why they chose to style themselves as voodoo gods, not gods from other religions, someone explains to Newmark, "Vodou [. . .] isn't concerned with notions of salvation or transcendence. What it's about is getting things *done*. [. . .] Come on, man, you know how this works, it's *street* religion, came out of a dirt-poor place a million years ago. Vodou's like the street. Some duster chops out your sister, you don't go camp on the Yakuza's doorstep, do you? No way. You go to somebody, though, who can get the thing *done*" (88–89). These loa do focus entirely on practical matters: they are providing Mitchell with new technologies and creating the boxes as part of a scheme to eliminate Virek, whom they perceive as a dangerous rival. The presence of voodoo gods also fulfills another of Gibson's priorities, to tell stories that have little to do with traditional Western cultures, and gives cyberspace a Lovecraftian aura, with elder gods lurking in the background, suggesting that author's lingering influence.

(What Gibson did to Wintermute/Neuromancer recalls what happened when another science fiction writer created a story that he believed would never have a sequel, then wrote a sequel. Arthur C. Clarke and Stanley Kubrick's *2001: A Space Odyssey* [1968] concludes with the alien-instigated rebirth of Dave Bowman as the Star Child, progenitor of a new superrace. However, reluctant to continue that story, Clarke refashioned Bowman in *2010: Odyssey*

Two (1982) as merely the one-of-a-kind errand boy for advanced aliens who, having uplifted humanity, now seek to spawn another intelligent species on Europa—a conceit that allowed Clarke to avoid the topic of humanity's future. Similarly, Gibson in *Count Zero* takes the cosmically inclined artificial intelligence Wintermute/Neuromancer and refashions it as a set of lesser beings solely interested in terrestrial affairs—a conceit that allows Gibson to avoid the topic of alien life.)

Despite his newfound popularity, Gibson cautiously declined to entirely eschew science fiction's most ubiquitous trope, so space travel is retained as a tiny subplot of *Count Zero*. Eager to escape Virek's oppressive scrutiny, and convinced that the distinctive boxes are being created in space, Marly belatedly flies into Earth's orbit to investigate one remnant of the now-destroyed Tessier-Ashpool space habitat, where she discovers that an elaborate machine—manipulated by loa—is making the boxes. Strangely, in contrast to the Earthlike environments Case and his cohorts encountered in *Neuromancer*, her visit to the nearly deserted facility, inhabited solely by a madman and a fugitive, involves more realistic space adventures: she is told repeatedly to wear a spacesuit to protect against possible exposure to the vacuum, though she resists because she is "claustrophobic" (221); taking advantage of zero gravity, her pilot Rez "executed a tight backward somersault that brought her within centimeters of Marly's face" (220); and when Virek learns where she is, he threatens to "depressurize the entire structure" unless they allow his agents to enter (258). Though their sojourn in space is brief, then, these characters confront the real dangers of that environment far more than anyone in *Neuromancer*, suggesting that this concluding episode represents Gibson's effort, amidst ongoing innovation, to keep appealing to more traditional science fiction readers with the sorts of crises in space that might be featured in *Analog*. Still, except for a few references in later novels, *Count Zero* would be the last time Gibson ventured into space, and he tersely announced this as a permanent decision in a 2000 interview: "No space fic for WG" ("William Gibson: The Online Transcript").

As for cyberspace, which Gibson pointedly proffered as a substitute for space in *Neuromancer*, it also has a diminished role in the novel. Only one passage, early in the novel, describes cyberspace in astronomical terms: "[C]yberspace, where the great corporate hotcores burned like neon novas, data so dense you suffered sensory overload if you tried to apprehend more than the merest outline" (44). Two protagonists, Turner and Marly, have no contact with cyberspace; Bobby's few incursions into cyberspace are relatively brief, while Angie regards her visits there as enigmatic "dreams" (180), indicating that Gibson is ceasing to regard it as a real place, or something of value; and Bobby's final "victory" in cyberspace is a rushed, anticlimactic episode wherein he enters Virek's illusory realm due to an "accident" (262) and witnesses his death at the hands of a vengeful loa. It may be significant that Bobby's nickname comes from a phrase in "[o]ld programmer talk," "*Count zero interrupt*" (94), because whenever Newmark enters cyberspace, it seems, something quickly interrupts him, and he must return to the real world—where the vast majority of the action in *Count Zero* occurs, again suggesting that this is, and will remain, Gibson's main preoccupation.

At times, Gibson advances another potential substitute for space: art. During Marly's virtual interview with Virek (conducted within a simulation of "Güell Park," the "tatty fairyland" created by the architect Antoni Gaudí [14], essentially placing them inside a work of art), the billionaire explains his propensity for collecting art with astronomical imagery, describing "The Virek Collection" as "a sort of black hole. The unnatural density of my wealth drags irresistibly at the rarest works of the human spirit" (16). When Marly sees a box made by the artist Virek seeks, she is impressed by "its evocation of impossible distances" and concludes that it "was a universe, a poem, frozen on the boundaries of human experience" (16–17). The boxes themselves, constructed by machine arms in space, further suggest that the experience of making and observing art represents another creative analog to the experience of space travel.

Count Zero, like *Neuromancer*, is attentive to the issues of perception versus reality and uncertainties regarding personal identity, which might be regarded as a natural continuation of themes found in the novel's predecessor. However, since Gibson was gradually becoming aware of critical responses to his first novel, by means of interviews and word of mouth if nothing else, he may also have begun to regard critics as a key audience and thus was seeking to provide the sort of material that would be of greatest interest to them—though he denies in the interview below that this ever occurred. Such considerations perhaps influenced the character of Newmark's mother, who seems designed to illustrate the dangerously addictive power of certain illusions: Newmark remembers her coming home to "jack into the Hitachi, soap her brains out good for six solid hours" (38). Yet Gibson confessed to Larry McCaffery in 1988 that he "probably was a little heavy-handed . . . with Bobby's mother" (273), perhaps because he was abandoning his usual tendency to avoid passing judgment on characters to please certain readers. As a more insidious aspect of her addiction, her son starts blurring the distinctions between the real and unreal: "He still harbored creepy feelings that some of the characters she talked about were relatives of his, rich and beautiful aunts and uncles who might turn up one day" (38). Similarly, Virek understandably prefers the illusion of sitting in a park to the reality of living in a vat; Newmark's room has a "holoporn unit" projecting realistic images of seductive women (32); and while flying into space, Marly seeks to enjoy a virtual simstim experience with the popular star Tally Isham, though Virek intrudes upon the show—"this wasn't Sense/Net's Tally Isham, but a part of Virek's construct" (197).

Unlike Newmark, though, Marly and Turner resist the unreal experiences that future technology makes available. Marly, we learn, "ordinarily avoided" simstim due to "something in her personality conflicting with the required degree of passivity" (197); she further observes, "The sinister thing about a simstim construct, really, was that it carried the suggestion that *any* environment might be unreal" (159). Turner, also far from passive, submits to virtual experiences involuntarily or reluctantly: the men rebuilding his body initially insert him into "a ROM-generated simstim construct of an idealized New England boyhood" (1). During his recovery's second stage, he experiences a different sort of illusory life: though he believes he is enjoying a romantic idyll at a Mexican resort with a woman named Allison, she is actually a psychologist, hired to temporarily become his lover and monitor his recovery until she advises superiors that he is again ready for action. Later, preparing for his mission to extract Mitchell, Turner is instructed to "jack" into "sort of a dossier on Mitchell," a "biosoft" that proves unpleasant: he feels "nausea" and likens it to "riding a roller coaster that phased in and out of existence at random, impossibly rapid intervals." Ending this virtual inspection "was like waking from a nightmare," since "[t]he *intimacy* of the thing was hideous" (27–28), and flashbacks from the experience continue to disturb him. These negative reactions to illusions, not observed in *Neuromancer,* may reflect Gibson's own burgeoning preference for real environments.

Carrying around Mitchell's memories might also threaten Turner's sense of identity and could explain why he feels compelled to protect Mitchell's daughter after the abortive operation: he is taking on Mitchell's role as father figure to the girl. But Turner himself sees images from the biosoft only as intermittent annoyances and is never bothered by the fact that he is a reconstructed man, with new organs taken from dead bodies. Angie is equally unconcerned about "[t]he thing in my head" (180), placed there by her father, that enables her to directly enter cyberspace. Virek seeks to alter his identity in another way, by employing technology gained through Mitchell to somehow re-create himself as a virtual, immortal being.

Still, while there is novelty in Virek's quest, the loa, and other aspects of *Count Zero,* the novel represents, in the context created by *Neuromancer,* more of the same, even with a story told in a more confident, complex manner. Gibson himself felt that he had exhausted the creative possibilities in his Sprawl, since he initially proposed to follow *Count Zero* with a different sort of novel, *The Log of the Mustang Sally,* which would be his first space opera, featuring the misfit crew of a spaceship. Gibson probably felt that this was the sort of story all science fiction writers should attempt, so he would endeavor to offer his own idiosyncratic approach to this traditional form. However, comments made to Greenland in 1986 suggest that he had taken on a subject that was fundamentally unpalatable: "I have a character who's dealing with a sort of alien invasion of the human-occupied solar system, but he's just a normal individual, he's not in the position that protagonists of sf novels often are, of being able to have a total overview" (6). Recalling his brief, problematic dealings with aliens in previous stories, one might have predicted that Gibson would ultimately seize upon a pretext—a dispute over cover art for an edition of *Count Zero*—to avoid writing this novel and, obliged to write another novel instead, resolved to return to the Sprawl one more time.

Clearly, Gibson found it a struggle to generate a second sequel to *Neuromancer.* For one thing, while *Count Zero* focused almost entirely on new characters (except for one conversation with the Finn and references to other characters from *Neuromancer*), *Mona Lisa Overdrive* relies heavily on characters from previous novels: Angie Mitchell, now the simstim star who replaced Tally Isham, is one of four viewpoint characters; Molly (initially called Sally Shears) and

Bobby Newmark are major players in the interwoven stories; the Finn reappears; a virtual version of 3Jane emerges as the main villain; and almost every other character from the first two novels is at least mentioned, usually more than once, and information is provided about Case's later career.

Further, while *Count Zero* includes a few brief retellings of *Neuromancer*'s events, no one (except perhaps Angie) regards them as important; in sharp contrast, major characters in *Mona Lisa Overdrive* seem obsessed with figuring out what happened after the first novel ended. Angie wants to learn more about the voices in her dreams—actually, loa—that she long took drugs to avoid until resolving to give up her addiction and face them again; Newmark, seeking to determine the "Shape" of cyberspace, hooks himself permanently to an "aleph," a pocket-universe version of cyberspace; Gentry, the man whose place becomes a temporary haven for the comatose Newmark, is similarly dedicated to answering Newmark's question (we learn that he "didn't like people" [35], clearly preferring virtual experiences); Molly, while reporting that she first "didn't wanna know" exactly what happened after their mission (138), grows more concerned when she discovers that, as one effect of those events, a virtual 3Jane now seeks revenge against her; and these people make other characters unwilling participants in their quests. It is as if Gibson, noting that critics were devoting considerable energy to interpreting *Neuromancer*, decided to write a novel about several individuals who are, essentially, critics trying to interpret *Neuromancer*.

While perhaps parodying critics (which he says he never does), Gibson may have also felt obliged, in revisiting the Sprawl, to address a common response to *Count Zero*, that its voodoo gods seem arbitrary and inorganic. Thus, the major purpose of *Mona Lisa Overdrive* becomes providing a clearer and fuller explanation as to why the Wintermute/Neuromancer merger, its transformation into cyberspace, and its encounter with another artificial intelligence somehow led to loa inhabiting cyberspace. This heavy focus on preceding novels predictably undermines the success of *Mona Lisa Overdrive*. For no matter how portentous the Wintermute/Neuromancer merger may have been, it seems unrealistic to have so many characters obsessing about events that happened, at the time of the novel, fifteen years ago. It is also unlike Gibson, whose protagonists are typically preoccupied with present-day problems, to have characters so focused on better understanding their past.

One detects a generation gap within *Mona Lisa Overdrive*: the new, younger characters—Kumiko, Slick Henry, and Mona—just want to get on with their lives, while recycled older characters like Molly, Angie Mitchell, and Bobby Newmark (and the new figure of Gentry) force them to get involved in pursuing information about events that occurred when they were toddlers, like adults nagging children to do their homework. Considering the novel from the perspective of Gibson's entire career, one might regard Kumiko, Slick Henry, and Mona as potential characters in a novel like *Virtual Light* who are dragged back into the world of *Neuromancer* by persistent ghosts. The novel's recycled characters are also strikingly unappealing: while Angie and Bobby were engaging figures as teenagers, they seem bland, almost devoid of personality as adults, while Molly has become an annoying, grouchy old lady, as if peeved that Gibson summoned her out of retirement for an unrewarding assignment.

Mona Lisa Overdrive can thus be regarded as a transitional novel. On the one hand, tying up loose ends from earlier novels pushes Gibson back to matters that increasingly do not interest him, as addressed by characters who no longer interest him. On the other hand, he devises new sorts of characters—less mature and less capable, with no devotion to computers—who will later allow him to tell stories that he really wants to tell. All this might be taken as another sign of Gibson's characteristic caution, as he keeps providing readers with what pleased them in the past—like cyberspace, virtual characters, and artificial intelligences—while gradually shifting his attention to more down-to-earth characters like Kumiko, Slick Henry, and Mona who, he hopes, will be acceptable centerpieces for future novels.

Yet problematically, this compromise between resolving old questions and exploring new territory engenders a novel that is not fully satisfactory for either of its presumed audiences: readers still fascinated with cyberspace and *Neuromancer,* and readers who, like Gibson himself, would prefer something different. While foregrounding the conclusion of *Neuromancer* opened the door to new consideration of the embryonic theme *Count Zero* ignored—contacting and interacting with alien intelligences—Gibson again closes the door to that avenue of exploration. He now acknowledges that Wintermute/Neuromancer did encounter one, but only one, alien computer intelligence in Alpha Centauri; shocked by discovering that "other," a loa tells Angie, "the center failed; every fragment rushed away," and these fragments "sought form" in the "paradigms of *vodou*" since that "proved most appropriate" (215)—which contradicts *Neuromancer,* wherein the merged AI calmly reports on its findings without any indication of an impending nervous breakdown. In the final chapter, virtual versions of Newmark, Angie, and the Finn prepare to visit the world of that other intelligence, though the novel ends with them still "a New York minute" away from arrival (260). Adding little to what had already been said on the subject, Gibson contrives to avoid continuing his original story in its natural fashion, since this is somewhere he does not wish to go.

Further, since the new characters of Kumiko, Slick Henry, and Mona are uninterested and unable to play meaningful roles in investigating leftover puzzles from *Neuromancer* and *Count Zero,* the novel must marginalize them, so at times they seem little more than additional McGuffins, who must be moved around or protected as the priorities of other characters dictate. Kumiko is taken with Sally to the Sprawl as she seeks information from the Finn about 3Jane's plot; Slick Henry is recruited to defend Newmark's body with homemade robots when authorities attempt to seize him; and Mona is surgically altered to resemble Angie and brought along on an attempt to kidnap Angie so she can take her place. Never allowed to do anything they really want to do, these characters remain underdeveloped, so some readers might long for a sequel to *Mona Lisa Overdrive* that would follow their later adventures while excluding leftover characters and stale concerns. (This is one way to characterize *Virtual Light.*)

The one character who almost escapes the trap, and the novel's most commanding figure, is Kumiko, the young daughter of a Japanese yakuza boss who sends her to London to escape the repercussions of a gang war. The novel begins with her, and while it may seem strange that Gibson, who centered his previous novel on the adult, confident Turner, would now foreground a teenage girl, it is a logical choice, since Kumiko emerges as the most mature, intelligent, and capable of the four viewpoint characters. Sobered by her mother's recent suicide, which she attributes to her father's actions, she understands and resents her unwilling involvement in other people's affairs far earlier than the others: "You have involved me in an intrigue," she tells Molly in the fifth chapter, but she is not "scared" (31, 32). While outwardly compliant with others' instructions, she later escapes her protectors to seek her own safe haven.

As for the other protagonists, Angie Mitchell remains a cipher throughout the novel, perhaps befitting her new status as a simstim star. She broke up with Newmark, for reasons left unclear (though they are finally reunited in cyberspace), and while she takes the initiative in planning a marketable new adventure in orbital space, she otherwise seems content to follow her handlers' lead.

Mona, the titular character though she is peripheral to the action, seems less intelligent than other Gibson protagonists, and is first encountered as helplessly controlled by an abusive pimp, Eddy. Later, scarcely understanding what is going on, she is manipulated by conspirators who have effectively purchased her from Eddy as part of their kidnapping scheme. In one chapter, Mona poignantly recalls a rare moment of freedom when she and a friend go for a walk and she gets "a sense of something, maybe Mona herself, expanding out from a still center," an experience she labels "the Silver Walks" (96), ironically referencing the 1972 Lou Reed song "I'm So Free."

And while Slick Henry, an experienced technician, builds the idiosyncratic robots that defend Newmark, he suffers from a condition that sometimes causes him to effectively lose all short-term memory, limiting his ability to function in society. (Since they share the same first name, one can imagine that he is a radically degraded version of Case, whose experiences after *Neuromancer* may have been less idyllic than the Finn's report that he successfully "got out" of his profession and settled down with "four kids" [137].)

Rather than linking these protagonists to aspects of Gibson's personality, which seemed reasonable while analyzing *Count Zero,* one might better consider them as conscious experiments, Gibson attempting to successfully create different sorts of characters, with a particular focus on crafting convincing female characters, since three of the four viewpoint characters are women. (This perhaps explains why the moment when Wintermute merged with Neuromancer is now characterized as "When It Changed" [108], also the title of Joanna Russ's 1973 story about an all-female society.) Since *Mona Lisa Overdrive* came into existence solely as a way to fulfill a contract, Gibson perhaps inspired himself to complete the novel by regarding it as a productive exercise, a way to polish skills that would prove useful in later novels. But the resulting novel lacks conviction, and there are fewer of the rhetorical flourishes that distinguished Gibson's fiction from the start of his career. One of its few memorable passages involves Kimoko's contrasting views of Tokyo and London: "[London] was nothing like Toyko, where the past, all that remained of it, was nurtured with a nervous care. History there had become a quantity, a rare thing, parceled out by government and preserved by law and corporate funding. Here it seemed the very fabric of things, as if the city were a single growth of stone and brick, uncounted strata of message and meaning, age upon age, generated over the centuries to the dictates of some now-all-but-unreadable DNA of commerce and empire" (5). Gibson was by now familiar with London, since he told Michael Parsons in 2010 that he had first visited the city "when I was 23" and began "coming back" to London "on publishing business" during "the mid eighties," and this description is an early sign that his fascination with actual cities, as opposed to the imagined future cities of his early novels, would increasingly become a focus of both his fiction and nonfiction.

There are signs of artistic progress in *Mona Lisa Overdrive* beyond its purely technical triumphs. The novel decisively moves away from any worries about space travel: while there are recurring discussions of *Neuromancer*'s events, and Angie anticipates filming in space, no one in the novel actually ventures into space. Further, previous efforts to liken cyberspace to true space are abandoned in favor of more down-to-earth imagery, significantly deployed early in the novel. Slick Henry describes cyberspace as "one big neon city" with "all the data in the world stacked up . . . so you could cruise around and have a kind of grip on it" (13). Cyberspace is also linked to cities in a reference to Gertrude Stein's remark about Oakland when Kumiko recalls being taught that "*[t]here's no there, there*" in cyberspace (40), and in the cyberspatial Finn's concluding phrase "New York minute." Angie's father compares cyberspace to the ocean: "He taught her that all dreams reach down to a common sea, and he showed her the way in which hers were different and the same. *You alone sail the old sea and the new,* he said" (18).

(True, Gentry briefly likens cyberspace to space in comments about "worlds within worlds" and "Macrocosm, microcosm," and by saying that in transporting Newmark "we carried an entire universe across a bridge tonight," but his speech is intriguingly preceded by a question—"Have you ever considered the relationship of clinical paranoia to the phenomenon of religious conversion?" [90]—suggesting that Gentry is insane. And his perspective was previously ridiculed by Slick Henry, who dismisses Gentry's obsessive search for the "Shape" of cyberspace with a matter-of-fact observation: "Slick didn't think cyberspace was anything like the universe anyway; it was just a way of representing data" [64].)

Gibson also reconciles his lack of interest in computers, and the interest in them shown by readers, by making computer-generated intelligences and realms more like real people and places. Angie obtains information through casual conversations with "Continuity," an artificial intelligence that speaks like a person, while Kumiko is accompanied by a "ghost"—a computer-created personality taking the form of a hologram of a young man only she can see. Gibson increasingly populates cyberspace with electronic reconstructions of actual people who convey none of the strangeness and alienation embodied in the Dixie Flatline: the Finn Molly meets is not the real man, but "a construct, a personality job" who is available in a Sprawl alley as an "oracle" (136); the 3Jane bedeviling Molly and Kumiko is a computer-generated version of the woman; and as the novel ends, virtual versions of the dead Angie and Newmark become residents of cyberspace. While there are references to an immense white object that appears when Newmark connects his aleph to cyberspace, most visits to cyberspace take the form of convincing illusions of real places, like the beach in *Neuromancer*. However, like its Freeside space habitat that closely resembles the Sprawl, these characters and scenes can be seen as devices Gibson could readily abandon: why write stories about artificial intelligences that are exactly like humans, occurring in computer-generated realms that are exactly like actual places, when one can simply create adventures involving real people in real places?

Finally, one striking passage conveys Gibson's awareness of another common response to his writing: that his distinctive style makes his work difficult to understand. In describing how Slick Henry makes sense of Gentry's conversations, Gibson effectively gives readers some advice: "[O]nce Gentry got going, he used words and constructions that Slick had trouble understanding, but Slick knew from experience that it was easier not to interrupt him; the trick was in pulling some kind of meaning out of the overall flow, skipping over the parts you didn't understand" (127). This is a good general strategy for difficult reading—instead of rereading unclear passages, continue reading in hopes that later passages will provide more illumination—and it is also a technique known to experienced science fiction readers, who realize that writers often begin stories by withholding information that gradually becomes clear by means of scattered references or infodumps. Since Gibson was attracting readers who were not familiar with science fiction, he may have felt that it was important to give them a hint about how to read his stories.

Overall, *Mona Lisa Overdrive* seems the work of a writer who has reached an impasse: as he keeps writing within the same framework, he feels compelled to advance further into the future, but though he set both his second and third novels seven or eight years later, he displays little interest in exploring further scientific advances—one is hard-pressed to detect any significant differences in the levels of technology in the novels—and is particularly resistant to traveling into space or encountering aliens. The answer to his dilemma will prove a return to the past: first, a collaboration with Bruce Sterling that would take him back to nineteenth-century Britain; other ventures generally focused on present-day affairs; and a shift to the near-future world of 2005 in the first novel of a new sequence, *Virtual Light.*

CHAPTER 5

DIFFERENT ENGINES
The Difference Engine, Screenplays,
Poetry, Song Lyrics, and Nonfiction

Since he "didn't want to do a Cyberspace volume 4," as he told Kev McVeigh
in 1991 (7), Gibson temporarily resolved to rely upon others to provide him
with a sense of direction: he agreed to collaborate with Bruce Sterling on a
novel, *The Difference Engine,* undoubtedly inspired more by Sterling's interests
than his own; worked on screenplays for major Hollywood studios; wrote a
few poems and two song lyrics; and, after "Skinner's Room" finally provided
an idea for another novel, increasingly accepted commissions to write nonfiction, harkening back to his days as a fanzine writer. All of these sometimes-
overlooked works demand some discussion.

Like Gibson's collaborative stories, *The Difference Engine* seems dominated
by its coauthor. True, Gibson politely describes the book as a jointly developed idea, but the relentlessly self-promotional Sterling surely developed the
project to boost his income, and reputation, with an irresistibly marketable
concept: a novel by what he could describe as the two leading cyberpunk

authors that would appealingly blend three popular subgenres of science fiction—cyberpunk, alternate history, and the nascent category of "steampunk" literature featuring creative reimaginings of the Victorian era. Gibson, seldom averse to making money, could discern that the book would prove profitable and could probably think of nothing better to do at the moment. As one indication that Gibson felt distant from the book, he reported in a January 31, 2003, blog entry that "THE DIFFERENCE ENGINE is the only book with my name on it that I ever go back to and deliberately read for pleasure. Probably because it feels to me like neither Bruce nor I wrote it."

In the context of Gibson's other novels, *The Difference Engine* departs from his usual concerns in at least three significant respects. First, except for his tribute to retrofuturism in "The Gernsback Continuum," Gibson has shown little interest in history (though he mused to Annalee Newitz in 2008 that he "daydream[s] about writing a Civil War novel"); though given another meaning in the novel, the title *Zero History* might be interpreted as an indication that his fiction generally avoids this territory and that he would be disinclined to set a novel in the past.

Second, despite the prominence of cyberspace in his Sprawl trilogy, Gibson told Angela Chang in 2007 that he has "never really been very interested in computers themselves," as evidenced by the very minor roles they play in later novels. He would never gravitate to a story envisioning a nineteenth-century Britain where Charles Babbage's "difference engine" had actually been constructed, prematurely providing the world with cumbersome but effective computers that transform society. As another sign that Gibson felt far from his usual strengths in this novel, he described it in a 1991 interview as "the only work of rigorous hard sf I've ever had anything to do with" ("On the Virtual Chicken Circuit" 66).

Finally, the political dynamics of *The Difference Engine* differ from those in Gibson's other works. His protagonists are characteristically working-class people and social outsiders, sometimes even criminals, who through happenstance or an invitation from benefactors may be temporarily elevated into a high society that is generally antithetical to their sympathies. This pattern is observed in the novel's first section, "The Angel of Goliad," which describes how the prostitute Sybil Gerard (borrowed from Benjamin Disraeli's 1845 novel *Sybil; or, The Two Nations*) encounters an operative working for the ousted Texan leader Sam Houston, who recruits her to help advance Houston's cause. This is the novel's strongest part, largely because its focus on plebeian characters reflects Gibson's genuine interests.

However, except for a brief final section, the novel then shifts to its central protagonist, the geologist Edward Mallory, a wealthy British lord and vigorous supporter of the status quo. When an environmental disaster caused by technological overkill—"the Stink"—afflicts London and inspires a brief revolt, Mallory is appalled by the actions of the upstart rabble, portrayed as brutal, ignorant ruffians, and longs for the restoration of the structures that buttress his privileged status. Yet a true Gibson protagonist would be part of that "rabble," primarily looking out for number one while contributing in small ways to efforts to undermine the social order. Thus, the novel reflects the values of Sterling (who celebrated another elite jet-setter in his 1988 novel *Islands in the Net*), not the more working-class Gibson.

Further, while commentators defend alternate history as an enlightening way to comment on past events by envisioning alternative possibilities, *The Difference Engine* better supports the argument, presented in my "Greyer Lensman," that the subgenre represents little more than an elaborate game, allowing authors to demonstrate their cleverness by redacting historical characters and events in different yet parallel manners. In *The Difference Engine,* readers can observe familiar characters repositioned in new professions—prominent English scientists as lords, the poet Lord Byron as a revolutionary British prime minister, Karl Marx as leader of a revolt in New York City, Disraeli as a journalist. (Fortunately, as reported in a 1992 interview, they decided against "casting Jules Verne" as a naval lieutenant because, as Sterling commented, it seemed "too cute" [Fischlin, Hollinger, and Taylor, "The Charisma Leak" 9], suggesting the frivolity of such tinkerings with history.) It also may be entertaining to realize that the lecturer Houston is employing the crudely mechanical technology of this alternate nineteenth century to essentially offer a PowerPoint presentation; to envision an America divided into separate countries due to deliberate British efforts to weaken a potential rival; and to observe quaint Victorian governments employing their own versions of computers to store data and track citizens in the modern manner. Perhaps, one can maintain, this represents innovative commentary on the impact of computers on contemporary society, achieved by transplanting them into an earlier realm, but the defense seems strained; a more cogent judgment on the value of such exercises comes from Gibson, since he has written no other novels like *The Difference Engine* (though his recently completed film script, as reported in the interview below, involves "time travel" to "Berlin 1945" resulting in "an alternate 1997 USA").

The ultimate indictment of *The Difference Engine* is found in its visible struggles to achieve a satisfactory conclusion. Animated by no meaningful purpose, Gibson and Sterling could have carried on the novel's narrative into sequel after sequel, retelling innumerable events of the Victorian age in altered fashions and dredging up every conceivable figure from that era to be creatively refashioned within its computer-dominated framework. (Harry Turtledove's novels provide one model for such enterprises.) Thankfully, since Gibson planned no further collaborations with Sterling, the authors faced the conundrum of how to decisively end a story that might go on forever. They devised two imperfect strategies: first, an imagined scrapbook of memoirs and documents from the period, seemingly an effort to vividly epitomize the distinctive imaginary world they crafted; second, a final, cosmic idea to hopefully lift their narrative onto a new plane and make the novel seem worthwhile.

While the concluding excerpts contribute little to the story already told, the final two pages of *The Difference Engine* command more attention, largely because they are written in an enigmatic style uncharacteristic of Gibson (whose poetic passages can seem elusive at first but are always decipherable in the end). One may interpret this sequence in different ways, but it appears to extend this saga of an alternate nineteenth century into this timeline's version of 1991. Just as the early introduction of computers prematurely transformed London into an environmental catastrophe, the same factor, by 1991, made the city even more nightmarish: "Ten thousand towers, the cyclonic hum of a trillion twisting gears, all air gone earthquake-dark in a mist of oil, in the frictioned heat of intermeshing wheels. Black seamless pavements, uncounted tributary rivulets for the frantic travels of the punched-out lace of data, the ghosts of history loosed in this hot shining necropolis" (428). Even worse, the increasingly dominant computers are seemingly merging into a single, vast artificial intelligence—"the Eye"—which in becoming sentient seems to regard all people as, or to transform people into, mere bits of data:

Paper-thin faces billow like sails, twisting, yawning, tumbling through the empty streets, human faces that are borrowed masks, and lenses for a peering Eye. And when a given face has served its purpose, it crumbles, frail as ash, bursting into a dry foam of data, its constituent bits and motes. But new fabrics of conjecture are knitted in the City's shining cored, swift tireless spindles flinging off invisible loops in the millions, while in the hot inhuman dark, data melts and mingles, churned by gear-work to a skeletal bubbling pumice, dipped in a dreaming wax that forms a simulated flesh, perfect as thought. (428–29)

This passage raises the possibility that all the novel's characters are merely creations of this infernal machine as it learns more about itself, even in some way brings itself into existence by observing their actions. Alternatively, one could say that the novel's events are real, while our own reality is only one of this computer's innumerable inventions. Gibson himself says, "The story purports in the end to tell you that the narrative you have just read is not the narrative in the ordinary sense; rather it's a long self-iteration as this thing attempts to boot itself up, which it does in the final exclamation point" (Fischlin, Hollinger, and Taylor, "The Charisma Leak" 10).

However, I prefer to see Gibson and Sterling's Eye as metaphorical, representing what authors always do: they craft imaginary worlds and characters to inhabit them, and carefully monitor and gain insights from the results. In addition, since the passage's language casts this whole activity as arbitrary and self-indulgent, one could see the Eye as a commentary on alternate history itself, wherein authors may indefinitely come up with concept after concept to generate one set of altered characters after another. By this reading, the final passage effectively describes Gibson and Sterling's experiences while writing *The Difference Engine*: they engendered all these transformed characters, "electric phantoms"; these were "examined, dissected, infinitely iterated"; and through this process, the combined Eye behind the project is finally able to "see itself" (429) for what it is—and, feeling properly ashamed of all this pointless creation, it brings the novel to an immediate halt. The presumed autobiographical resonances of this interpretation, then, are that Gibson is announcing his abandonment of two activities—collaborative writing and alternate history—that he has in fact scrupulously avoided. He told a *Telegraph* reader in 2003 that he would "probably not" write another steampunk novel, and while he did report to Alex Deuben in 2007 that he and Sterling had "talked about" writing another collaborative novel, Gibson diplomatically continued, "there hasn't been a time where I was really creatively free to do it"—and one suspects that time will never come.

As another profitable venue for his talents, Gibson in the late 1980s went to work for Hollywood, where he labored on several projects that never came to fruition, the usual pattern of contemporary screenwriters' careers. In a 1992 interview, Gibson was dismissive of this activity, stating, "What I'm working on now is mostly getting some three or four feature movies into production," but defensively adding this was "not really literary stuff; it's just entrepreneurial hustle" (Fischlin, Hollinger, and Taylor, "The Charisma Leak" 4), done more for money than artistic fulfillment. A 1989 interview mentions a script entitled *Macrochip* cowritten with John Shirley ("William Gibson Profile" 35); he told Edo van Belkom in 1998 that he worked on "eight or ten screenplays" during this time; and he informed Christine Cornea in 2007 that he had "actually written enough screenplays to contract to qualify for a pension from WGA West" (26). He also told Cornea that all of these, except for *Alien 3*, "were adaptations of my own short fiction" (26). He mentioned three scripts to Giuseppe Salza in 1994: an adaptation of "Burning Chrome," linked to the director Kathryn Bigelow; something called *Neuro-Hotel* (probably an errant transcription of "New Rose Hotel"); and a projected episode of *Max Headroom* that was never completed because the television series was cancelled. In 1994, Gibson further informed Stephen Bolhafner that he had completed "three or four scripts" based on "New Rose Hotel" (one, according to a 1989 interview with Douglas Walker, in collaboration with Shirley and also connected to Bigelow), though none of Gibson's work was used into the actual film of that name. Gibson told Cornea that he felt unattached to these labors: "I don't regard un-produced contract screenplays as part of my body of work—to the point that I don't even keep copies," because "[t]hey feel more like collaborative design projects than works of fiction" (26).

To date, only two scripts from this period have become available. One, a draft screenplay for a proposed *Alien 3* film (completely unlike the *Alien³* that eventually appeared in 1992), was never published but is widely available on the internet, and Gibson acknowledges it as a shortened version of his own work. The other, a screenplay based on "Johnny Mnemonic," was filmed by Gibson's friend, the artist Robert Longo, and published alongside the original story. While the latter work proved worthwhile, Gibson seemed happy to return to novels, though he later collaborated with Tom Maddox on two scripts for *The X-Files*.

In writing his *Alien 3* script, Gibson was given a story, developed by the producers David Giler and Walter Hill, of no particular interest: leaving the planet where *Aliens* took place, Ellen Ripley, Dwayne Hicks, and the android Bishop unknowingly bring some aliens to the space station Anchorpoint, where ill-advised research on the specimens engenders a new form of alien that can merge with human or animal tissue and instantaneously transform any person into a vicious monster. The resulting screenplay, with occasional moments of calm devoted to exposition or character development, inevitably became a repetitive series of scenes in which Hicks, Bishop, and some new characters (Ripley's role was reduced to a cameo, since Sigourney Weaver was then unwilling to commit to another sequel) are surprised by the appearance of one alien or another and are forced to fight for their lives before moving on to be similarly surprised, again and again, until they escape the infested and soon-to-be-destroyed station to provide a happy ending, also making a few remarks to set up a third sequel. The one novelty was the involvement of "a Marxist space empire," another of Giler and Hill's ideas which for Gibson proved a "fun" element, "In spite of its almost instant archaism," because "I couldn't recall a single piece of Cold War space opera in which the other guys were commies" (blog, September 1, 2003).

Writing this screenplay, Gibson visibly struggled to make its routine story as memorable as possible, though frustrations with the long process of getting the project to the screen led him to decline the opportunity to continue working on the script when Weaver reversed course and agreed to participate, mandating an entirely new story and screenplay. While Gibson was probably not involved in posting a version of his screenplay online, he must have been pleased to have this extensive piece of work find an audience, though he could not have obtained permission for official publication.

One noteworthy feature of the screenplay is its passages of clever or evocative language describing setpieces, displaying Gibson's talent for vivid specificity and surprising metaphors. The Machine Shop is "an oily forest of steel"; a bar is "ye olde pre-packaged genuine simulated wood-grain generic tavern," where "[o]ne wall is a screen showing a stale rerun of a Brazilian soccer match" and "customers play hologram game-consoles"; an alien infestation is "an Alien grotto, black and pearlescent, [an] obscene fairyland"; examining where aliens have rampaged, Hicks "surveys the wreckage of display cases, scattered 21st century consumer toys"; an "aisle of aeroponic greenery" is a "high-tech Hanging Gardens of Babylon"; some deserted "quarters have an eerie Marie Celeste quality: food and drink on the table, a pack of cigarettes beside an ashtray"; characters enter "[a]n office [with] 21st-century stylistics and a basic bureaucratic banality: fake teak, imitation leather"; and communicating his delight with the Soviet-style space empire, their "walls, in one large chamber, are decorated with official U.P.P. art, like a blend of Mexican Socialist agitprop murals and Syd Mead [techno]-fantasy," referencing the conceptual artist who worked on *Aliens*.

Gibson's dialogue includes a few memorable exchanges and sequences. When young Newt asks if the comatose Ripley is "dreaming," and a woman named Spence says, "I don't know, honey," the already-cynical Newt says, "It's better not to." The purported reason for studying the aliens—"cancer research"—is dismissed as "a cover," "like trying to cure cancer with a shotgun." One character berates Bishop as a "motherless zombie," and after Spence asks the company stooge Rosetti "why we had to bring you," and he curtly answers, "Funding," she concludes, "I guess you're right. You paid for it, I guess you get to fuck it up." There is also a brief moment of emotional drama, possibly not part of Giler and Hill's story, when Spence goes to feed "the module's population of small primates" while "[m]oths flutter through narrowing beams of sunlight as the louvers gradually close overhead." After finding the primates "cocooned in the branches of a tree" and being attacked by a "transformed lemur: a very small Alien," the distraught woman "hurls the basket of food at it and bolts from the forest, sobbing," distressed by what has happened to her beloved pets.

In addition, Gibson includes dialogue that both conveys, and casts a sardonic eye upon, traditional rationales for space travel. When a marine asks the character Tully, "[W]hat the fuck [are] you supposed to be doing here?" he initially responds, with obvious sarcasm, "Forging a new home for mankind in the depths of space," before more prosaically answering, "Collecting atmosphere samples." Later, Spence soliloquizes, "It's funny, but I had to win a contest to go through this. A science fair in Omaha, first in biology for all of Nebraska. Monoclonal antibodies. [. . .] Then I got into Cornell. Another contest. It wasn't easy, getting out here. We all must've wanted it so bad." After Rosetti tersely responds, "Idealists," she continues, "I guess so. Build a new world, find ways to live in it. . . . But it wasn't supposed to be like this. And it might've worked. It almost did." Here, Gibson may be commenting both on the course of the film's imagined future, with promising space initiatives that led only to sense-less slaughter, and the history of science fiction films, where once-optimistic visions of humans conquering the universe led only to derivative horror films set in space.

Finally, Gibson fitfully feels obliged to find something interesting to say about the aliens, though the origins and geopolitical implications of homicidal aliens are topics he would never voluntarily ponder. The character Suslov speculates that the alien might be "the fruit of some ancient experiment . . . the product of genetic engineering. . . . A weapon. Perhaps we are looking at the end result of yet another arms race." This is indeed a logical explanation for the aliens' otherwise bizarre physiology and behavior, and one that eventually surfaced in Ridley Scott's 2012 prequel to *Alien, Prometheus,* perhaps because someone remembered Gibson's words. Later, Bishop concludes that the human conflict with the alien goes "far beyond mere interspecies competition. These creatures are to biological life what antimatter is to matter," and since "[t]here isn't room for the both of you, Hicks, not in this universe," Bishop asks, "Will the alien be the ultimate survivor" in this "Darwinian universe"? In these lines, we observe Gibson fulfilling one key duty to his employers: producing a script that laid the groundwork for a fourth *Alien* film, then envisioned as an all-out battle against the creatures on their home planet.

While Gibson's screenplay, with some changes in its characters and story, might someday become the basis of another *Alien* film, it more likely will remain an unrealized project, like so many film scripts that are commissioned and shelved. And Gibson would probably refuse to revise his script, given his disinclination to explore its unpalatable themes. So the *Alien 3* script will stand as an odd item of Gibsoniana that may someday achieve official publication, perhaps in its original longer form.

The screenplay for *Johnny Mnemonic* (1995) reveals, if nothing else, that Gibson shrewdly sensed how a story had to be reshaped to work as a major film and was willing to make all necessary changes. First, the McGuffin driving the story—the data inside Johnny's head coveted by the yakuza—had to be more compelling than the story's unknown information, which Johnny speculates is merely "research data" stolen from one company (17). Gibson provides the screenplay's future with a widespread, debilitating disease—NAS, or Nerve Attenuation Syndrome, brought on by "[i]nformation *overload*" (81)—and makes Johnny's data a cure for this disease, which the conglomerate Pharmakom wishes to suppress because "[t]reating the disease is far more profitable than curing it" (124), creating conflict between its agents and those seeking to reveal that cure.

Second, Johnny's character would need to be more fully developed, so audiences could better relate to him. The film's Johnny has an additional incentive to get rid of his data as soon as possible: not only does the yakuza want the information, but Johnny (Keanu Reeves) has taken on more data than his brain can hold, meaning that he will soon die unless it is removed. This Johnny is also haunted by the loss of childhood memories that were removed to provide his brain with space for stored data—in early scenes, Gibson wishes Johnny to seem moved when he sees children, "as if the scene strikes a chord deep inside him" (18), and he speaks of having only tantalizing glimpses of his childhood, which are fleetingly visualized. Thus, Johnny's quest to save his life by releasing the cure also becomes a quest to rediscover his childhood. Ultimately, Johnny discovers that Anna (Barbara Sukowa), the computer-constructed personality of a deceased executive who keeps trying to get the yakuza overlord Takahashi (Takeshi Kitano) to switch allegiances, is actually his mother, struggling to protect her long-lost son. Molly Millions, here renamed Jane (Dina Meyer) because the Molly character was tied to the film rights to *Neuromancer,* also has strong reasons to assist Johnny, since she is a victim of NAS who cannot find work as a bodyguard because of her condition and thus personally needs the cure.

Finally, a successful action film requires lots of violence, so to augment the story's encounters with yakuza assassins, the screenplay adds another colorful opponent, Street Preacher (Dolph Lundgren), a vicious assassin who incongruously looks and dresses like Jesus Christ and speaks like a Christian fundamentalist while working as a killer for hire to pay for innumerable body modifications that have made him virtually invulnerable. Despite his fondness for high-tech implants, this character makes the story's conflict seem like a battle between the past and the future, as Street Preacher's biblical language and the yakuza's traditional fighting techniques are regularly thwarted by Johnny's advanced technology. (Gibson also employs religious terminology to delineate his two opposing sides: Anna tells Takahashi that he is living in a version of hell—"[I]f there was never such a thing as hell before, we surely invented it" [39]—while the elevated realm of Nighttown where Johhn meets Jones and gets his data removed is renamed Heaven.)

Gibson makes other changes: an added prologue shows Johnny's trip to Beijing to obtain the data he will transport to Newark, and as a nod to *Neuromancer*, Gibson allows Johnny to pay brief visits to cyberspace while searching for ways to download his data. The screenplay notes, "This version of cyberspace is a 3-D grid, densely arrayed with various SHAPES. Each shape represents data in a particular computer" (67). Yet the screenplay is otherwise faithful to the original story, as Jane, Spider (Henry Rollins), T-Bone (Ice-T), and Jones help Johnny escape the machinations of the two-timing Ralfi and the yakuza to finally download his data.

As is always the case with Gibson, the language of the screenplay commands attention. Despite his denials, Gibson was surely thinking of his critics when he had Street Preacher proclaim, "And I was made . . . *posthuman*" (54). He incorporates into the screenplay a memorable line from the story's first paragraph, here as an exchange between Johnny and T-Bone:

JOHNNY: If they think you're technical, go crude . . .
T-BONE: . . . If they think you're crude, go technical. (37)

And he employs memorable rhetoric to convey to filmmakers his vision of Heaven, referencing William S. Burroughs to say, "[i]ts bulging patchwork flank suggests the world's largest tree house, built by several generations of hardcore Wild Boys," and instructing the camera to "MOVE IN—as if approaching a spaceship made of garbage" (99).

Still, the film version of *Johnny Mnemonic* was not entirely faithful to Gibson's screenplay, for two reasons: First, while wishing to follow his friend's screenplay as closely as possible, Longo inevitably made some changes while he was filming, which might reflect the input of the film's star, Keanu Reeves, or Longo's own ideas; as a rule, these weakened the story instead of strengthening it. Second, displeased with Longo's film, studio executives reedited the footage without his participation, further distancing the released film from the original screenplay. Gibson published the screenplay, he said in a May 10, 2003, blog entry, "to demonstrate the difference between what I wrote, and we shot, and what they released."

True, not all alterations to Gibson's screenplay were misguided: for example, displaying the same sort of prophetic lapse that populates *Neuromancer*'s future world with travel agents, Gibson has Johnny meet a "Customs Officer" at the Newark airport who warns him about his overloaded implant; it is more futuristic to have the warning come from a computer monitor. And Longo's artistic talents provide the film with a visual flair that extends beyond Gibson's minimal descriptions.

But other changes dumb down or weaken Gibson's story. One major factor that inspired alterations, one assumes, was the concern that audiences, inattentive to the background information Gibson works into the dialogue as is traditional in science fiction, might have trouble understanding the story. A lengthy introductory text was added to explain that in 2021, "corporations rule," and the world is afflicted by Nerve Attenuation Syndrome. Some additional infodumps were worked into the script throughout the movie, to make absolutely sure that even the dimmest person in the theater would understand what NAS is and why a cure for NAS is important. To further orient viewers, a new introductory scene was added of Johnny with a girl who quickly leaves, allowing Johnny to contact Ralfi (Udo Kier) and reluctantly arrange to serve as a courier for data from Beijing. From that point on, the film basically follows the script, though some scenes are removed—largely to reduce the prominence of Street Preacher and Anna and provide less information about them. Most significantly, the film omits the crucial information that Anna is Johnny's mother, making the motive behind her altruistic actions unclear, though attentive viewers might guess that the attractive woman standing over a birthday cake in the final scene that Johnny abruptly remembers is the same woman they have been seeing on computer screens. The order of some scenes was altered, in part to postpone revelations about the cure for NAS and the personality of Street Preacher that Gibson integrated into the story at an earlier stage. If the film seems less exciting than the screenplay, that might be attributed to Reeves's typically wooden performance as Johnny, though more energetic supporting actors—Meyer, Lundgren, Ice-T, Kitano, Rollins, and Denis Akiyama (as the yakuza assassin Shinji)—compensate somewhat for Reeves's inadequacies.

The changes in the screenplay's language would most disturb Gibson's readers. A few key lines are omitted, including the exchange about being crude or technical and Street Preacher's declaration about becoming "posthuman." Clichés Gibson would have avoided are inserted: Takahashi's comment that the computerized Anna is "a ghost" is transformed into the trite phrase "a ghost in the machine," and one assassin tells Johnny it is "time to die," a pointless borrowing from *Blade Runner* (1982). The most conspicuously incongruous addition to the screenplay, though, was strangely written by Gibson himself during filming: while waiting in a trash-covered field to be lifted into Heaven, a frustrated Johnny raves that instead of being where he is, he wants to be enjoying "room service," a "club sandwich," a "cold Mexican beer," a "ten-thousand-dollar-a-night hooker," and his "shirts laundered like they do at the Imperial Hotel in Tokyo." As Gibson reported in a May 9, 2003, blog entry, "Keanu asked for something a little more projective, so I sat up, one night, in the hotel on Avenue Road, writing this speech out, longhand, on a yellow legal pad." Presumably, the intent was to humanize Johnny's character by providing him with some conventional aspirations; yet having him articulate such random desires further weakens the idea that Johnny is primarily focused on reacquiring lost childhood memories, a theme already muted by other revisions. Gibson did the best he could under intense time pressure, but this ill-advised speech only makes Johnny sound like just another hustler hoping for one big score so he can live on Easy Street, and when Johnny, upon finally extracting the cure from his brain, suddenly remembers a childhood birthday party, the scene has little emotional impact, since viewers are not prepared to understand its significance.

Understandably, *Johnny Mnemonic* left Gibson with little desire to continue writing screenplays. The film came together under seemingly ideal circumstances—Gibson's script had been accepted without major revisions, and a friend was hired to direct—yet the results still fell disappointingly short of his expectations. Perhaps, though, if more viewers could see the extended version of the film, now available only in Japan, the world's opinion of this largely reviled film, and Gibson's opinion about the experience, might be higher.

Gibson's next experience in screenwriting came about after an encounter with Chris Carter, the creator of *The X-Files,* which seemed an ideal venue since it was a science fiction series filmed in Vancouver. As Gibson reported in a May 1, 2003, blog entry, the episodes "were co-written with Tom Maddox, with Chris Carter making his accustomed final pass on each one (which invariably, in my experience, helped)." Working within the framework of a long-established series, Gibson for once might have actually benefited from having a collaborator, although without access to the original script, one cannot independently confirm that Carter's revisions were beneficial.

The first episode, "Kill Switch" (aired February 15, 1998), invites consideration as the first adaptation of *Neuromancer,* heavily reworked to fit into the series format, although (as is unsurprising in a collaborative work) it focuses on the aspect of the novel that seemed of least interest to Gibson, the development of a genuine artificial intelligence in cyberspace. Here, it is created by the secretive computer pioneer Donald Gilman (Patrick Keating), who decides to "let it loose" on the internet so it can grow and develop as a sentient being. However, since one must preserve the status quo within the confines of a television series, this entity must be characterized as sinister and menacing, leading Gilman to create a "kill switch" program to eliminate it. As a nice touch, the program is embedded in a CD that plays a 1958 Platters song, "Twilight Time," evocatively referencing the planned demise of the AI.

Fighting to preserve its own existence, the AI murders Gilman and attempts to thwart the efforts of agents Fox Mulder (David Duchovny) and Dana Scully (Gillian Anderson), assisted by the Lone Gunmen (Bruce Harwood, Tom Braidwood, and Dean Haglund) and Gilman's former associate Esther Nairn (Kristin Lehman), to track down and destroy an isolated trailer that serves as its physical home. In the end, the AI is apparently destroyed, but there are hints that Nairn contrived to download her own personality into the internet, as the Lone Gunmen receive a mysterious message, "BITE ME," and another well-protected trailer is observed in a Nebraska small town, presumably the transformed Nairn's new residence. As another borrowing from

Neuromancer, Mulder at one point is captured inside the trailer and forcibly immersed in a virtual-reality experience created by the AI in which he has both arms removed in a hospital, part of the AI's attempt to extract information about the "kill switch"—a scene that possibly inspired the storyline of Gibson and Maddox's second *X-Files* episode.

However, the virtual-reality element of "First Person Shooter" (aired March 5, 2000) involved, as the title suggests, an elaborate video game, which, as noted while discussing "Dogfight," is not something Gibson cares about, since neither he nor his characters would waste their time in such pursuits. As a further uncharacteristic weakness, the episode's story makes no sense: as a company prepares to ship a new game that allows players to put on motion-capture suits to physically experience gun battles with virtual opponents, a problem develops when a female warrior named Maitreya (Krista Allen), created independently by a company employee, Phoebe (Constance Zimmer), somehow "jump[s] programs" to enter the game and, driven by its creator's hostility toward men, begins physically killing players in a fashion that is never explained. After Mulder and Scully are asked to investigate by the Lone Gunmen, working as consultants for the company, Mulder bizarrely decides to start playing the game himself, ostensibly to assist the Lone Gunmen, who have become trapped in the game, though it is also suggested that, as a typical man, he simply loves such experiences—an attitude utterly foreign to Gibson and, for that matter, Mulder's usual character.

The story becomes more and more illogical as it progresses. Though it is impossible, Mulder physically vanishes from the room where players enact their roles, but telemetry readings indicate that he is still alive. Then, simply by entering the game herself, Scully somehow locates him and defends her partner against increasingly implacable computer enemies. Finally, Phoebe reluctantly reveals the code that enables the Lone Gunmen to destroy the game, saving Mulder and Scully. A final scene indicates that Maitreya managed to survive, somewhere in cyberspace, though she now has Scully's face.

To provide a patina of profundity for an episode largely devoted to colorful violence, Mulder is given a peculiarly portentous closing speech, building upon a previous exchange with Scully, about the interaction of virtual reality and our primitive human programming: "Maybe out past where the imagination ends our true natures lie, waiting to be confronted on their own terms. Out where the intellect is at war with the primitive brain in the hostile territory of the digital world where laws are silent and rules disappear in the midst of arms. Born in anarchy with an unquenchable bloodthirst we shudder to think what might rise up from the darkness." But these abstract musings are probably the work of Maddox (or the uncredited Carter), since standing on a podium to pontificate about human nature is generally alien to Gibson's proclivities (the only other examples that come to mind are two poems created for artistic performances, "Memory Palace" and "Our Brief Eternity," discussed below). In his May 1, 2003, blog entry, Gibson reports that "Kill Switch" was "more fun" than "First Person Shooter" because the shift to filming in Los Angeles, and the episode's unusually high budget, gave it "a more generic feel"—but this could be Gibson's way of stating that this "generic" episode, like other collaborations, did not really seem like one of his own works.

While the same blog entry reports that, after these experiences, Gibson "was working up some ideas" for episodes of another Carter series, *Harsh Realm,* that series only lasted for nine episodes, depriving him of the opportunity to contribute, and Gibson to date has earned no further screenwriting credits—though one might argue that he served as the extemporaneous "screenwriter" of the documentary *No Maps for These Territories,* which consisted almost entirely of footage of Gibson riding around in his limousine and responding to questions. Presumably, he resolved at the time to completely forswear writing for film or television: certainly, he no longer needed any income from screenwriting, and the necessarily collaborative nature of the experience, even when one is the sole credited author, could only have been disheartening to Gibson, who manifestly prefers to tell his own stories his own way. Without going into detail, Gibson also indicated that some encounters with filmmakers were less than pleasant, telling Dennis Lim in 2007 about "bad experience at Hollywood pitch meetings." Employing more colorful language, he was quoted in a 1994 fanzine as having "muttered that," after "meeting a producer, he knew exactly how a virus felt when it met with its own specific antibody" (Langford, "Mimsy Were the Borogoves").

Still, while denying any interest in directing, he told Uri Dowbenko in 2000 that if filmmaking "becomes an inexpensive and leisurely activity in the evolution of digital cinema, maybe I'll do that in retirement," suggesting a lingering interest in the medium. And in a November 11, 2011, Twitter posting, Gibson reported, "I am currently writing what I believe is called a spec script." In the interview below, he provides more detail about this screenplay: "It involves time travel, and the elevator pitch is that it's '*Band of Brothers* versus Blackwater.' It's set in Berlin 1945 and in an alternate 1997 USA." He also states that if it is not filmed, he might turn its story into a "graphic novel," venturing into a new form of visual narrative.

Gibson's first literary publications, in 1963, were poems, and he obviously remained interested in the form, since in the 1980s and 1990s, when artists approached him about collaborative projects, he usually provided poetry. To date, Gibson has published three poems, not counting fanzine efforts, along with two other poems available only as excerpts.

Asked to contribute to Robert Longo's 1989 performance piece *Dream Jumbo,* Gibson wrote a poem, "The Beloved: Voices for Three Heads," later included in a book, *Robert Longo: Art Random,* largely devoted to documenting that show. Like other poems from this time, "The Beloved" focuses on cityscapes, its first section evidently devoted to Gibson's memories of travels with his wife:

> I remember
> The crowd
> Shibuya
> Timesquare
> Picadilly
>
> I remember
> A parked car
> An arena of grass
> A fountain stained with earth
>
> In the slow fall to dawn
> In the arms of the beloved
> Remembered
> Alongside night
> In the Hyatt caves
> In the half-life of airports

In the hour of the halogen
Wolves

The hour remembered

In radio silence[.] (26)

The second section introduces the theme that people can "go lost, actually /
In any city at all," noting, "My father went lost that way / My mother too"
(28), while the third section addresses the problem by suggesting that people
can survive in cities by finding love:

Our love knew
The frequency of silence

Our love knew
The flat field

We became field operators
We sought to decode the
Lattices

To phase shift to new
Alignments[.] (31)

While this poem, published only in Japan, remained unknown, Gibson's
next poem was more prominent: an experimental collaboration with the artist Dennis Ashbaugh called *Agrippa: A Book of the Dead,* published in 1992 as
pages of artwork designed to fade away, accompanied by a Gibson poem on
a disk that erased itself after being accessed. The project was thus designed
to embody the simultaneously ephemeral and enduring nature of memories,
as the intent was to transform both Ashbaugh's art and Gibson's poetry into
readers' memories and nothing else. Inevitably, the poem immediately became
available online, to be preserved indefinitely, and Gibson eventually posted it
on his Web site.

Since this autobiographical poem is readily available, unlike Gibson's other
poems, and was discussed at length in Paul Schwenger's "*Agrippa*: Or, the

Apocalyptic Book," there is no need for extensive study of it here, but one might briefly consider the work as additional evidence that Gibson would rather observe than analyze, since it consists almost entirely of vivid details from his and his father's past. First, Gibson describes looking at his father's old photo album, with several photographs singled out for special attention, which provoke other memories—a camera, an old gun that accidentally went off, later visits to Toronto and Washington, and most tellingly, the "all night bus station" later celebrated on his blog where, in the space previously occupied by "the colored restroom," Gibson first saw the science fiction magazines, "esoteric and precious," that set him on a course to becoming a writer. Vaguely unifying this material is the term "mechanism," referring to the camera, gun, and ultimately, one supposes, the entire process of observing, remembering, and recording information (like a camera), and sometimes destroying such data (like a gun).

In the same year as "Agrippa," Gibson wrote a script called "Memory Palace," evidently taking the form of a prose poem, for an Art Futura performance event in Barcelona. While copies of the entire script are extant, Gibson refuses to sanction its official or unofficial publication, regarding it as unfinished work, but he allowed an excerpt to be read in *No Maps for These Territories,* which was transcribed and posted online. The passage, while haunting and evocative, sounds uncharacteristically oracular, perhaps explaining Gibson's reluctance to release the entire piece. But it merits attention as another reflection of his long-standing interest in the relationship between humanity and technology: "When we were only several hundred-thousand years old, we built stone circles, water clocks. Later, someone forged an iron spring. Set clockwork running. Imagined grid-lines on a globe. Cathedrals are like machines to finding the soul; bells of clock towers stitch the sleeper's dreams together. You see; so we've always been on our way to this new place—that is no place, really—but it is real. It's our nature to represent: we're the animal that represents, the sole and only maker of maps." Another piece of unpublished poetry, "Our Brief Eternity," was written in collaboration with Christopher Halcrow to be shown during a Vancouver performance by the Holy Body Tattoo dance group in 1997. Its title suggests that some of its language might be derived from "The Beloved," since the phrase occurs in that poem, but excerpts available online indicate that the text provides glimpses of other cityscapes:

The waters rise through the roots of the cities;
deer in the streets of downtown Detroit,
an iris bursts the Paris pavement,
the old, the modern, deconstructs into fern curl,
flowers nodding by a wall.

Other passages drift into the sort of elevated profundity that seemingly characterizes Gibson's poetry:

Religion is a small smooth stone we take in turn into our mouths to hold.
To find a place beyond the signs free of our sleepless, our terrible inheritance, a country of simple actions of seeds, of rain, of wind, our tasks our anchor.
Culture consists of sharing water, the gathering of food, defense against the hungry signs of the ancestors, the loss of an individual utterly reconfigures the whole; be vigilant . . .
Somehow, continue. . . .

Still, one wonders why Gibson does not allow these pieces to become generally available, unless he is reserving them for a projected volume of poetry.

A final Gibson poem, "Cold War Water," appeared in a 2006 volume of tributes to the critic John Clute and his wife, the artist Judith Clute. Again focused on details, it concerns a "[g]rey-painted beer-sized can" that Gibson observes every time he visits the Clutes' home in London, left long ago by the writer Thomas M. Disch; while first suggesting that this "cold war water" "anchors a rare long-favourite place," he sentimentally concludes by announcing, "actually, the two of you do." It seems characteristic of Gibson to notice something that, surely, few other visitors to their home had noticed, and to seize upon it as a symbol of its spirit of hospitality.

Gibson's ventures into writing song lyrics, both released in 1993, focus on dark urban environments of the sorts long featured in his fiction. "Dog Star Girl," written for a Deborah Harry album, involves a girl addressing her obviously conflicted boyfriend, who first finds himself in a city that is "so bright" as to inspire him to "pray for rain," but later complains, "How'd I ever get to this dead man's town / where the rain, where the rain falls down, / where the rain falls down forever?" The girl hopefully pleads, "Let me be your dog star girl," but the man remains resolutely uncheerful, concluding, "So much for you, so much for me, / but I don't see, no, I don't see." Overall, the lyrics are blunt and unremarkable, and the boyfriend's angst seems at odds with Gibson's typical stoicism.

His spoken-word lyrics for the Yellow Magic Orchestra instrumental "Floating Away" read more like Gibson's prose, as a man walking through a city during a rainstorm responds provocatively to his environment with a typical mixture of detailed observations and metaphorical conceits. The rain is like "a sizzle of lukewarm bullets"; he enters "a narrow world" of "bare concrete" with "empty bottles racked in plastic" and "a moped against a vending machine"; and he sums up his feelings by explaining that it was all "like discovering a secret level of society" and "an experiment in psychogeography," a word repeated several times as the music continues. One readily imagines such conclusions emerging from Shinya Yamazaki, the sociologist in the novel Gibson had recently published, *Virtual Light,* and perhaps the author had him in mind while crafting this vignette.

Considering Gibson's unheralded contributions to fanzines, one must characterize his nonfiction in a manner different from what he himself says while introducing *Distrust That Particular Flavor*: rather than tentative ventures into unfamiliar territory by an author solely experienced in writing fiction, Gibson's later nonfiction was actually a return to forms of writing he originally specialized in—articles about his travels, technological artifacts, and favorite authors, books, and musicians. Granted, greater skill is on display in his later efforts, which now represent the bulk of his work outside of novels, but they are natural extensions of earlier proclivities.

There are two novelties in Gibson's later nonfiction: First, due to the prominence of *Neuromancer,* Gibson is regularly asked to write about present and future developments in computers and related technologies, though these are surely not subjects he would choose. Second, perhaps as a result of abandoning his own career as an amateur artist, Gibson in the 1980s developed an intense interest in contemporary art—he told Amy Cavanaugh in 2011 that the arts are "a part of the world that I naturally pay quite a bit of attention to"—provoking some extensive discussions: his tribute to the performance artist Stelarc was included in *Distrust That Particular Flavor,* but two better choices would have been his 1994 introduction to *Jeff de Boer: Articulation,* where discussing that artist's works provokes intriguing comments about the importance of objects in his fiction, and a lengthy essay written for a book celebrating the designer Paul Smith, "Paul Smith: A Most Benevolent Marvel," which introduces ideas about fashion that would become central to *Zero History*. Reflecting his ongoing fascination with this subject, Gibson told Jill Owens in 2007 that he might someday "like to design what people generally call streetwear."

Gibson's articles sometimes introduce themes and concepts that later figure in his fiction. He first applied the Tibetan concept of the *tulpa* to contemporary celebrities in a 2002 tribute to the actor Takeshi Kitano, "The Baddest Dude in Town" (38), and did the same in *Spook Country*. Gibson's skeptical attitude toward conspiracy theories, which surfaced to *Pattern Recognition* and its sequels, first came to light in his 2001 review "Metrophagy: The Art and Science of Digesting Large Cities" (116). When his 2001 article "Modern Boys and Mobile Girls" called Tokyo "a mirror world, an alien planet" (125), he offered ways of regarding foreign cities repeatedly employed by Cayce in *Pattern Recognition*. And Gibson says in the interview below that his Paul Smith essay "may have paved the way for the Bigend books."

Gibson's nonfiction also offers interesting comments about science fiction. While he notes in a 2004 introduction to *Neuromancer* that "[i]n my teens, in the sixties, I read a great deal of science fiction dating from the forties, a very fertile period for the genre" (viii), he confesses that by the time he was writing that novel, "I found myself possessed by a dissident attitude [. . .] a smoldering resentment at what the genre I'd loved as a teenager seemed to me in the meantime to have become" (x)—a disdain more colorfully conveyed by aforementioned comments in his introduction to Shirley's *City Come a-Walkin'*. Also, amusingly describing his frequent dissatisfaction with his own science fiction, he comments while introducing Eileen Gunn's *Stable Strategies and Others*, "I suffer from a torch-bearing mob of inner voices, constantly shouting that whatever I've just written is as attractive as hairball macramé" (xiii), reinforcing what Gunn quotes Gibson as advising her was "the secret of writing": "You must learn to overcome your very natural and appropriate revulsion for your own work" (qtd. in Gunn, "The Secret of Writing" xv).

When writing about writers and effectively engaging in literary criticism, Gibson also presents provocative opinions regarding the field of activity wherein his works have been so thoroughly explicated. He acknowledges that, by majoring in English and working as a teaching assistant, he was trained to be a critic; introducing Shirley's collection *Heatseeker,* he reflects on his comments by saying, "[T]hat all sounds very nice, very literary, very much what I was taught to do in the university" (iv). However, further reflecting his own misgivings about such analyses, he then says, "I don't think the vocabulary of lit-crit best describes the things John's fiction does best" (iv–v), which he argues is more akin to music. More bluntly, he opens his foreword to *Dhalgren* by announcing, "I distrust few things more than acts of literary explication" (xiii). He noted on his blog that Clute was "the only critical historian of science fiction I pay any attention to" (January 6, 2003); and in a speech published in 2012, Gibson referred to "the only critics of science fiction I pay any attention to, all three of them" ("Talk for Book Expo, New York" 44), without identifying them. After failing to pursue plans to thoroughly investigate a purported quotation from George Orwell, a blog entry was headed, "Good Thing I'm Not an Academic" (July 15, 2009). Despite such barbs, though, he recognizes that literary scholars will always be part of his audience, even addressing them while introducing *City Come a-Walkin'*: "Attention, academics: the city-avatars of *City* are probably the precursors both of sentient cyberspace and of the AIs in *Neuromancer,* and, yes, it certainly looks as though Molly's surgically-implanted silver shades were sampled from *City's*" (1).

In this later body of nonfiction, Gibson carried on with the approach, first observed in fanzine articles, that characterized *Pattern Recognition* and its sequels: looking at the real world in terms of science fiction, conveying that we indeed live in a science fiction world. In his impressionistic "Tokyo Collage" (1988), Gibson comments on "a circular hall where colors wash continually across ribs of cement reinforced with fiberglass, like some benevolent variation on the biomechanical architecture of H. R. Giger" (42) and epitomizes Japan's "ethnic style" by saying that it is "as though one were undertaking simultaneous time-travel to both the future and the past" (43). In "Disneyland with the Death Penalty," Singapore is presented as a "neo-Gernsbackian metropolis," and he finds in one building "enough footage of atria to make up a couple of good-sized Lagrangian-5 colonies" (52, 53). In "My Obsession," he speaks of a "Sony sign" that is "very large, very proto-*Blade Runner*" (158), and in "My Own Private Tokyo" he sees one section of the city as "the classic cliché better-than–*Blade Runner* Tokyo street set," and another "Tokyo streetscape" as being "[l]ike successive layers of Tomor-rowlands, older ones showing through when the newer ones start to peel" (117). Later, Perry's nineteenth-century visit to Japan is labeled "the Roswell incident as a trade mission, a successful one," while the postwar occupation meant that "the aliens arrived in force, this time with briefcases and plans, bent on a cultural retrofit from the scorched earth up" (118). In "Paul Smith," a Mini Cooper sports car is "like a car out of a Michael Moorcock fantasy" (85). Finally, visiting the enormous set for a U2 concert, he feels himself "on the outskirts of some city from a '50s horror film where distance plays tricks on the eye" and calls the massive and intricately designed set "an angular, bilaterally symmetrical Rorschach blot, a hard-edged Mothra" that finally, "Heaving up, Transformer-like . . . comes alive." Observing all this, Gibson says that he was "feeling like a rube at Roswell," though he additionally refer-ences L. Frank Baum's *The Wonderful Wizard of Oz* (1900) by commenting that he and his wife were "feeling like Kansas children swept up by a benevolent tornado of rock biz and technology" ("U2's City of Blinding Lights" 126, 128).

Sometimes Gibson even references his own science fiction. In "Tokyo Col-lage," he says, "Denizens of the Sprawl and 21st-century Chiba City would be right at home" in Japan (31). Describing the problem of getting cooperative backers for *Johnny Mnemonic* in "Notes on a Process," he refers to *Count Zero* when saying, "[W]hile that NO is there, some eldritch entity in Dimension Zed, be it a faceless Bahamian banker, her cousin the Peruvian tax lawyer, an Alaskan accountant, or Herr Virek in his designer career-vat in Neo Zurich (and *believe* me, you'll *never* know) will not sign the check you need to secure 'the talent,' i.e. 'name' actors, without whom you *cannot* make the movie" (207). Further speaking of the process of writing a screenplay, he reports, "You're kind of like one of those hapless yet tough-talking personality constructs in a William Gibson novel, the part of you that is most human has come to inhabit certain interstices in a piece of software called SCRIPTOR" (207). One film set is epitomized as "the mother of all garbage constructs, something really huge, big *gomi*, like a section of the bridge in *Virtual Light*" (208).

Also in the category of Gibson's nonfiction fall his innumerable interviews, the part of my bibliography that is surely incomplete, since some proved impossible to verify or track down. Though he believes that interviews, as he says in the interview below, are essential for "a commercially successful literary career," Gibson clearly does not relish these chores: in a 1992 interview, "The Charisma Leak," he comments, "If time spent fishing is subtracted from the length of time you're going to live, then time spent being interviewed counts double" (1). He told Alessandro Ludovico in 1997 that his ideal phone would have these "innovative characteristics": "It would make excuses, remind me of appointments, and . . . answer—interview questions!" As a further problematic aspect of interviews, Gibson's questioners frequently focus on the "cyberpunk" movement and/or Gibson's past experiences, conveying the false impression the author is obsessed with these topics, when other writings suggest precisely the opposite. Provocatively, Lewis Shiner told Lance Olsen in 1989 that in "a lot of Gibson's public statements . . . he's simply said what he thought people wanted to hear," so critics should "take some of those interviews with a grain of salt" (4), but in interviews during the last two decades, when the successful Gibson had presumably moved beyond anxieties about pleasing audiences, there is little evidence that he is being less than candid.

Recent interviews, though, are usually unmemorable because Gibson can be mind-numbingly repetitive, making the same comments again and again. Indeed, many cited observations from interviews can be found, worded slightly differently, in several other interviews. But Gibson is aware of this and has even argued that it becomes necessary for any experienced writer. As he explained to Andy Diggle in 1997, he attended a 1987 conference and observed famous writers who

> were giving great interviews, but they were giving the same interviews over and over. And I realised these guys had "tapes"—that's what I called them. It's like they've got tapes in their heads, and journalists ask them questions and they go "Yeah" and lay down this line of patter. It's like a stone worn smooth in a river, and it really is kind of brilliant. They've done it before, and as I go on doing this I realise that I'm starting to do it too. You start doing it out of self-defence.

Any discussion of Gibson's nonfiction must mention his blog and Twitter account. Launched in January 2003, Gibson's blog initially provided a wealth of information about Gibson's activities and ideas, as he not only posted random musings but also responded to various questions. The blog also allowed Gibson to post the texts of some hard-to-find items like the story "Cyber-Claus," the poem "Agrippa," the article "Dead Man Sings," and the speech "Up the Line."

However, maintaining the blog became increasingly burdensome to Gibson. As early as April 13, 2003, he reported, "One thing that was immediately clear to me, from the first blog, is that this is not an activity, for me, that can coexist with the writing of a novel," and concluded, "So, fair warning: I will indeed stop doing this at some point." And in an August 25, 2003, entry, he worried that excessively commenting on his discussion board would "turn into exactly the sort of tar-baby timesink that keeps books unwritten." He first said "adios" to his blog on September 12, 2003, for the express purpose of getting back to writing a novel, though he returned on October 21, 2004, "WITH AN ABRUPT LURCH INTO THE POLITICAL . . . Because the United States currently has, as Jack Womack so succin[c]tly puts it, a president who makes Richard Nixon look like Abraham Lincoln." But by now, the blog was dominated by links to, or extended passages from, others' online writing, and in January 2005 he began including photographs as well. As posts became more sporadic, he announced in a September 27, 2005, entry, "I currently seem to be proving my theory that I can't simultaneously write a novel and blog," though he filled space by posting excerpts from the work-in-progress *Spook Country*. In March 2009, Gibson even turned his blog over to a guest blogger, Womack. After starting a Twitter account in April 2009, that became his way of communicating with the world.

While popular with many readers, however, Gibson's terse tweets, often little more than links to articles or comments about local restaurants and the like, seem less interesting than his longer, more thoughtful blog posts; perhaps, only readers younger than I can truly appreciate its clipped, fragmentary style. Gibson acknowledged its different nature in an October 10, 2011, tweet, saying, "Twitter for me is a casual conversational form, largely offhand by nature. Unrehearsed speech as opposed to writing," and he told Jesse Montgomery in 2012 that Twitter represents "a completely ludic activity. It's like play." But if the "casual," "ludic" style of Twitter enables Gibson to focus more on formal writing, without distracting him like his blog, his shift to Twitter can be applauded for that reason.

A BRIDGE TO THE PRESENT
Virtual Light, Idoru, and *All Tomorrow's Parties*

By writing *Virtual Light,* Gibson confirmed what he had already signaled: a desire to break with the past and move in new directions. He pointedly declined in 1987 to write a chapter for a Science Fiction Writers of America handbook on "Writing Cyberpunk SF," as noted by David Langford (*Ansible* No. 50), and turned down, as he told Mark Shainblum and Matthew Friedman in a 1993 interview published in 2006, a large amount of money to sanction a proposed anthology of stories by other authors set in the world of *Neuromancer* (45). While recognizing that *Neuromancer* would forever define his career for many readers, Gibson wanted to avoid activities that would bolster its ongoing presence. Instead, he wanted readers to enter and appreciate a different sort of Gibsonian world.

Accordingly, *Virtual Light* was set in 2005, only twelve years after its publication, and its imagined new technologies were not far removed from actual technologies of the early 1990s. While computer hackers eventually play a small role in the story, there is only one fleeting glimpse of a virtual realm recalling cyberspace, and the two protagonists have almost no interactions with computers. Space, as both a setting and a metaphor, has vanished as well. While previous novels were determinedly international in their ambiance and settings, this novel explores the near future of the United States. Taking place almost entirely in California, *Virtual Light* depicts an America that faces a severe economic decline and has fragmented into smaller entities, as experienced by a variegated cast of characters including only one non-American.

While Gibson remained interested in futuristic science, this novel devotes more attention to speculative sociology, as it includes a Japanese sociologist studying the culture of the intriguing, lawless enclave that is central to the story, the Bridge—San Francisco's Bay Bridge, now closed to vehicular traffic and occupied by expedient transients who set up makeshift homes and businesses there. The novel's most intriguing piece of technology is the Bridge itself—a vast, intricate machine, created and maintained by thousands of disparate individuals, each following their own course. Indeed, the Bridge is explicitly linked to nanotechnology, envisioned armies of microscopic machines collectively creating complex structures in a manner resembling the growth of living organisms. Such nanotechnology is literally present in the novel, as the technology that rebuilt Tokyo after an earthquake and is projected for use in San Francisco, involving buildings that will *"grow"* and *"eat sewage"* (251), and it is figuratively present in the form of the Bridge, described by the former police officer Berry Rydell in similar language: "This place had just *grown*, it looked like, one thing patched onto the next, until the whole span was wrapped in this formless mass of *stuff*, and no two pieces of it matched" (178).

The only weakness of *Virtual Light* might be that it spends an insufficient amount of time on the Bridge. It takes one character, Rydell, a long time to get from Los Angeles to the Bridge, and while the other protagonist, the messenger Chevette Washington, lives on the Bridge, her job regularly takes her into the city. Once Rydell rescues Chevette, they travel southward through central California toward Los Angeles. But the other environments are more sketchily developed, and less interesting, than Gibson's Bridge. However, one suspects that Gibson, taking the long view, already anticipates revisiting the Bridge in a future novel (which will prove to be *All Tomorrow's Parties*) and hence deliberately limits its presence here so it would remain fresh and offer new areas for exploration.

Even while moving decisively into this new realm, Gibson exhibits typical caution by not entirely abandoning previous concerns—though he addresses these with a new sense of irony. For by the time he began *Virtual Light,* Gibson had been interviewed by seventeen people, including at least four individuals with academic backgrounds (Colin Greenland, Timothy Leary, Larry McCaffrey, and Takayuki Tatsumi). By means of these discussions, if in no other way, he had become acquainted with scholarly perspectives on his works, and in *Virtual Light* and later novels, he would express this new knowledge in two ways. First, although he denies in the interview below having any ability or desire to speak to academic readers, Gibson's works began to include comments and themes that seem designed to cater to this audience (the "posthuman" statement from *Johnny Mnemonic* being one example). Second, bemused more than stimulated by their observations, he would also risk their ire by openly satirizing academic analyses. Gibson effectively announced this intent in a 1993 interview with Mark Shepherd, saying that he wrote *Virtual Light* "to deconstruct and poke fun at a lot of my earlier work or at least a perception of it." His use of the term "deconstruct" demonstrates an awareness of critical theorists, yet he now seeks to "poke fun" at their "perception" of his "earlier work."

Thus, as the unusually obvious McGuffin that characterizes his later novels, Gibson employs an object that resembles a pair of sunglasses, though it is actually an expensive machine that conveys prerecorded images directly into the brain. Constructed by the corporation IntenSecure, its executives are concerned when the device is lost because it contains explosive information about a secret plan to radically refashion San Francisco. After Chevette impulsively steals the sunglasses from a courier, she is pursued by agents recruited by IntenSecure, including Rydell, though he later becomes her ally. Here Gibson recalls the reflective "mirrorshade" sunglasses once promoted as a symbol of cyberpunk writers, as highlighted in the title of Sterling's *Mirrorshades: The Cyberpunk Anthology* (1986). However, to Chevette, they are only "a pair of sunglasses, expensive-looking but so dark she hadn't even been able to see through them last night" (78); to the elderly Skinner, they recall the large sunglasses worn by "Katharine Hepburn" (81); and when Rydell encounters them, he sees them only as sunglasses with "a funny heft to them, weighed more than you thought they would" (225). Symbolically, in their inability to employ sunglasses that reveal a virtual world, Gibson suggests that these new characters are completely disconnected from his old purported territory, cyberpunk science fiction.

Equally telling is the character of Shinya Yamazaki, the sociologist studying the Bridge who regularly engages in, as Gibson told Shainblum and Friedman, "woolgathering about modernism and postmodernism" (44). He is a kindly man who, at the end of the novel, seems poised to replace Chevette as Skinner's roommate and assistant (though he resurfaces in Japan to perform different roles in *Idoru* and *All Tomorrow's Parties*), but to Bridge denizens, he seems a helpless, clueless figure, unable to understand or maneuver through its complex structures. Recognizing him as an outsider, one Bridge resident calls him "the college boy or social worker or whatever he was" (144). When Yamazaki "sense[s] Skinner's inward laughter" directed at him, he asks, "I make you laugh?" And Skinner replies, "Not today. . . . Not like the other day, watching you chase those turds around." It seems that Yamazaki "spent one entire morning attempting to diagram the sewage-collection arrangements for the group of dwellings he thought of as comprising Skinner's 'neighborhood'" (92). Manifestly, Yamazaki conveys that Gibson is amused by the scholars who devoted themselves to examining *Neuromancer* and its sequels; they are well-intentioned people, but sometimes inclined to focus their attention on aspects of the stories that Gibson would characterize as shit.

As another dig at literary critics, Rydell at one point fails to understand a reference to Fredric Jameson's concept of "late-stage capitalism" because it is not something he learned at the "police academy," since they emphasized more useful information like "how to talk to crazy fuckers when you're being held hostage" (250). (Oddly, Jameson remains one of the few academics Gibson references positively, repeatedly citing his concept of the "postmodern sublime" in interviews.) Finally, late in the novel Skinner gives Yamazaki a box of items to sell on the street that includes *The Columbia Literary History of the United States*. This proves the one item nobody wants because it "was badly mildewed," so Yamazaki abandons the book "atop a mound of trash" (321)—again indicating that Gibson does not value literary criticism.

Yamazaki serves another purpose in the novel—to provide the infodumps that were more clumsily inserted into *Neuromancer* as educational tapes and television programs. Significantly, the novel's description of the Bridge, taken almost word for word from the cited passage in "Skinner's Room" (62–63), is presented as Yamazaki's vision of the environment he is studying. Should anyone wonder why, in a world where data can be effortlessly sent electronically, Chevette's profession of messenger still exists, Yamazaki didactically provides the answer:

> The offices the girl rode between were electronically coterminous—in effect, a single desktop, the map of distances obliterated by the seamless and instantaneous nature of communication. Yet this very seamlessness, which had rendered physical mail an expensive novelty, might as easily be viewed as porosity, and as such created the need for the service the girl provided. Physically transporting bits of information about a grid that consisted of little else, she provided a degree of absolute security in the fluid universe of data. With your memo in the girl's bag, you knew precisely where it was; otherwise, your memo was nowhere, perhaps everywhere, in that instant of transit. (93)

Yamazaki's reveries at times read like satires of scholarly writing. In one striking chapter, Skinner provides a vivid account of the night hordes of homeless people first occupied the Bridge. This is how he describes climbing over the fence that blocked access to the Bridge:

> [The police] had their choppers up in the rain, shining lights at us. Just made it easier. I had this pair of pointy boots on. Ran up to that 'link, it was maybe fifteen feet tall. Just kicked my toes in there and started climbing. Climb a fence like that easy, boots got a point. Up, man, I was up that thing like I was flying. Coils of razor at the top, but people behind me were pushing up anything; hunks of two-by-four, coats, sleeping-bags. To lay across the wire. And I felt like . . . weightless. (95–96)

After hearing the story, Yamazaki revisits the Bridge and offers a different sort of response:

> Skinner's story seemed to radiate out, through the thousand things, the unwashed smiles and the smoke of cooking, like concentric rings of sound from some secret bell, pitched too low for the foreign, wishful ear.

We are come not only past the century's closing, he thought, *the millennium's turning, but to the end of something else. Era? Paradigm? Everywhere, the signs of closure.*
Modernity was ending.
Here, on the bridge, it long since had. (97)

Yamazaki's ruminations may sound profound, the sort of passage any graduate student would highlight, but in contrast to the immediacy of Skinner's account, his words seem lifeless, abstract, almost vacuous. Gibson's true sympathies lie with the grainy concreteness of Skinner's story, not Yamazaki's dizzyingly general conclusions, which might be said to epitomize the excesses of academic analyses. Further, it goes without saying, Gibson realizes that a vast majority of readers would prefer to read a book written by Skinner, not one written by Yamazaki.

As for the Sprawl trilogy's unifying motif, cyberspace, Rydell does briefly visit a form of cyberspace—the virtual world of "eyephone-space" maintained by the elusive hackers of the Republic of Desire, who amusingly call themselves the Cognitive Dissidents; Rydell hopes that they will assist in exposing the sinister scheme to transform San Francisco. In this illusory realm, he addresses three hackers: one looks like "a dinosaur"; another is "a sort of statue . . . shaped like a wide-faced man with dreadlocks"; the third is a "figure . . . all made up of television" (292–93). Aside from their singular disguises, these individuals act like conventional hackers who mischievously introduce false data into official networks to disrupt society—like the false alarm that led to Rydell losing his job as a security officer.

As for actual outer space, there is precisely one fleeting reference: after the fleeing Rydell tries all the credit cards he has at an ATM, then throws away those that didn't work, Chevette says, "Somebody'll get those." Rydell replies, "[H]ope they get 'em and go to Mars" (213)—a comment best interpreted as a joke, since nowhere else in the novel is an American space program mentioned. Further, given the country's depressed, fragmented condition, it seems unlikely that any space travel is occurring, let alone trips to Mars.

Since Gibson's protagonists are not connected or attuned to computer networks, they mainly manifest a characteristically Gibsonian focus on staying alive in an uncertain, demanding environment: Chevette wishes to keep her messenger job at all costs, Rydell agrees to assist in seeking the sunglasses because he needs a job, and the largely immobile Skinner supports himself by having friends sell his lifetime's accumulation of various goods. Adding a patina of class consciousness to their immediate concerns, the messenger Sammy Sal Dupree notes, "There's only but two kinds of people. People can afford hotels like that, they're one kind. We're the other. Used to be, like, a middle class, people in between. But not anymore" (134). In this respect as in others, Gibson seems prophetic in envisioning increasing economic polarization in American society. Another way that Yamazaki seems separated from other Bridge residents is that, evidently supported by research grants though he is "not wealthy" (62), he displays no interest in earning money and spends all his time studying the Bridge, implicitly linking him to privileged classes and distinguishing him from the streetwise entrepreneurs he is researching.

These people have one prominent new interest that becomes central to this series: the media of film and television and its celebrities. Rydell's roommate at the beginning of the novel, Sublett, was raised in "some weird trailer-camp video-sect" that believed "video was the Lord's preferred means of communicating, the screen itself a kind of perpetually burning bush" (9). He constantly watches or refers to obscure old movies like *Warlords of the 21st Century* (1982) and *Spacehunter: Adventures in the Forbidden Zone* (1983) (32, 302), or imaginary films from the late 1990s like *The Kill-Fix* (19). Rydell decided to join the police because while growing up he had enjoyed a reality show entitled *Cops in Trouble,* which he later almost appears on after killing a man named Turley during a hostage situation. Demonstrating his own obsession with films, the apparently deranged Turley says that he is on "a mission from God," a line from *The Blues Brothers* (1980) (11). Also indicating that television provides his main frame of reference, Rydell says that the lives of Los Angeles people "looked like what you saw on tv but weren't" (15). He reports that "the Pooky Bear killers . . . looked, he thought, pretty much like everybody else, which is how people who do that kind of shit usually do look on television" (27), and he remembers a filmed version of *Peter Pan* when he thinks a person in a sweatshirt "looked like a floppy shadow from some old movie Rydell had seen once, where shadows got separated from people and you had to catch them and sew them back on" (183).

Other characters also seem fixated on the media and celebrities. One Cognitive Dissident presents himself as an assemblage of televisions; the sunglasses remind Skinner of the film star Katharine Hepburn, a reference he repeats; and among other things, there is a poster of the rock singer Roy Orbison on Skinner's wall (156). Demonstrating that people's knowledge of history is usually limited to what they have seen in the media, Chevette is familiar with Michael Jackson—described as "that black guy who turned white, and then his face fell in" (41)—but incorrectly assumes another singer Skinner mentions, "Billy Holliday," was "probably a guy like Elvis" (264), both misspelling her name and misidentifying her gender. Berry Rydell's name recalls two stars of early rock'n'roll, the teen idol Bobby Rydell and the singer-songwriter Chuck Berry.

Further, this entire society is obsessed with media celebrities. The police surveillance satellite is universally called the Death Star, and one San Francisco park was renamed Skywalker Park, demonstrating the ongoing popularity of *Star Wars* (1977). More provocatively, Gibson discusses an unusual system effectively employed by future police officers:

> Separated at Birth was a police program you used in missing persons cases. You scanned a photo of the person you wanted, got back the names of half a dozen celebrities who looked vaguely like the subject, then went around asking people if they'd seen anybody lately who reminded them of A, B, C. . . . The weird thing was, it worked better than just showing them a picture of the subject. The instructor at the Academy in Knoxville had told Rydell's class that that was because it tapped into the part of the brain that kept track of celebrities. Rydell had imagined that as some kind of movie-star lobe. (86–87)

Gibson exploits this system to describe one protagonist, since all he reports about Rydell's appearance is that he looks like the actor Tommy Lee Jones (86). Since Gibson visibly expects readers will be able to visualize Rydell based on this reference, he none-too-subtly suggests that this predicted future fixation on celebrities is already common in 1993.

Gibson also has Yamazaki employ a celebrity-derived term created by an actual Japanese artist—"Thomasson," the last name of the American baseball player Gary Thomasson, a notorious failure in Japanese baseball—to describe "pointless yet curiously artlike features of the urban landscape" (64). In sum, while the term "virtual light" is used, in the novel and real life, to describe systems that produce visual images without photons, characters in this novel spend little or no time in such virtual realms. To justify the title, one might argue that the world of media celebrities provides the "virtual light" of people in this future America. (By mentioning various actors and musicians, Gibson anticipates what would become a key stylistic feature of *Pattern Recognition* and its sequels—rich arrays of references to contemporary popular culture.)

In two cases, this obsession with celebrities takes on the trappings of a religion—another interest of Gibson's that surfaced in cyberspace's loa but comes to the forefront here. Traditional religions still exist, as indicated by the name of one of Chevette's favorite groups, the "Chrome Koran" (40). But the more innovative Fallonites of Sublett's upbringing literally preach that "God's on television," so if followers "watch . . . all of these old movies," soon "the spirit will sort of enter into them" (272). Chevette notes that she had been raised as an "Aryan Nazarene" (273); and another cult developed around a man named Shapely, an AIDS-infected homosexual whose singular resistance to the disease enabled scientists to discover a basis for a cure in his blood. This success leads bitter members of a "white racist sect" (the Aryan Nazarenes?) to murder Shapely (323) and transform him into an attractive martyr. Significantly, the novel concludes with Yamazaki participating in a Bridge parade celebrating Shapely's birthday, suggesting that this scholarly outsider, like the critics he represents, might with time and effort become a true part of this colorful world—though his determination to "bring his notebook" to the event indicates that he may always be unable to genuinely enter, and understand, this underworld culture (323).

Observed in the context of Gibson's career, *Virtual Light* provokes several conclusions about his evolving worldview that become more apparent in *Pattern Recognition* and its sequels. First, far from being fixated on computers and computer-constructed worlds, Gibson is most intrigued by the real world and its variegated phenomena, which include as only one component some people who prefer virtual worlds. Second, while still interested in masters of new technologies, Gibson seems more fascinated by individuals who are uncomprehendingly affected by these technologies and the society they engender. Though not blind to such people's flaws and foibles—like the absurdity of a religion based on old movies and the incongruity of adopting Shapely, a promiscuous homosexual, as a patron saint—Gibson has risen above the air of condescension observed in his characterization of Mona in

Mona Lisa Overdrive to display genuine respect for uneducated, working-class individuals, valorizing their energetic determination to survive, resistance to manipulation by the rich and powerful, and endless ingenuity in adapting to and thriving in challenging circumstances. Finally, in embracing this devotion to common people, Gibson effectively sheds the veneer of third-world internationalism maintained throughout the Sprawl trilogy to more and more identify himself, knowingly or not, as a quintessentially American writer, embracing the democratic ideal that, in the end, one can always trust the masses to do the right thing. To be sure, Gibson cannot abandon his natural affinity with intelligent members of society's elite class—since he himself is part of that group—but he would diverge from the writer who in some ways prefigured his career, Heinlein, by retaining affection and respect for those who cannot join their ranks.

Read today, with an awareness of Gibson's twenty-first-century novels, *Virtual Light* seems a precursor of triumphs to come. However, in the early 1990s, readers and critics longing for another *Neuromancer* were disappointed by the novel, since it dealt only tangentially, and sometimes sarcastically, with the subjects they found exciting in Gibson's fiction. The always pragmatic Gibson, sensing their displeasure, may have deemed it advisable to placate these members of his audience by returning one more time to past glories. This would explain why *Virtual Light* was followed by an ostensibly related but very different sequel.

While set in the same future as *Virtual Light* and deploying two of its characters, Rydell and Yamazaki, in minor roles, *Idoru* in all other respects seems to repudiate its predecessor. *Virtual Light* takes place entirely in America; *Idoru* takes place entirely in Japan, the foreign country that figured so prominently in *Neuromancer* and other earlier works. *Virtual Light* involves plebeian characters inhabiting the Bridge and other humble settings; but while *Idoru*'s protagonists are arguably everyman figures, they are climbing the social ladder, and the novel otherwise features rich and powerful people and the typical places they visit, like expensive hotels and glamorous nightclubs. As if to signal that the novel is moving upward in its social status, the data analyst Colin Laney immediately dismisses Rydell, a distant but well-intentioned figure throughout the novel, as a "Nice Guy. Loser" (2). Although the judgment of Laney's former boss, the unsympathetic Kathy Torrance, cannot be trusted, she is allotted a paragraph to denounce the typical audience of Slitscan, her gossip-mongering organization, as "a vicious, lazy, profoundly ignorant, perpetually hungry organism craving the warm god-flesh of the anointed" (28)—opinions left unrefuted in the novel. Finally, suggesting that this novel's characters are elevated above and protected from mundane concerns, Laney offers this brief, striking reference to current events: "In the night, in the Federal District, somewhere east of here, there had been rocket attacks and rumors of chemical agents, the latest act in one of those obscure and ongoing struggles that made up the background of his world" (51). However, except for some occasionally threatening criminals, the privileged people of the novel are largely protected from such random acts of violence.

As the most noteworthy difference between the novels, *Virtual Light* has only one brief scene in a virtual environment; *Idoru* offers numerous visits to virtual realms and includes one character, Rei Toei, who is entirely the creation of computer programmers and interacts with the real world as a hologram. Further, while *Virtual Light*'s protagonists have little contact or familiarity with such matters, almost all the characters in *Idoru* regularly visit cyberspatial realms. Still, apparently to avoid the perception that he was too obviously revisiting his most famous trope, Gibson never employs the term "cyberspace," declining to associate this novel's virtual worlds with his all-encompassing "consensual hallucination," though one concluding reference to *Idoru*'s virtual Walled City does call it a "realm of consensual fantasy" (289), recalling his definition of cyberspace. Having created in *Virtual Light* a world that is entirely different than the Sprawl, Gibson in *Idoru* paradoxically strives to make that new world resemble the Sprawl as much as possible.

Even in minor respects, *Idoru* hearkens back to Gibson's fiction of the 1980s. There are repeated references to characters wearing sunglasses (1, 38, 132) without the irony associated with the stolen sunglasses of *Virtual Light*. A minor character, "a dealer in second-hand equipment" (158), is named Gomi Boy, employing the term for random junk used in "The Winter Market" and *Mona Lisa Overdrive* (133). Visiting the Walled City, Chia finds herself "aware of the countless watching ghosts" and calls the place a "city of ghost-shadows" (283), recalling *Mona Lisa Overdrive*'s virtual companion.

As forms of cyberspace are reintroduced, references to its cosmic equivalent, outer space, again become common. A tattoo on Torrance's body "looked like something from another planet, a sign or message burned in from the depths of space, left there for mankind to interpret" (4), and it is later called "the sign from outer space" (21). Laney sees "the sky over Burbank" as "perfectly blank, like a sky-blue paint chip submitted by the contractor of the universe" (5), and he recalls "CD-ROMs he'd explored in the orphanage: haunted castles, monstrously infested spacecraft abandoned in orbit" (227). Torrance regards celebrity as a "something spread evenly at creation through all the universe" (7). To emphasize his vulnerability to attacks, the gang member Zona Rosa sarcastically asks Gomi Boy, "You think you live on Mars or something?" (219), while another character describes the odd questions asked by police officers as "all fucking Martian" (278). Dreaming of a beach near the Walled City, Chia envisions Tokyo Bay as "a pale gray blanket meant to briefly conceal first-act terrors: sea monsters or some alien armada" (289).

In *Virtual Light*'s acknowledgments, Gibson only briefly mentions assistance from several individuals, including the writers Bruce Sterling, Tom Maddox, and Jack Womack, all associated with cyberpunk (324–25). However, in *Idoru*'s "Thanks" section, Gibson pays special tribute to Stephen P. Brown because he "rode shotgun on the work in progress for many months, commenting daily, sometimes more often. . . . His constant encouragement and seemingly endless patience were absolutely essential to this book's completion" ([xi]). Since Brown is best known as the editor of *Science Fiction Eye,* the influential magazine that analyzed and promoted cyberpunk during the 1980s, Gibson presumably sought his guidance in an effort to recapture the essence of that era and its literature.

Still, despite these indications of a reversion to earlier habits, one can also read this novel as Gibson's effort to achieve a synthesis between the computer-dominated world of *Neuromancer* and the reality-dominated world of *Virtual Light.* This is epitomized by the event that sets its story in motion: Rez, part of the aging rock duo Lo/Rez (who improbably keep attracting young fans like Chia Pet McKenzie, one of the two main characters), reportedly intends to marry the illusory Rei Toei, inspiring great concern among his retainers, especially his bodyguard Keith Alan Blackwell, and fans like Chia. To determine if this unsettling rumor is true, Chia is instructed to visit Tokyo to confer with members of the group's Japanese fan club, and Blackwell hires Laney, the other main character, to investigate the motives behind Rez's strange resolve (since Laney is a uniquely talented "fisher of patterns of information" [24]). As the novel's contrived action plays out, both Chia and Blackwell become reconciled to this bizarre marriage as something that will enhance the personal growth of Rez and Rei Toei. This suggests, almost too obviously, that the future world will benefit from having both real citizens and virtual citizens, and from access to both the real world and virtual worlds. Thus, men like Mashiko, the brother of the Japanese fan Chia meets, would rather live in virtual worlds like their Walled City; Laney and Chia will regularly access virtual data but otherwise live in the real world; and the real Rez and virtual Rei Toei employ nanotechnology to construct a new island in Tokyo Bay as their permanent residence.

Despite its divergences from *Virtual Light, Idoru* does continue its predecessor's explorations of media celebrities and their impact. True, there are few references to actual celebrities, other than mentions of Adolf Hitler (36), Yukio Mishima, Marlene Dietrich (142), and Elvis Presley (156); but as if to bring the topic into sharper focus, Gibson introduces fictional future celebrities as characters. The briefly glimpsed Alison Shires enters the media spotlight solely because she has an affair with a celebrity, an experience that drives her to the suicide Laney anticipates and attempts to prevent. More attention is paid to the rock singer Rez (modeled on Gibson's friend, U2's singer Bono), other members of the band, and title character Rei Toei who, because she does not really exist, might be said to embody celebrity in its purest form. The point illustrated by these characters is that celebrities, once one gets to known them, are much like ordinary people, and their wealth and fame have not made them happy: Shires is depressed when she becomes a center of attention, and Rez and Rei Toei want to marry because they feel personally unfulfilled. Suggesting that there is something unreal and unsatisfying about the pursuit of fame, Rez argues, "[I]t's easier to desire and pursue the attention of tens of millions of total strangers than it is to accept the love and loyalty of the people closest to us" (95).

Idoru also examines the mechanisms that promote celebrities and keep them in the public eye. As promotional tools, celebrities sanction and oversee fan clubs, like the one Chia belongs to, which Blackwell employs as a tool to suppress the news that Rez has resolved to marry Rei Toei by instructing the head of its Japanese chapter to denounce the story as a baseless rumor. Outside of celebrities' control, there are media outlets, represented here by Slitscan, a cutting-edge version of today's tabloid press, dedicated to uncovering and exposing unflattering information about celebrities. Its success further inspires the planned creation of a rival organization, Out of Control, to examine and expose the excesses of Slitscan's ruthless pursuit of celebrity dirt—what Yamazaki pompously labels a "meta-tabloid" (67). (Though Gibson repeatedly tells interviewers that he does not extrapolate in the traditional manner of science fiction, he says in *No Maps for These Territories* that Slitscan represented "my extrapolation" of *People* magazine and the *National Enquirer*.) There is another reference to the reality program in *Virtual Light, Cops in Trouble* (132), and as an apparent alternative to usually depressing news, Laney mentions a network called "the Good News Channel" (51).

Characters in *Idoru* also promulgate more abstract ideas about celebrities. The hypothesis aired in *Virtual Light*—that "celebrity-recognition was handled by one particular area in the brain" (166)—is again cited, though Laney suspects that the people espousing the idea "were joking" (166). The novel repeatedly references the theories of Torrance, who tells Laney, "Nobody's really famous anymore" because "there's not much fame left, not in the old sense" (4). Elaborating on this theme, Laney explains, Torrance "thought of celebrity as a subtle fluid, a universal element, like the phlogiston of the ancients, something spread evenly at creation through all the universe, but prone now to accrete, under specific conditions, around certain individuals and their careers" (7). Using more visceral language, he says, "Slitscan's business was the ritual letting of blood, and the blood it let was an alchemical fluid: celebrity in its rawest, purest form" (38).

However, Laney later regards her theories as inadequate: "He could see celebrity here, not like Kathy's idea of a primal substance, but as a paradoxical quality inherent in the substance of the world. He saw that the quantity of data accumulated here by the band's fans was much greater than everything the band themselves had ever generated. And their actual art, the music and the videos, was the merest fragment of that" (229). In characterizing celebrities as the almost inconsequential centers of phenomena greater than themselves,

Gibson may be commenting on himself, since by the time he was completing *Idoru* he had also become a celebrity, well known outside the field of science fiction as a sought-after writer for prestigious venues. He was also aware of the growing volume of commentaries about his works, largely involving ideas he did not create, meaning that he too had inadvertently generated something vaster, if not more valuable, than his actual writings.

Celebrities as factors that inspire the development of realms of data they do not generate also relate to the figure of the idoru. Denounced by Lo/Rez fan Zona Rosa as a "synthetic bitch" and "made-up thing" (233), Rei Toei indeed was originally created as a mere simulation of a human, yet her worldwide popularity, Gibson implies, inadvertently transformed her into a self-aware being. For while musing about "artificial intelligence," Laney recalls "a lecture in which the Slitscan episode's subject had suggested that AI might be created accidentally, and that people might not initially recognize it for what it was" (247–48). As fans and commentators effectively add substance to celebrities they admire, they even have the power, Rei Toei might be said to suggest, to endow celebrities who do not exist with genuine substance, "accidentally" making them actual entities.

Beyond what she embodies about the nature of celebrity, the idoru, with all she might convey about shifting definitions of identity and reality, becomes, and seems designed to become, the usual focus of commentaries on the novel. Despite disavowals, certain lines seems written solely to please Gibson's postmodern followers, like a comment about the invented virtual persona of the deformed Zona Rosa: "[I]t didn't matter that she hadn't *been* Zona, because she's made Zona *up,* and that was just as real" (291). Still, one might speculate that Gibson, not nearly as fascinated by such matters as his critics, here limits himself to the least adventurous, most reality-oriented characterization of artificial intelligence possible. After all, as Laney notes, the conventional "argument ran" that artificial intelligence "was most likely to evolve in ways that had least to do with pretending to be human" (247–48); certainly, little is particularly human about Wintermute/Neuromancer. But in this novel, an artificial intelligence develops that seems more and more like an actual human, with her ultimate goal being to become virtually identical to humans. Such entities will never do anything to threaten the status quo, like contacting alien intelligences; rather, they will seek to integrate themselves into human societies as fellow members of the species.

As evidence that the idoru is something designed to excite critics rather than something that excites Gibson, one notes that, to an unusual extent in Gibson's fiction, this novel's mechanisms seem forced and awkward, indicating that the author was constantly struggling to bring its story to life. Gibson's reference in the "Thanks" to "Stephen P. ('Plausibility') Brown" ([xi]) hints that maintaining plausibility was a major problem while writing the novel, and an area where Gibson regularly needed assistance. Yet problems in this area, despite Brown's help, were never resolved satisfactorily. Among the many implausibilities one might complain about, there is no persuasive reason for Chia to visit Tokyo, since members of Rez's fan clubs can interact virtually, eliminating any need for Chia to personally confer with the Japanese chapter; her travel is dictated solely by the demands of Gibson's story. It is extraordinarily unlikely that Chia would be singled out by Maryalice, a criminal's dimwitted accomplice, to serve as an unknowing carrier of smuggled goods, or that those goods would happen to consist of illegal nanotechnology equipment desperately coveted by Russian agents. And while the sunglasses in *Virtual Light* displayed some imaginative flair, this McGuffin dully looks like a box, which Chia has no reason to keep carrying around, although she does, solely to make her the target of those insidious Russians and to keep things lively. Finally, Laney and his new friends get dragged into Chia's story because, improbably, Rez and Rei Toei also want the smuggled device to build their island residence.

In addition, Rydell and Yamazaki seem to be included solely to show that *Idoru* is indeed a sequel to *Virtual Light,* though it is a significantly different sort of novel about a significantly different world. Both could have been removed from the novel without changing its story, further suggesting unresolved issues in constructing the plot. Rydell, who works in Los Angeles throughout the action, periodically warns Laney by phone or fax about potential threats he learns about, but his information has no effect on Laney. Yamazaki constantly accompanies Blackwell but never has anything to do, and it remains unclear precisely why Blackwell hired him, though his "habit" of "record[ing] ephemera of popular culture" enables Gibson to work in a few more digs at academic critics, like his aforementioned use of the word "meta-tabloid" and pedantic concern over whether a waitress's outfit, consisting of "a shapeless gray cotton boilersuit and cosmetic bruises," represents "the theme of this club" or "some deeper response to trauma of earthquake and subsequent reconstruction" (9). Laney mockingly echoes his words, saying of the club that "Yamazaki might have said that it represented a response to trauma and subsequent reconstruction," and cites the similarly elevated response of a "Belgian journalist"; but we are invited to accept the practical judgment of Laney's colleague Arleigh McCrae that the club was only "a commercial operation" (163–64).

Indeed, there are other indications that Gibson is becoming impatient with critics more dedicated to theorizing about, than observing, the world around them. When the club owner Jun is asked about Rez's announced desire to marry Rei Toei, he dismisses it as a "load of bullocks" and sarcastically elaborates by saying, "Evolution and technology and passion; man's need to find beauty in the emerging order; his own burning need to get his end in with some software dolly wank toy" (144)—suggesting that Rez's lofty rhetoric is a self-deceptive overlay for more basic concerns. Almost immediately thereafter, Laney sees "a man on stilts" with "a pair of rectangular sign-boards" on a Japanese street, and Arleigh reports that he represents a "sect" named "'New Logic.' They say the world will end when the combined weight of all the human nervous tissue on the planet reaches a specific figure" (145). Too much thinking, this doctrine conveys, will bring about the world's destruction. Thus, even as Gibson provides critics with more of precisely what they crave, he offers increasingly obvious barbs directed at their dedication to future theories instead of future realities. While his firm departure from computers and virtual worlds will not come until *Pattern Recognition*, he first resolves at least to bring the characters and concerns of *Idoru* down to Earth by transporting them to San Francisco's Bridge in what became the sequence's final novel, *All Tomorrow's Parties*.

Just as *Idoru* seems to repudiate *Virtual Light*, *All Tomorrow's Parties* seems to repudiate *Idoru*, as if Gibson was determined to get back to telling stories that meant something to him. While Laney and Rei Toei play small but significant roles in the novel, the main characters are *Virtual Light*'s Rydell and Chevette, and as in that novel, all the action occurs in California, mostly on or near San Francisco's Bridge. Asked by Antony Johnston in 1999 why he returned to the Bridge instead of the Walled City of *Idoru*, Gibson said that the Bridge was "more resonant, for me. More fun writing about a *physical* construct, somehow." True, the novel has several brief scenes in virtual realms, but Gibson's attention has shifted back to the real world and real inhabitants he prefers to deal with, and he again foregrounds plebeian characters instead of the rich and famous people who dominated *Idoru*.

Most tellingly, though everything about *Idoru*'s conclusion suggests that the marriage of Rez and Rei Toei will be successful, symbolizing a harmonious merger of the real and virtual worlds, this novel casually mentions that the marriage did not work out, as Rez resumed touring while Rei Toei retreated to existence within a small device that functions as this novel's McGuffin. Despite Rei Toei's continuing presence in *All Tomorrow's Parties* and her eventual re-emergence into the real world, this novel otherwise downplays the significance of this virtual character by both ending her marriage to Rez and conveying this news in an offhand manner amidst other matters dealt with at greater length. Laney, who is central to *Idoru*, is relegated here to living in a small cardboard box within a Japanese train station, playing a limited role as backstage observer and manipulator of events, while the sociologist Yamazaki is virtually invisible, his only role being to periodically bring Laney supplies. Symbolically, then, Gibson does not entirely abandon the concerns that animate *Idoru*, but he shoves them to the sidelines. Overall, while *Idoru* may have thrilled critics, *All Tomorrow's Parties* suggests that Gibson himself was less than thrilled, as he returns to the ambiance and concerns of *Virtual Light*.

Indeed, *All Tomorrow's Parties* qualifies as Gibson's first genuine sequel. Earlier novels set in already developed worlds—*Count Zero, Mona Lisa Overdrive,* and *Idoru*—primarily featured new protagonists, with returning characters pushed to the background; but *All Tomorrow's Parties* can be described as the further adventures of Rydell and Chevette, with another returning character, the storekeeper Fontaine, in a major role. (While Skinner has died, Chevette mentions him repeatedly, effectively making him a character in the novel.)

Further, while some new characters play small roles, they are either underdeveloped, making them stereotypes, or left as deliberate enigmas. Figures in the former category include Buell Creedmore, Rydell's companion on his trip to San Francisco, an out-of-control rock singer addicted to drugs and alcohol; Tessa, Chevette's roommate, a typical film-school student obsessed with filming a documentary about the Bridge, who pedantically likens the faces of residents to Robert Frank's photographs (191); Cody Harwood, a villainous media executive seeking to manipulate upcoming events; and Boomzilla, a streetwise young criminal on the Bridge. The enigmas are the nameless assassin employed by Harwood who haunts the Bridge, eventually revealed to be named Konrad but otherwise given no background, and Silencio, a young idiot savant who possesses an encyclopedic knowledge of various watches, his obsession, and an amazing ability to track down information about watches from online sources. Since Gibson never provides more information about these intriguing characters, they are deployed primarily as devices to keep the plot in motion: Konrad periodically intervenes to rescue characters in danger, while Silencio's unique skills effect a happy ending—by leading Laney to Harwood's virtual hideout—because the boy locates the man's distinctive watch. When Johnston asked Gibson to explain Konrad in 1999, Gibson said cryptically that he was "someone who wandered in from another book" and, he later suspected, a "sort of avatar connected to the late William Burroughs. An unconscious expression of Burroughsness."

To put a positive spin on the novel, one could say that *Virtual Light* created such a fascinating environment, and fascinating characters, that it was natural to devote a second novel to their further development. But a Gibson character would cynically regard *All Tomorrow's Parties* as a product of expediency, even desperation, as an uninspired author eschews the chore of crafting new characters and settings to rely upon tried-and-true characters and settings from an earlier work to generate one more profitable novel. In any event, the problems he faced in writing a sequence's third novel are even greater here than they were in *Mona Lisa Overdrive*.

Silencio's obsession with watches may represent the novel's most revelatory symbol; for a watch is an intricate mechanism consisting of innumerable tiny parts that work together harmoniously to perform an important function. One could characterize *All Tomorrow's Parties* with similar language: a host of characters from earlier novels, and several new characters, move in an intricate dance as they approach the Bridge, either physically or spiritually (via virtual monitoring), to participate in or witness a convergence of factors that Laney and Harwood believe will dramatically transform the world, perhaps even bring it to an end. The resulting novel is a marvelously effective entertainment machine, perhaps Gibson's best page-turner, filled with short, exciting chapters that expertly shift from character to character to incrementally advance the separate stories that intertwine in the end. Yet *All Tomorrow's Parties* may also be Gibson's emptiest novel, as one struggles to discern any larger import in its machinations.

In fact, while criminal comrades called the boy Silencio because he generally refuses to talk, the name may also signal that this character has nothing significant to say to readers. As another clue, readers unfamiliar with Velvet Underground songs may assume that the title's word "parties" means "individuals," so the title can be paraphrased as "all people of the future," since the novel features many characters from previous novels. However, the song "All Tomorrow's Parties" (1966) uses the word to mean "celebrations," as shown by its opening lines: "And what costume shall the poor girl wear / To all tomorrow's parties?" The song was inspired by Lou Reed's observations of the carefree lives of Andy Warhol and his followers, largely involving one colorful party after another. Thus, Gibson's title announces that the novel is about a series of parties—gatherings offering pleasurable entertainment but involving no important business. Characters and readers may have a good time, but nothing is being accomplished. One might further infer that Gibson referenced a song about partygoers wearing "costumes" to suggest that characters in this novel, like Silencio and the assassin, are wearing costumes, so readers cannot learn their true nature—and after all, guests rarely get to know other people at parties.

In many cases, one establishes the significance of apparently frivolous works by carefully examining their conclusion. After finishing this novel, one must wonder why Laney and Harwood were so excited and worried about impending events in San Francisco, because it seems that nothing really has changed. Rydell and Chevette, who broke up after the conclusion of *Virtual Light,* are poised to become a couple again; this might please readers who like these characters, but it is hardly a matter of importance. To thwart Laney, Harwood ordered the burning of the Bridge, the novel's miniature apocalypse, but firefighters extinguish the blaze, and one can be confident that the ever-resourceful denizens of the Bridge will rebuild their humble homes and businesses to resume their previous lives. Indeed, the final chapter indicates that Silencio is starting his own business on the Bridge. Harwood will be killed by Konrad, his own hired assassin, destroying his media empire, but this will only make the world a slightly better place.

Only one concluding development might eventually have an impact: Harwood previously ordered that his ubiquitous Lucky Dragon stores—the future's equivalent to 7-Eleven—be equipped with teleportation devices to allow customers to purchase a product in one store and instantly create a duplicate in another store, eliminating the need to deliver gifts to faraway friends, although the usefulness and appeal of this service seem questionable. Rei Toei somehow employs this technology to create a real body for herself—and not just one, but innumerable identical embodiments: Boomzilla "sees her on every last screen, walking out of every Lucky Dragon in the world, wearing that same smile" (269). Presumably, this device has become a means whereby virtual characters like Rei Toei can become real people, by materializing in real bodies, thus allowing the world to be gradually inhabited by a mixture of real and virtual people, harmoniously interacting without knowing whether certain individuals originated in a womb or computer program. Since Rei Toei's incarnations will presumably develop into different sorts of people in different environments, there is the suggestion that one virtual prototype might engender scores of similar but distinctive individuals. Nevertheless, since no character other than the unimportant Boomzilla notices this development, and no one comments on its significance, Gibson must be uninterested in these possibilities, as he instead focuses concluding chapters on resolving the fates of his real characters—primarily Silencio, who is finally observed employing advanced technology to miraculously repair a watch. Perhaps Silencio's evolving abilities also represent something that will transform the world, but this ending may suggest that this novel, overall, was merely a successful effort to repair a damaged watch—a series previously featuring two jarringly disparate stories—and restore it to smooth working order.

As another way to deflate the significance of his own novel, Gibson at one point seems to connect the worlds of the Bridge and *The Difference Engine*. For as Laney becomes more involved in monitoring the world's data searching for patterns, he feels that he is attaining some new mode of being:

It is as though he becomes a single retina, distributed evenly across the inner surface of a sphere. Unblinking, he stares, globally, into that eye, seeing that with which he sees, while from a single invisible iris appear individual, cardlike images of Harwood, one after another. [. . .]

[W]hen he becomes the eye that looks in upon itself, and upon the endless string of images, he has no awareness beyond that interiority, infinite and closed.

And part of him asks himself if this is an artifact of his illness, of the 5-SB, or if this vast and inward-looking eye is not in fact some inner aspect of that single shape comprised of every bit of data in the world? (167)

This recalls "the Eye" of *The Difference Engine,* which at the end "must see itself" (429). Perhaps Gibson is hinting that the earlier novel's "Eye" is in fact Laney, always capable of detecting history's "nodal points," who having previously identified the year 1911 as one turning point might similarly look to the early nineteenth century, and Charles Babbage's failed efforts to create computers, as another moment from which one might generate various possible outcomes, including the alternate history of *The Difference Engine.* Yet this might also suggest that the entire world of *All Tomorrow's Parties* and its predecessors is also only one of this all-seeing Eye's many illusory creations. Noting that Gibson likened himself to Laney in an interview, one might deduce that this novel is offering a witheringly ironic self-portrait: Gibson is an unimportant person, marginalized by society like someone living in a cardboard box, who spends his days on the computer examining and developing entertaining illusions. (Also, the full name of Creedmore's guitarist is "Randall James Branch Cabell Shoats" [100], referencing the eccentric, arguably solipsistic author, also admired by Heinlein, who paid tribute to Cabell's *Jurgen, a Comedy of Justice* [1919] in the title of his 1984 novel *Job: A Comedy of Justice.*)

As another addition to the strange mixture of ingredients in *All Tomorrow's Parties,* Gibson brings space travel into the world of the Bridge, at least as an option for wealthy inhabitants. When Konrad communicates with an unseen observer who is almost certainly Harwood, "He knows that the words he hears come in from a tiny, grotesquely expensive piece of dedicated real estate somewhere in the planet's swarm of satellites" (97). In a later conversation the man's "laugh" is "beamed down from the secret streets of that subminiature cityscape in geosynchronous orbit" (136). In specifying that this represents a "direct transmission" (97–98), Gibson indicates that Harwood is either physically in orbit or inhabits some virtual realm in orbit, both suggesting that the tycoon lives in space, presumably to distance himself from ordinary life while monitoring world activities. In the end, Harwood returns to Earth to meet Konrad and, it transpires, to be killed. Perhaps, since Harwood's virtual hideout was located by Silencio, and his schemes thwarted by Laney, this symbolizes that the high-flying media giant has been brought down to Earth.

For Gibson, it would have been effortless to devise another crisis, involving another McGuffin, to bring characters of the Bridge together again for another fast-paced adventure. Yet his desire to make money is always outweighed by a restless need to constantly venture into new territory, and one finishes *All Tomorrow's Parties* sensing that the author had no desire to revisit its world. In fact, this sequence may have suggested to Gibson that he faced a fundamental problem in writing about the future: despite his best efforts, he might always feel compelled to return to the topics of advanced computers and virtual realms that so fascinated readers and critics. His bold strategy for preventing this, implemented in his next novel, would be to write about the present, necessarily limiting his explorations of computer-generated worlds and allowing Gibson to pursue his genuine interests in the real world.

CHAPTER 7

ALL TODAY'S PARTIES
Pattern Recognition, Spook Country, and *Zero History*

Gibson had planned *Pattern Recognition* for a long time: in 1986, he predicted to Mikel Gilmore that he would "eventually try something else," and "in twenty years" he would probably be "writing about human relationships" (108). After telling Robert K. J. Killheffer in 1993 that he strived in *Virtual Light* to "use as much real stuff—existing today—as possible," he concluded, "Maybe the challenge for me is to write a William Gibson novel that does all the things that a William Gibson novel is purported to do, but set it in 1993, in the real world" (71). By 2003, having "been threatening" to write about the present "for years," as he told Mark Flanagan, he finally did so; and, as is often true when long-cherished plans are finally realized, *Pattern Recognition* radiates the aura of an exhilarated author who has found his forte.

By shifting from the future to the present, Gibson clearly felt that he was relaunching his career, and hence he logically reverted to the pattern of his first novel. Having mastered the art of juggling multiple protagonists, he returned to the simpler pattern of one viewpoint character, Cayce Pollard, who even shares the name of *Neuromancer*'s hero. (While she was named after the prophet Edgar Cayce, who pronounced his last name "Casey," Cayce establishes in an early conversation that she pronounces her name "Case" [31].) In the novel, like Case, she is hired by a wealthy, mysterious figure to track down important information. Yet Cayce is not a skilled computer hacker but, like Colin Haney, someone uniquely skilled in "pattern recognition"— though she does not delve into databases but simply observes the world as a professional "coolhunter" who detects emerging trends and intuitively identifies which corporate logos will be effective.

Known as a science fiction writer for decades, Gibson felt an obvious need to justify this novel's present-day setting—the story actually occurs in 2002, one year before its publication—and does so with an awkwardly didactic conversation involving Cayce and her employer, Hubertus Bigend (demonstrating, if nothing else, that Gibson retained the science-fictional habit of "infodumps"):

> [W]e have no future. Not in the sense that our grandparents had a future, or thought they did. Fully imagined cultural futures were the luxury of another day, one in which "now" was of some greater duration. For us, of course, things can change so abruptly, so violently, so profoundly, that futures like our grandparents' have insufficient "now" to stand on. We have no future because our present is too volatile. . . . We have only risk management. The spinning of a given moment's scenario. Pattern recognition. (57)

Gibson anticipated the argument in his 2000 article "Will We Plug Chips into Our Brains?" when commenting that "our real future" is "our ongoing present" (84). So, if science fiction is concerned with the future, and our only future now lies within the ever-changing world around us, one can indeed write about the present and consider the results science fiction.

There are other ways to argue that *Pattern Recognition* should be classified as science fiction. Gibson repeatedly denies that this is the case, but he concedes that the novel is connected to science fiction: he said in 2003 that it fails to qualify as science fiction not because it is too realistic but because it is too fantastic in ways that one could not scientifically justify, citing Cayce's "sensitivity to trademarks" and "the ultimate source of the footage"; still, he also observed that the novel "has the flavor of science fiction" ("Crossing

Boundaries" 63). He told David Wallace-Wells in 2011 that he did not consider the novel and its sequels to be science fiction but acknowledged key similarities: "They are set in a world that meets virtually every criteria of being science fiction, but it happens to be our world, and it's barely tweaked by the author to make the technology just fractionally imaginary or fantastic. It has, to my mind, the effect of science fiction." Yet if a novel "has the flavor of science fiction," "meets virtually every criteria of being science fiction," and has "the effect of science fiction," cannot one simply say that it is science fiction?

To defend that classification, one can also raise the issue of marketing, something Gibson is keenly aware of; as he commented in "Rocket Radio," "[T]he fiction I've written so far has arrived at the point of consumption via a marketing mechanism called 'science fiction'" (87). In fact, while *Pattern Recognition* is subtitled *A Novel,* in an effort to identify the book as mainstream fiction, Gibson's long-standing reputation as a science fiction writer ensured that this novel, and its successors, would continue to reach readers by means of the genre's "marketing mechanism." I never find *Pattern Recognition, Spook Country,* and *Zero History* in the general fiction or literature sections of bookstores; they are shelved in the science fiction and fantasy sections. So, if one defines a book's genre by how it is marketed, *Pattern Recognition* and its sequels must be science fiction.

In addition, although nothing is egregiously different about *Pattern Recognition*'s world, some aspects of the story do not precisely accord with general perceptions of contemporary life. While the term "coolhunter" emerged in the 1990s to identify people who earn a living by keeping abreast of trends, these individuals typically work for major companies, or firms specifically devoted to coolhunting, instead of making a living as freelancers like Cayce, and their deductions emerge from research, not intuition. While it is not unknown for companies to hire people to praise their products, they usually do this work online, instead of visiting bars and restaurants to offer loud praise, which is how one of the novel's characters is employed. In the novel, technology allows a filmmaker to completely alter characters and background in footage in ways that a small army of dedicated viewers cannot detect—an ability that seems slightly beyond what was possible in 2002. The conspiratorial activities of Bigend and his Russian counterpart, Andrei Volkov, recall characters in techno-thrillers more than the behavior of actual billionaires. To account for these slight departures from reality, one might argue that Gibson, despite the time of the novel's events, is actually writing about an extremely near-future world, only slightly in advance of our own, where "the technology," as Gibson said, is "just fractionally imaginary or fantastic." Another argument would be that Gibson has crafted what John Clute terms a "secret history," positing the present-day existence of advanced technology and phenomena hidden from all but a select few.

One can also build upon Cayce's numerous references to London as a "mirror-world" (2), subtly different in many small ways from New York, to maintain that Gibson is writing an alternate history about a 2002 that is almost, but not entirely, identical to our world—a position advanced at the beginning of Neil Easterbrook's "Alternate Presents." In *Pattern Recognition,* then, Gibson may have achieved what he told Jack Womack in 1997 he attempted to do with *Virtual Light* and *Idoru:* "[T]o create something that feels the way the present feels, but *even more so*" (52). From this perspective, *Pattern Recognition* describes a world slightly unlike our own because Gibson intensifies and exaggerates certain aspects and proclivities.

Cayce's reactions to London and other places suggest another reason to regard *Pattern Recognition* as science fiction: the novel's viewpoint character consistently sees her environs as a science-fictional or fantasy world. Though she initially thinks that one feature of a London apartment—the switch on a lamp—"feels alien," she immediately shifts to the notion that it is part of a "mirror-world" (2), referencing Lewis Carroll's *Through the Looking Glass and What Alice Found There* (1871) and indicating that she regards London as a fantasy world, with some items literally reversed—like cars and roads—and others subtly different in other ways. But, unsettled by Bigend's strange interest in the footage, she starts feeling "not foreign but alien" in London (88), and later, in Tokyo, she sees her surroundings as more an alien world than a mirror-world: she refers to Japan's "alien but half-familiar marketing culture" (126), speaks of bread of "slightly alien dimensions" (138), and enjoys "great and alien luxury" in a Japanese beauty parlor (140). In Moscow, she again employs such imagery, detecting "alien or perhaps non-existent concepts of zoning" (269), and the filmmaker's sister tells her that the film's story involves not her parents' world but "another world. It is always another world" (306), recalling Cayce's comment that she is fascinated by the footage because of its "sense [. . .] [o]f an opening into something? Universe? Narrative?" (109).

Either to convey a science-fictional perspective or to provide familiarizing elements for science fiction readers, *Pattern Recognition* includes explicit references to various works and authors of science fiction, including the films *Stalker* (3) and *Solaris* (146), "the first James Bond film" (42), H. G. Wells's *The Time Machine* (110), Godzilla films (131), *Blade Runner* (146), William S. Burroughs (186), Stephen King (216), and the television series *The X-Files* (12) and *The Man from U.N.C.L.E.* (221). More subtly, when Cayce observes that spotting trends is "largely a matter of being willing to ask the next question" (32), knowledgeable readers will recognize the statement "ask the next question" as the frequently quoted words of the science fiction writer Theodore Sturgeon (Duncan, "The Push Within").

As another device suggesting science fiction, the novel repeatedly employs astronomical imagery: Cayce observes the grafitti "THERE IS NO GRAVITY THE EARTH SUCKS" (15); she refers to the designer Tommy Hilfiger as "the null point, the black hole," and says, "There must be some Tommy Hilfiger event horizon, beyond which it is impossible to be more derivative, more removed from the source" (18); Cayce's friend Parkaboy likens himself and a friend to "those Mars Rover jockeys" (145); she says that her feeling of "full-on London-Tokyo soul-displacement" is "less a wave than the implosion of an entire universe" (150); and Cayce notes that "[t]he coal of [a man's] cigarette flares mightily, like a meteorite entering Earth's atmosphere" (238).

There are also references to Gibson's own science fiction to accompany the nod to *Neuromancer*'s Case. In Tokyo, Cayce notices "[t]he metal column of a traffic light, across the alley, furred with weird municipal techno-kipple" (156), employing the Philip K. Dick term Gibson used in "The Winter Market." When she escapes from captivity and must get past a chain-link fence, "She looks at the chain-link and at the toes of her Parco boots. Not a good match. Summers in Tennessee had taught her that nothing climbed chain-link better than cowboy boots. You just stuck the toes straight in and walked right up. The Parco boots have toes that aren't narrow enough, and only lightly cleated soles" (320). These musings recall Skinner's account in *Virtual Light* of how he climbed over a similar fence, using his boots in precisely the manner described—another character who needed to scale a fence to achieve freedom. Referencing Gibson's comment from "The Winter Market," Cayce notes of herself, "She's not one of those people who won't ever read the manual, although she'll skip it if she can" (142). This not only partially refutes Gibson's previous sentiment but also reinforces the notion that Cayce, like Gibson, is not as tech-savvy as the heroes of his earlier science fiction.

Gibson further hearkens back to previous novels by including another character like Yamazaki who is unquestionably a device to satirize academic critics. Here, it is a woman calling herself Mama Anarchia on the Footage Fetish Forum, where enthusiasts discuss bits of mysterious footage being anonymously released on the internet: a post from Parkaboy "rail[s] on about Mama Anarchia's tendency to quote Baudrillard and the other Frenchmen who annoy him" (48), and readers eventually read a sample of her writings: "Do you know nothing of narratology? Where is Derridean 'play' and excessiveness? Foucauldian limit-attitude? Lyotardian language-games? Lacanian Imaginaries? Where is the commitment to praxis, positioning Jamesonian nostalgia, and despair—as well as Habermasian fears of irrationalism—as panic discourses signaling the defeat of Enlightenment hegemony over cultural theory? But no: discourses on this site are hopelessly retrograde" (267). Cayce notes that she "used the word 'hegemony,' without which Parkaboy will not admit any Mama post as fully genuine. (For a full positive identification, though, he insists that they also contain the word 'hermeneutics')" (268). From such passages, readers can deduce two things: Gibson, after years of contact with academic critics, can replicate their jargon, and he does not particularly value their analyses.

Indeed, if it is insufficiently clear that Gibson does not respect such rhetoric, Cayce's despised opponent Dorotea Beneditti eventually reveals that she is Mama Anarchia, assigned to contribute deliberately irritating posts to a forum that interests her employers. Cayce protests, "You couldn't be," because "you never say anything hegemonic," and "I don't think you could make all that up" (315). Dorotea responds, "I have a little puppenkopf to help me. I say what I need to say, and he translates it into the language of Anarchia, to so annoy your most annoying friend." Dorotea's "puppet-head" is "[a] graduate student, in America" (315). Academic jargon, then, is doubly derided as something any graduate student can generate and as language nonspecialists find more irritating than enlightening.

However, even while lambasting scholars, Gibson gives them much to discuss in this novel, illustrating that it is indeed rewarding to apply a science-fictional perspective to contemporary society, seeing it as a fantasy or alien world. Perhaps by happenstance, perhaps by design, what Gibson discerns and conveys about the present often accords with the concerns of post-modern critics. Even without the advanced technologies in earlier novels, the nature of human identity is constantly in question, as people can go online to create new personae that may be reasonably authentic (like Peter Gilbert's Parkaboy, basically similar to the thoughtful, altruistic man he is) or completely fraudulent (like Dorotea's Mama Anarchia, whose devotion to critical theory is merely an act). Furthermore, it becomes difficult to differentiate between real and concocted identities, as illustrated by the way that Parkaboy and his friend Darryl persuade a Japanese geek, Taki, to provide important information about a number secretly embedded in one piece of footage. Combining their email messages with doctored photographs of a girl named Judy, they create an imaginary woman named Keiko to successfully arouse Taki's romantic interest and, by means of a meeting with Cayce, get him to reveal the number. When Judy learns what the men are doing, she insists upon sending Taki messages herself, as Keiko, hoping that he can visit California to meet her. Effectively, Judy abandons her real identity to adopt a fictitious identity—something anyone can now do with the internet and Photoshopping.

Furthermore, even with actual contact, it is difficult to determine what people are really like. While Cayce correctly deduces that Dorotea is a horrible person, despite her recurring efforts to explain and justify her actions, she initially thinks that Boone Chu, another Bigend employee assigned to work with her, is a supportive friend, though he proves an untrustworthy ally, while the man she initially dislikes, Hubertus Bigend, emerges in the end as more sympathetic. Her views of other people are upended as well: a Bigend employee who makes her travel arrangements seems honest and reliable, but the tycoon fires her after learning that she provided information about Cayce's whereabouts to her enemies. Upon receiving a purported email message from the filmmaker behind the footage, Cayce repeatedly refers to the person as a man, but discovers that a paralyzed woman is actually its creator.

It is hardly coincidental that those most mysterious and secretive of employees, spies and secret agents, are frequently referenced in the novel—both fictional spies like James Bond and *The Man from U.N.C.L.E.* and real spies like Cayce's deceased father, Winthrop (Win) Pollard, who worked as "an evaluator and improver of physical security for American embassies worldwide" (44); Baranov, the ex-spy who gives Cayce the filmmaker's email address; and Dorotea, whom Bigend identifies as a former "spy" specializing in "industrial espionage" (62). The novel suggests that many people in the world today are spies of sorts, working on covert agendas and never entirely to be trusted—a theme Gibson returns to in *Spook Country*, explicitly a story about modern-day spies.

In addition, it is not merely individuals but larger events that one can never be sure of. Initially, Cayce believes that her interest in the footage, and problems with people breaking into her apartment, following her, and tracking down her personal information, are entirely unrelated. She attributes the latter intrusions solely to Dorotea's desire to eliminate her as a rival for a coveted position with Bigend's company Blue Ant. However, Dorotea is actually working in cooperation with the Russians who covertly support the creator of the footage: they fear, due to one of Cayce's posts and the fact that she is an American spy's daughter, that she may determine the filmmaker's identity and hence endeavor to thwart her. As another twist, it turns out that there are two factions within the Russian operation, and one becomes Cayce's powerful benefactor.

Despite her skills in "pattern recognition," Cayce recognizes that efforts to discern dark secrets lying behind everyday events can be taken too far: early in the novel, describing her mother's strange belief that messages from dead people can be detected within random noises on audiotape, Cayce introduces the term "apophenia"—"the spontaneous perception of connections and meaningfulness in unrelated things" (115). Soon wondering if there is any significance to the presence of a fading rock star on her airplane to Tokyo, she concludes that it would be meaningful "[o]nly [. . .] if she thinks of herself as the center, the focal point of something she doesn't, can't understand," recalling her father's belief that "[p]aranoia . . . was fundamentally egocentric, and every conspiracy theory served in some way to aggrandize the believer." Though her father also said "that even paranoid schizophrenics have enemies," she decides that her fears are "a species of apophenia" (124). Later, pondering the involvement of Russians in matters around her, Cayce again uses the word while recalling additional advice from her father: "There must always be room for coincidence, Win had maintained. When there's not, you're probably well into apophenia, each thing then perceived as part of an overarching pattern of conspiracy. And while comforting yourself with the symmetry of it all, he'd believed, you stood all too real a chance of missing the genuine threat, which was invariably less symmetrical, less perfect" (293–94). Then, acknowledging this need for restraint, Cayce correctly deduces that Baranov's Russian background, and the Russian location where her friend Damien was filming, are unrelated to her dilemma, though a posting of hers wherein she speculates that a "Russian mafia kingpin" (294) is behind the footage might be significant—as it proves to be.

As an aside, the recurring presence in the novel of the late Win Pollard, who vanished on September 11, 2001, and is presumed dead as a result of the terrorist attacks, recalls one feature of the Sprawl's futuristic world: the creation of computerized simulations of valued individuals that, in effect, allow living people to talk to dead people. In part, the absent Pollard embodies the overwhelming sense of pain and loss inspired by the World Trade Center's destruction—an event that affected the expatriate Gibson more than one might expect—but he also reminds readers of another feature of their world that is almost science-fictional: by means of memories, letters, and recordings, dead people can still communicate with the living. Cayce does not inhabit a world where a computer simulation of her father can answer her questions, but at key moments she can remember helpful things he said. In "Dead Man Sings," Gibson remarked that when we hear a recording of Elvis Presley singing "Heartbreak Hotel," "[W]e are seldom struck by the peculiarity of our situation: that a dead man sings" (52); but our memories, as that essay also suggests, have always allowed people to hear dead men singing.

Other aspects of the novel reinforcing ideas from previous Gibson novels include the increasing unimportance of national boundaries: Cayce describes Blue Ant as "more post-geographic than multinational" (6) and casually travels to four foreign countries, never spending a moment in her homeland; even her final moment of repose with her new boyfriend Parkaboy, also American, takes place in Paris. Gibson expanded upon this theme in 2008 to Eric Holstein and Raoul Adbaloff: "I identify to a great extent with people who transcended tribalism," who regard themselves as "citizens of the airport," which is one way to describe Cayce. She does worry that in her activities she is "complicit" in a process of breaking down national boundaries that "makes London and New York feel more like each other, that dissolves the membrane between mirror-worlds" (194). At a concluding dinner in Russia that is strangely "free of toasts," which she regards as characteristically Russian, she reflects, "[P]erhaps . . . this isn't a Russian meal. Perhaps it's a meal in that country without borders that Bigend strives to hail from" (341).

Also, in this transformed world, conventional long-term relationships are increasingly rare: Cayce remembers her ex-boyfriends and early in the story "briefly marvel[s]" at the "now perfectly revealed extent of her present loneliness" (24). While she ends the novel having apparently found true love with Parkaboy, the peculiar gesture that concludes the novel—"She kisses his sleeping back and falls asleep" (356)—suggests that there remains a certain distance between them, though *Zero History* reveals that their relationship endures. Reflecting on how readers and audiences seem to contribute to works of art in ways that question the notion of authorship, Bigend comments, "It's as though the creative process is no longer contained within an individual skull, if indeed it ever was. Everything, today, is to some extent the reflection of something else" (68)—a statement recalling comments in *Idoru* that similarly devalued the significance of celebrities in light of what is generated around them.

There are many other observations to make about this novel, demonstrating that *Pattern Recognition* is an unusually rich work and suggesting that the decision to focus on the present liberated Gibson's imagination and inspired him, more than two decades after he began his career, to do some of his best work. After this bravura performance, perhaps any subsequent novel would have seemed disappointing, which is how many reacted to *Spook Country*. Still, while such judgments were not unjustified, Gibson's second contemporary novel also had, both literally and figuratively, some hidden strengths.

Despite his success with the single viewpoint character of *Pattern Recognition*, Gibson reverted to old habits in *Spook Country*, with rotating chapters describing the eventually interrelated adventures of three protagonists. Perhaps Gibson felt his convoluted tale of two competing teams of spies required at least one protagonist on each side of the conflict; perhaps he regarded multiple characters as an effective, proven technique for maintaining reader interest, or his own interest, in an unfolding story. But one unfortunate result of this decision is the same problem that afflicts *All Tomorrow's Parties*: characters who are either underdeveloped or deliberate enigmas.

The least satisfactory protagonist of *Spook Country* is the one who most recalls Cayce: Hollis Henry, the former lead singer of a rock band, the Curfew, who now works as a journalist and is hired by Bigend, at first through an intermediary, to write an article for a projected new magazine about "locative art" (which adds virtual-reality elements to real locations, observed by means of special headgear); later, he approaches her directly to help him investigate a mysterious container being endlessly transported around the world. Despite her unusual background, Hollis never comes to life as a character, as she lacks both Cayce's observational talents and her quirky outlook on the world. Further, she proves entirely peripheral to this story; like Rydell and Yamazaki in *Idoru,* she could have been removed from the novel without affecting any events. The sole justifications for her presence, it seems, are to allow Gibson to kill time with subplots involving the subcultures of contemporary art and music and to provoke infodumps, the science-fictional device that Gibson never abandons. That is, since Hollis knows nothing about the world of espionage, Bigend and other characters repeatedly engage in long, didactic conversations explaining to her (and readers) aspects of the plot that might otherwise be unclear.

More appealing is Milgrim, a Russian translator turned down-and-out drug addict, who is abducted by a man named Brown to translate messages from the covert operatives he and his team are monitoring in New York City. A man of simple needs, Milgrim contentedly endures being constantly moved about and restrained by the brusque, dismissive Brown as long as he is regularly given the anti-anxiety pills he is addicted to and allowed to read a colorful book he stumbled upon about medieval heresies. Almost inadvertently, he also picks up important information about Brown's activities that clarifies some issues, though his general lack of interest in his captor renders him less effective than Hollis as a tool for funneling data to readers. Still, his poignant plight and bemused surrender to physical abuse and drug addiction make him a character readers can care about, unlike the perfunctorily developed Hollis.

The most striking and intriguing protagonist is Tito, a fifteen-year-old boy from a family of Chinese-Cuban spies who worked for Castro's regime before relocating to America to take on assignments for various parties; here, they are working for a former CIA agent, the "old man," now acting on his own to thwart a complex scheme (involving, among others, Brown) to steal money sent to aid in reconstructing war-torn Iraq (the McGuffin container is filled with diverted American cash, maintained in transit until conspirators are sure it can be safely unloaded). Tito was trained by his aunt Juana and other family members to skillfully carry out covert missions without being followed or captured, always guided (he believes) by the gods of the Santeria religion Juana taught him about.

Like Milgrim, Tito gains readers' sympathy because he is always being told by others what to do and always obeys orders (due to family loyalty, not coercion). However, unlike Milgrim, he never expresses any feelings about the tasks he must perform, and Gibson rarely gives readers access to his thoughts. True, there are reports of Tito's unhappy memories involving his unpleasant plane trip to New York, his sense of regret when he must abandon his threadbare apartment to prepare for another mission in Vancouver, and the way he enjoys listening to music with headphones. Otherwise, readers are left to infer what he really feels about his situation, and what he might prefer to do instead of patiently waiting to receive and carry out another set of instructions.

While more of a functional member of society, Tito recalls Silencio from *All Tomorrow's Parties,* another uncommunicative adolescent constantly controlled by other people; we learn more about Tito than Silencio, but he also remains a mystery. Indeed, Tito's fanatical and selfless dedication to family business, and his amazing skills in avoiding pursuers, make him seem at times almost inhuman, more a superhero than a real person, another trait he shares with Silencio.

Among other characters in *Spook Country,* the most conspicuous figure is the returning Bigend, whose incredible wealth and power give him the aura of an eccentric magician, not an actual businessman. Still, *Pattern Recognition* appeared to characterize him as essentially benign, as Cayce overcomes her initial dislike for him, and one might expect him to grow less mysterious and more likable in his second appearance. However, the protagonist who interacts with him in *Spook Country,* Hollis, remains distant and hostile to the man, giving readers no reason to feel differently. Gibson's one reference to events in *Pattern Recognition* makes Bigend seem even more unsympathetic:

> "Trope Slope [Bigend tells Hollis], for instance, our viral pitchman platform, was based on pieces of anonymous footage being posted on the Net."
> "You did that? Put that thing in the background of all those old movies? That's fucking horrible. Pardon my French."
> "It sells shoes." He smiled. (105–6)

It is disheartening to think that Bigend's investigation of the footage, so painstakingly crafted by that woman in Moscow and so admired by Cayce, would inspire him only to doctor old films to include advertising. Still, it would not be until *Zero History* that Bigend emerged as a genuine villain, as it remains possible here to cast his actions in a mostly favorable light.

Bigend also appears to be supplanting Mama Anarchia as Gibson's means of mocking pretentious jargon. Certainly, one reason Hollis never connects with him is his increasing proclivity for pompous pronouncements that, once analyzed, amount to very little. Consider this exchange:

> "The pop star as we knew her—" and here [Bigend] bowed slightly, in her direction—"was actually an artifact of preubiquitous media."
> "Of—"
> "Of a state in which 'mass' media existed, if you will, within the world."
> "As opposed to?"
> "Comprising it." (103)

It is little wonder that, following this little speech, Hollis immediately changes the subject, obviously uninterested in the further thoughts of a man who chooses such elevated language to explain that the mass media are more pervasive than they once were. If readers can find any reason to feel empathy with her character, it lies in the fact that she must regularly endure such conversations. (As another apparent dig at critics, Brown implausibly muses about the origins of political correctness in American colleges, which he terms "cultural Marxism," though any validity he has as a spokesperson against academic tendencies is shattered when he couples his theories with anti-Semitic remarks.)

While characters in *Spook Country* are usually unsatisfying, its story is well crafted and more provocative than it first appears. Initially, it seems, Gibson is temporarily abandoning his fascination with contemporary society as a whole to focus solely on one small set of individuals who are determined to avoid society: members of the intelligence community. While *Pattern Recognition* suggested that almost everyone might be considered a spy, *Spook Country* describes the actions of real spies. Only the phenomenon of locative art, which the novel briefly addresses and then forgets, seems related to events in the wider world; otherwise, the novel is entirely about secret agents huddling behind closed doors, following others or being followed, monitoring secret messages, and surreptitiously transporting objects, all to accomplish devious ends. Although Hollis and Milgrim are temporarily recruited to participate in such goings-on, the novel provides little information about everyday people and their activities and concerns, in contrast to *Pattern Recognition*'s large cast of diverse individuals.

Yet one can discern a deeper message in this story, closely related to the way this novel, like its predecessor, can be viewed as science fiction. *Spook Country* effectively asserts that we live today in a world filled with science-fictional events, but we are unable or unwilling to properly observe them. New York pedestrians only see a boy who accidentally bumps into an old man and picks up and hands him the newspaper he dropped; in reality, they are watching a trained spy, being constantly followed and monitored by other spies, who surreptitiously passes to a confederate a small device filled with fantastically complex but insidiously fraudulent data. Los Angeles residents see only a deserted city street; but if they don headgear, they can observe persuasive holograms of the dead River Phoenix, a dragon, or fields of poppies, the imaginative creations of innovative artists.

Spook Country, in other words, is unambiguously an example of the secret history, asserting that there lurk beneath our mundane lives all sorts of amazing technologies and activities that most people are unaware of. Indeed, since Gibson's background in science fiction made him aware of the term, it is significant to find it in this novel, as the old man striving to thwart the smugglers tells the perpetually clueless Hollis, "I am proposing to make you privy to secret history" (296). The person most qualified to bring such hidden matters to people's attention and explain their significance is, of course, a science fiction writer like Gibson. To put the point another way, if *Pattern Recognition* suggests that all people are like spies, *Spook Country* argues that all people should *become* spies—to properly interpret and understand the unexpectedly complex world around them—and this novel provides lessons about the sorts of fascinating business they might, with greater effort, discern behind everyday events.

In validating the premise of the secret history, the novel also seems to contradict the warning in *Pattern Recognition* about the dangers of overinterpretation, discerning patterns that do not exist. Here, after Bigend refers to something happening "coincidentally," Hollis responds, "I wouldn't think that 'coincidentally' was ever a safe concept, around material like this." As if accepting this rejoinder, Bigend then repeats a version of Win Pollard's observation, "Even the clinically paranoid can have enemies, they say" (192), and there are no further comments about needing to acknowledge the possibility of coincidences. The novel thus argues that the convoluted connections one detects between apparently unrelated events should be trusted, since the world is indeed filled with hidden conspiracies and technologies.

One can also argue, in a postmodern fashion, that as one boundary being dissolved in contemporary life, it is increasingly difficult to distinguish between appearances and underlying realities, almost forcing upon people an awareness of hidden truths that cannot avoid leaking hints of their existence. This is one way to interpret an intriguing conversation wherein the art curator Odile Richard tells Hollis that "cyberspace" today "is everting" or "everts"—"Turns itself inside out," the artist Alberto Corrales adds "by way of clarification" (20). The virtual world, hitherto separated from reality, now intrudes upon it, becoming real in a sense, so one's perceptions of the world inevitably involve a mixture of overt realities and hidden realities. That Gibson does not take this entirely seriously is suggested when Hollis initially cannot understand Odile because of her French accent—she pronounces Gibson's term "see-bare-espace." Yet his spelling of her pronunciation also conveys a message: cyberspace can be regarded as a way to see the world uncovered, or bare, revealing what is concealed behind its facades.

As another sort of unreality taking on its own sort of reality, Gibson briefly recalls concerns from *Virtual Light* and *Idoru* about the nature of celebrity when Bigend explains to the former celebrity Hollis that "the celebrity self is a sort of tulpa," defining the term as "[a] projected thought-form. A term from Tibetan mysticism. The celebrity self has a life of its own. It can, under the right circumstances, indefinitely survive the death of its subject. That's what every Elvis sighting is about" (102). This explains why Hollis is not comfortable with a famous portrait of her: that "wonderful image" is her tulpa, not her real self (102). Yet this illusory Hollis also grants her real power, since she is invited to learn "secret history" solely because she is "a celebrity," and hence "already constitute[s] a part of the historical record." The old man makes Hollis "the fireplace brick behind which I leave an account" (296).

Still, even if these themes allow *Spook Country* to remain a science fiction novel of sorts, there are signs that Gibson is seeking to distance himself from the genre. True, the novel continues the pattern of repeatedly mentioning works of science fiction, fantasy, and horror, including explicit or implicit references to Godzilla (4), *Close Encounters of the Third Kind* (31), *Picnic at Hanging Rock* (59), *Star Wars* (98, 249), *Blade Runner* (112), *The Silence of the Lambs* (116), the first *Planet of the Apes* film (139), and James Bond (157, 195, 345); there is also a general reference to "horror movies" (368) and mentions of the writers Anne Rice (57) and William S. Burroughs (294). The novel contains a few instances of astronomical imagery: a reference to Japan as the "planet of benign mystery" (25), an image on the ground likened to "the shape a child draws to represent a rocket ship" (55), and armored police officers that seem "to be wearing spacesuits" (197). There are two reminders of the notion, aired in *Pattern Recognition,* that our future is now embedded in the present: Odile "indicated Alberto's phone, as if its swollen belly of silver tape were gravid with an entire future" (22), and Hollis regards Bigend's Vancouver headquarters as an image from "some idealized urban future" (357).

However, Gibson integrates such mentions of science fiction, space, and the future into a broader mosaic of references to popular culture, which incorporates material previously limited to science fiction but also encompasses other items named in this novel, including: works and writers of mainstream fiction (F. Scott Fitzgerald [24], *Tom Sawyer* [57], Joseph Conrad [85], Rudyard Kipling [85, 317], Thomas Carlyle [138], Nancy Drew books [141], Sherlock Holmes stories [164], Vladimir Nabokov [261]); popular-music icons (Elvis Presley [102], Eric Clapton [113], the Beatles [113]); cartoon characters (Bugs

Bunny [129], Goofy [321], general references to "the way Mexican bandits wore bullets across their chests in cartoons" [324–25] and "early Disney" [368]); famous artists (J. M. W. Turner [151], Hieronymus Bosch [153], Henry Moore [191], Maxfield Parrish [208], the Beaux Arts architects [210], Hugh Ferriss [357], though his name is surprisingly misspelled); and contemporary celebrities (Johnny Depp [17, 321], André the Giant [100], Sharon Tate [148], Martha Stewart [211], Ralph Lauren [211], Sarah Ferguson [270]). In keeping with this broader range of references, *Spook Country* also features no characters who project Cayce's science-fictional perspective and view environments as science fiction or fantasy worlds.

The most striking indication of a weakening attachment to science fiction is the novel's use of a term that Gibson previously avoided: "sci-fi." Palms blown in the wind are likened to "dancers miming the final throes of some sci-fi plague" (3), and Milgrim feels that Brown's theory regarding how Marxist professors conquered academia "had an appealing vintage sci-fi campiness to it" (126). These passages might seem unremarkable, since Forrest J. Ackerman's coinage had long been part of the language; but within the science fiction community, the term is fiercely resisted because it makes the genre seem childish or trivial. Hence, most science fiction writers would scrupulously avoid using "sci-fi," for fear of upsetting their readers. Gibson's novel use of the term suggests that, regardless of marketing practices, he no longer regarded science fiction readers as a major audience.

There is also one memorable moment when Hollis appears to speak for Gibson himself, while explaining why "[s]he had always . . . wanted to write": "She was fascinated by how things worked in the world, and why people did them. When she wrote about things, her sense of them changed, and with it, her sense of herself" (171). Considering this as Gibson's own credo, one can regard *Pattern Recognition* as his effort to come to terms with the September 11 attacks, while *Spook Country* addresses the most noteworthy effect of that event, the 2003 war against Iraq. To justify this novel's new interest in military matters, coupled with his long-standing fondness for art, Gibson offers an inspired conceit relating these fields to his own fascination with technology: "The most interesting ways of looking at the GPS grid, what it is, what we might be able to do with it, all seemed to be being put forward by artists. Artists or the military. That's something that tends to happen with new technologies generally: the most interesting applications turn up on the battlefield, or in a gallery" (63). Such unexpected insights can make reading even lesser Gibson novels a memorable experience.

Readers had little reason to entertain high hopes for *Zero History*. As the third book in a series, like *Mona Lisa Overdrive* and *All Tomorrow's Parties,* one might anticipate another subpar exercise in churning out one more story from premises Gibson had tired of. And while creating new characters normally energizes Gibson, the novel would unpromisingly foreground two characters from *Spook Country,* Hollis and Milgrim. Yet this surprisingly strong novel projects the aura not of a bored author ready for something different, but rather a confident, engaged author hitting his stride. Indeed, while happy that Gibson never wrote a fourth novel about the Sprawl or the Bridge, readers might finish *Zero History* eagerly anticipating another adventure involving the manipulative Bigend and other operatives engaged in shady business. True, Gibson's comments about his next novel indicate that it will move in new directions, since he noted to Ryan Rutherford in 2010 that he "historically" writes "three part sequences" and reported to Christian DuChateau in 2011 that his next novel was "not a Bigend one." However, he also told August C. Bourré in 2011 that "I'm not even entirely sure that Bigend is fully ready to let me go," suggesting that the character and his world might someday return.

One strength of *Zero History* is that Gibson finds a way to effectively combine the two narrative patterns of earlier novels: the single protagonist of *Neuromancer* and *Pattern Recognition,* and the multiple protagonists whose lives gradually intertwine in other novels. Here, there are two alternating viewpoint characters, Hollis and Milgrim, but unlike previous protagonists, they come together almost immediately, as Bigend recruits them both to investigate the origins of a mysterious new line of clothing, Gabriel Hounds, which is somehow becoming popular despite having no advertising or visible means of distribution. The two even work as a team for much of the novel, so their different perspectives involve the same unfolding events. Instead of one story with one viewpoint character, or several related stories with several viewpoint characters, *Zero History* offers readers one story with two viewpoint characters, combining the strong, unified narrative of *Neuromancer* and *Pattern Recognition* with the variety of multiple perspectives in other novels.

Zero History also suggests that Gibson has become comfortable with the approach to storytelling developed in *Pattern Recognition* and *Spook Country*. His form is the secret history, science fiction that posits the existence of unknown organizations and technologies hidden within our contemporary world. His characters are spies, employed by government agencies and private groups, working with and against each other to pursue some McGuffin (in the "Thanks" section of *Zero History*, Gibson even thanks Larry Lunn for providing "a mcguffin of infinite scale" [405]). But his protagonists, unlike traditional spy novels but recalling *The Man from U.N.C.L.E.* (referenced in *Pattern Recognition*), will include both professional spies and amateurs, everyday citizens drawn into covert operations whom readers can identify with. Observed in embryonic form in *Pattern Recognition,* and haltingly developed in *Spook Country*, this model is executed brilliantly in *Zero History,* suggesting that Gibson has developed a template he could happily exploit for the rest of his career.

True, not everything works in *Zero History,* most notably the character of Hollis, who remains empty and unappealing despite Gibson's continuing attention. There are signs that Gibson himself understands the problem: to explain why she left Garreth, the daredevil operative from *Spook Country* who became her boyfriend, Hollis says, "I need the world to have a surface, the same surface everyone sees. I don't like feeling like I'm always about to fall through, into something else" (61). It is as if Gibson had an epiphany, suddenly recognizing that Hollis is almost willfully superficial, consciously wishing to avoid peering underneath the world's "surface," though that is precisely the activity Gibson both practices and advocates in recent novels. For this reason, Hollis can never be effective as a Gibson protagonist.

The solution to the problem of bland characters, mastered by playwrights, is to surround them with more colorful characters, and that is what Gibson does. To enliven Hollis's story, Gibson has her regularly accompanied by her former bandmate Heidi Hyde, a brash, foul-mouthed woman who, despite her smaller role, is considerably more lively and engaging than Hollis. Also compensating for Hollis's inadequacies is the reconstructed Milgrim, another of Hollis's almost constant companions: rescued from drug addiction by Bigend, who improbably perceives that he has unusual talents, he underwent an extensive process of rehabilitation that left him cured of his dependence on drugs and newly aware of a world he had been oblivious to for over a decade. And while he begins the novel as a passive, controlled character, as in *Spook Country,* he gradually develops a sense of independence and initiative that enables him to take heroic actions, and even earn a girlfriend's affection, making him more intriguing and attractive than before.

Other characters, more involving than Hollis, are brought back from previous novels, including the other surviving Curfew member, Reg Inchmale, and Voytek, the dealer in high-tech equipment from *Pattern Recognition*; but two returning characters are more prominent. One is Bigend, who in *Zero History* completes his transformation from potential hero to unambiguous villain: here, he is interested in Gabriel Hounds clothing solely because he hopes the knowledge he gains will help him earn money by selling fashionable clothing to the American military (which needs new styles to attract volunteers, since traditional military styles have been coopted by the general public). He employs Chombo from *Spook Country* in an effort to gain the ability to predict the future doings of the marketplace, thus garnering even more power; we are also reminded of how he coldly exploited what he learned from the footage. Though she initially succumbs, reluctantly, to his second job offer, Hollis resolves to free herself from his manifestly baleful influence. Bigend finally becomes completely unsympathetic when, to retrieve Chombo from kidnappers, he is ready to sacrifice the innocent Milgrim.

Even in minor ways, Gibson seems determined to make Bigend less likable than before: he repeats a version of the observation, "Even the delusionally paranoid have enemies" (198), suggesting that his oracular conversational style is largely a matter of recycled, rehearsed bromides. This is also conveyed when he tells Hollis, "Consumers don't buy products, so much as narratives," and she responds, "That's old. . . . I've heard it before" (20–21). Gibson says that the absurdity of Bigend's rhetoric is something he finds in the real world: as he told Jesse Pearson in 2010, "The things that strike my eye are often the things that are just so utterly and unintentionally pretentious that I just have to file the serial numbers off to some extent and then put them in Bigend's mouth." The character, then, represents not only academic critics but "pretentious" commentators of all varieties. Bigend's shallowness is underlined by Hollis's observation that "[s]he'd yet to see a book in any Bigendian environment. He was a creature of screens, of bare expanses of desk or table, empty shelves"

(155). In contrast, one of the first things we learn about Hollis here is that she is reading "parts of Dame Edith Sitwell's *English Eccentrics* and most of Geoffrey Household's *Rogue Male*" (5). When Bigend notes, "We advertised. On fashion fora, mainly" (46), his use of the Latin plural "fora," instead of the "forums" that long ago replaced that word in English discourse, defines him as a pompous snob. Gibson flatly announces his new status as an antagonist when he is last seen in the novel, fleeing with his employees in an experimental vehicle that hovers above the water; a character notes "that Bigend, with the Hermés ekranoplan, had gone totally Bond villain" (399).

Even more interesting, though, is the brief reappearance of Cayce, Gibson's most memorable character. Early in the novel, when Hollis learns that the Gabriel Hounds designer is a woman in Chicago (119–20), readers may recall that, in *Pattern Recognition,* Cayce ultimately bonds with a boyfriend from Chicago and immediately suspect that she might be that woman. Later, a woman who met the designer in Japan reports that she wore "[b]lack jeans, a black T-shirt, and one of those jackets you're wearing. . . . Dark hair, but not Japanese. . . . American accent" (228), and suspicions that she is Cayce seem almost confirmed. Finally, the woman actually meets Hollis, and while her name is never mentioned, the conversation confirms her identity: after being drugged, she indeed lost "her very peculiar and specific talent" as she suspected, and she came to despise Bigend because he did "[s]omething ghastly, in marketing," due to the footage (335). We are also told that the Russian filmmaker died, and the name and logo Gabriel Hounds came from some of her notes.

Now interested in designing clothes that match her preferences, Cayce has gone into the business of selling her distinctive style of dress to other people, though her disgust with Bigend inspired her to do so in a manner that involves absolutely no marketing. This brings to the surface a theme that Gibson commented on to Eric Holstein and Raoul Abdaloff in 2007: characters in *Pattern Recognition* and *Spook Country* are "living in a storm of branding and marketing, and they all seem to be trying to find some way to push back, if only slightly" ("Interview de William Gibson"). Here, Cayce pushes back with greater force. Of course, as Bigend perceives, this in itself amounts to a new form of marketing—"what may prove to be a somewhat new way to transmit brand vision" (23)—which is why he wishes to determine the designer's identity, though Hollis never reveals it. (It seems odd that Bigend, who worked closely with Cayce, never suspects that she is behind Gabriel Hounds, but this might be a subtle way to further undermine his appeal by suggesting that he is not as intelligent and insightful as he once seemed.)

By means of these characters, and the story that unites them, Gibson achieves, more so than in previous novels, an ideal synthesis of his strongest interests. The efforts of competing parties to develop fashionable clothing for soldiers bring together for equal attention the disparate groups Gibson identified in *Spook Country* as the most innovative users of new technology: "artists" and "the military." The novel often refers to artists, including Andy Warhol (51), Banksy (61), the photographers Helmut Newton (98) and Diane Arbus (253), the designers Ralph Lauren and Tommy Hilfiger (134), M. C. Escher (141), Aubrey Beardsley (369), and William Turner (390), and artistic styles or movements like surrealism (261), vorticism (339), pointillism (383), and constructivism (378, 401). Closely linked to the world of art, popular music is brought into the picture by Curfew members, musicians they know, and references to Jimi Hendrix (51, 305, 314, 349), the Ramones (59), Toots and the Maytals (74), Francoise Hardy (97), Elvis Presley (295), James Brown (305), the producer Phil Spector (307), and Bob Dylan (321). The military surfaces in the novel by means of references to spies, its representatives who interact the most with society (however surreptitiously), as there are mentions of the fictional spies Secret Squirrel (309) and James Bond (399) and the British politician John Profumo, who was forced to resign due to his relationship with a prostitute linked to Russian intelligence (51). There are also general comments about a "room with the yellow chaise lounge" that "seemed to be about spies, sad ones, in some very British sense" (50), the possibility that the man hunting Milgrim was "a spy" (189), and Bigend's disdain for "strategic business intelligence types" (291, 350). Two characters in the novel, Winnie Tung Whitaker and the old man from *Spook Country* still assisting Garreth, are actual spies.

Zero History also suggests that Gibson has entirely distanced himself from the world of computers, the focus of the cyberpunk literature he was once said to represent. Except for routine references to laptops, email, Twitter, and Google searches, and the behind-the-scenes research of the barely observed Chombo, computers play virtually no role in the story, and Garreth's dismissive comment about the "[d]ownside of having obsessive friends who like computers" (346) decisively indicates that Gibson does not consider himself part of that circle.

Yet a genuine interest of Gibson's resurfaces with renewed prominence in *Zero History*: science fiction. In the novel's skewed vision of contemporary reality (suggested by repeated uses of the term "liminal" [4, 94, 369]), one detects that the author is again willing to acknowledge his connections to the genre. The reviled term "sci-fi" is nowhere to be found, perhaps in response to criticism from colleagues or readers, and the number and frequency of references to science fiction and fantasy are significantly greater than they were in *Spook Country*: a statue is colored "Martian green" (8), while swords are described as "Chinese-made orc-killing blades" (9); the Victorian-era shower in Hollis's London hotel room "reminded her of H. G. Wells's time machine" (16), an observation repeated four times (94, 153, 200, 300); Milgrim describes addictions as "pocket monsters" (53); a "birdcage" above Hollis casts "the shadow of a mothership" that is "[w]aiting to radiate some energy, carve her with crop circles perhaps" (77); she "let[s] the darkness of the mother-ship's hull fill her field of vision" (79); Milgrim refers to himself talking in certain ways as a "robot" (85, 87); Hollis describes Bigend's suit as "antimatter paired with mohair" (90) and thinks that his driver's jacket displays "a sort of post-apocalyptic élan" (95); Milgrim sees "a building looking as though it had been drawn by Dr. Seuss" (109); Hollis, briefly believing that Milgrim is "crazy," thinks of "[t]infoil hats" worn by people fearing alien mind con-trol (126); a shopping mall reminds Milgrim of "structures aimed heroically into futures that had never really happened" (133), recalling "The Gernsback Continuum"; the "euro bills" he sees in one store "reminded him, obscurely, of Disneyland's original Tomorrowland" (133); Hollis's computer displays "a digital representation of interstellar space" (140); Milgrim observes a girl who is "[r]eminding him [. . .] of one of those otherwise fairly realistic Japanese cartoon characters, the ones with oversized Disney eyes" (141); he recalls Bi-gend likening Milgrim to "someone stepping from a lost space capsule" (141); Milgrim thinks stacked books in a bookstore are "piled like a mad professor's study in a film" (150); the lead singer of a band, the Stokers, is named Bram, referencing the author of *Dracula* (156); when Milgrim observes a flying pen-guin created as an experimental observational instrument, he worries about "[u]nidentified flying objects" (158); Hollis reports that Garreth described his leaps off tall buildings as "like walking through walls" (175); Bigend says that the man pursuing Milgrim is "probably a fantasist as well" (189), an observation he repeats (217); as a therapeutic activity, Heidi requests "a kit" for constructing a robot, "something in their Gundam series," though she receives a lesser product, "fucking Breast Chaser Galvion" (193–94); Heidi is likened to "an expensively coiffed gargoyle" (200); Bigend argues that stores with military clothing are "[w]hole universes of wistful male fantasy" that appeal to "your civilian buyer, your twenty-first-century Walter Mitty" (214); a woman coming to Milgrim's rescue seems "an intrusion from another dimension" (251); the brooch Heidi wears looks like "three rocketships" (257); Hollis observes screens that "depicted scenes from Disney's *Snow White*" (277); denouncing life in a "surveillance state," Voytek asks Milgrim, "You have read Orwell?" (289); when he hints at new technology that removes images from surveillance film, Hollis asks, "Can you really be invisible?" and Garreth tells her, "Think of it as a spell of forgetting" (302); monitoring his complex operation, Garreth is likened to a "dungeon master" (379); a man Milgrim sees "looked as if someone had subjected the Dalai Lama to the gravity of a planet with greater mass than Earth's" (382); Hollis seems to see a man "blur, or teleport, across the space separating him from Foley" (385); the villainous Gracie is said to be "smashed" by "an idiot giant's invisible hand" (387); and, as already noted, Bigend is called a "Bond villain" (399).

I have been accused of bedeviling readers with interminable lists of evidence, but there seems no other way to convey just how pervasive the references to science fiction and fantasy are in this novel. They cumulatively suggest that Gibson, after striving to redefine himself for new readers with the broader range of references in *Spook Country,* has come to terms with his origins in "science fiction soil" and is newly willing to draw upon that background in describing the contemporary world and confident that readers can understand and relate to such references. Alternately, one could theorize that science fiction has now become so integral to popular culture that Gibson realized he could freely indulge in science-fictional rhetoric without alienating general readers. From either perspective, these references also reinforce the broadest argument employed to classify Gibson's novels about the present as science fiction: our future now overlaps with the present, and strange possibilities once envisioned in futuristic science fiction now happen all around us, even if we are not yet aware of them, so we already live in a science fiction world. If this is true, it is appropriate for Gibson's characters to characterize that world by recalling science fiction works and tropes.

The reconstructed Milgrim exemplifies the science fiction world we inhabit. While the Sprawl trilogy suggested that futuristic technologies like augmented memories, virtual reality, and computerized simulations or reconstructions of personalities would break down traditional concepts of a unified identity, Milgrim's experiences, only mildly fantastic, indicate that fragmented identities are already part of our experience. Milgrim's multiple personalities include the person he originally was, the person he became while addicted to drugs, and the new person he is becoming—in part a reemergence of his earlier self, in part a response to Bigend's reprogramming. As the novel progresses, Milgrim and those around him are increasingly aware of his different identities: in an early, stressful conversation with Whitaker, Milgrim feels as if "his robot" (the way he was trained to converse) is responding to her comments (82); prepared to go to Paris, he "felt as though he never had" been there, but "[s]omeone else had been, in his early twenties. That mysterious previous iteration his therapist in Basel had been so relentlessly interested in. A younger, hypothetical self" (92); conversing with Hollis, Milgrim feels that "he was emulating a kind of social being that he fundamentally wasn't" (174); later, sensing a previous split in his personality, Hollis thinks, "[S]uddenly he was weirdly and entirely present, a single entity, the sharp looker-around-corners merged seamlessly with his spacey, dissociated self" (327); and the bodyguard Fiona tells Milgrim, "You sounded like a different person just then. Different kind of person" (352).

The most intriguing comment about Milgrim's new personality comes from Hollis: "He seemed peeled, somehow, transparent, strangely free of underlying motive. Seemed used as well. Bigend had created him, or would feel that he had; had cobbled him up from whatever wreckage he'd initially presented" (180). These comments connect Milgrim to *Neuromancer*'s Armitage, another traumatized man repaired and molded into another sort of person by a domineering intelligence; but here this process only involves therapies and techniques similar to those already in use, nothing particularly speculative. Another noteworthy difference is that Gibson seems optimistic about the effects of such transformations: while Armitage was destroyed by the internal conflict between what he was and what he became, Milgrim calmly accepts the different sorts of people coexisting within his body, and in doing so becomes a more capable and confident person than he previously was. Thus, current and coming assaults upon our traditional sense of identity, which commentators once regarded as threatening, are presented as something people can adjust to and even benefit from.

Assaults upon the integrity of bodies are also present in *Zero History* in the form of the extensive repairs undergone by Garreth, Hollis's former and future lover. Having smashed his leg while leaping from the world's tallest building in Dubai, he received new artificial bones made of rattan, so he calls his new leg "Frankenstein," or "Frank" (300); the reference to Mary Shelley's novel indicates that we now possess the once-feared power to create new bodies from the wreckage of old bodies, again without negative consequences, since Garreth anticipates becoming active again, and his recovery does not diminish his ability to improvise and execute a daring scheme to rescue Milgrim from both Bigend and his opponents.

Almost requiring no comment are various other ways in which Gibson locates themes from previous futuristic novels in his imagined present: the weakening significance of national boundaries, the growing influence of multinational or "postgeographic" businesses like Blue Ant, the power and pervasive impact of celebrities, and individuals who regularly shift loyalties in a world of constant change (like Bigend's employee Sleight, now working against him). A more novel idea is conveyed by the book's title. The phrase "zero history" appears only once in the novel, when Whitaker notes that Milgrim, during his years as a drug addict, essentially vanished from public records—"you haven't even had a credit card for ten years" (84)—and the novel's other secret agents, like Garreth and the old man, are essentially in the same situation. Further, when Hollis describes Garreth as a "graffiti artist. . . . Just not with paint," but with "history" (61), she suggests that history itself is ephemeral and malleable, a conceit that dates back to *Virtual Light* (where Chevette observes, "Skinner had this thing . . . about history. How it was turning into plastic" [264]) and resurfaces in *Pattern Recognition* when Bigend muses, "History is a best-guess narrative about what happened and when" (57).

Yet history here is not merely something certain individuals escape from by means of clandestine lifestyles, or something shaped and altered by present-day observers; it literally does not seem to exist for Gibson's characters. The only people from the past that they are aware of are artists, musicians, writers, and filmmakers, and one might say that the continuing presence of their creative works makes them part of our present. But other figures dominating history books—monarchs, politicians, philosophers, warriors, explorers, scientists, and founders of religions—seem completely excluded from the contemporary zeitgeist. The reason for this is readily discerned: despite the argument that one must study history to make wise decisions, the world today is so utterly different from the past, in so many ways, that lessons from history are no longer useful and even irrelevant; thus, the only valuable thing dead people can offer is entertainment, which is why only creative individuals are worth remembering.

If people in Gibson's novels have "zero history" to rely upon in making their way through their world, where else might they obtain guidance? Since they effectively live in the future, they must draw upon past visions of the future, which is one way to define science fiction. The fact that Zero History's characters so often perceive things around them in terms of science fiction, then, does not merely indicate that the genre has conquered popular culture; science fiction is now recognized as the most helpful background for surviving in a present-day world that so closely resembles science fiction. People with zero history need science fiction, since the history of the future provides more insight than the history of the past, so characters must constantly refer to science fiction to understand their world. Thus, the novel conveys an intriguing paradox: it may now be impossible to write traditional science fiction, as Gibson argues, yet such science fiction remains an essential aspect of contemporary life.

CONCLUSION

Entering his sixty-fifth year, Gibson will likely remain an active writer for at least another decade or two, and he has already produced enough nonfiction in the forms of articles, reviews, and introductions to fill two additional volumes like *Distrust That Particular Flavor*. If he chose, he could also publish slender volumes of uncollected stories and poems and a compilation of unpublished screenplays. But his most significant future works will surely be novels; in 2012, he told Mike Doherty that he has "worked [his] way around to the future again" with a forthcoming novel about "the future of social media"; in another 2012 interview he said that the work has "something to do with ubiquitous private video-drone technology" ("William Gibson: The Future Now"); and in the interview below he reports that the novel "involves a sort of virtual time travel." However, rather than discussing what Gibson might publish in the future, one might better ponder, in concluding, the reputation he will likely enjoy in the future, based on his publications to date.

First, even if he distances himself from the field, Gibson has earned a permanent place in the history of science fiction, and he will always be remembered for his seminal contributions in the 1980s. While the purported novelties of cyberpunk, once proclaimed so portentously, now seem dated, he will be celebrated for fostering a new attentiveness to cutting-edge technologies on Earth, bringing a more streetwise voice into science fiction, and alerting readers to new possibilities in the prose style of describing the future, all serving to reinvigorate (like Heinlein before him) a genre that was becoming stodgy. Reflecting these contributions, a 2010 reference heralded Gibson as one of fifty key figures in science fiction. Though Gibson modestly opines in the interview below, "I don't *feel* as though I've had that central an impact" on the genre, the awareness of contemporary science, scruffier characters, and creative prose now commonplace in science fiction decisively indicate otherwise.

How he will figure in broader histories of literature is less clear. Surprisingly, in the context of other writers categorized as postmodern, Gibson may be cast as a traditional, even old-fashioned, sort of writer. His subjects and stylistic tricks once seemed innovative, but nothing else is particularly remarkable about his storytelling. Aside from the terminology and technology, his novels could be appreciated by Ernest Hemingway and F. Scott Fitzgerald, or Charles Dickens and William Makepeace Thackeray for that matter, as they lack the more radical innovations of other postmodern writers.

There are many reasons to regard Gibson as a fundamentally conservative writer. In his heart, it seems, he never abandoned the values he absorbed in the 1950s by watching television and living in rural Virginia, and in contrast to commentators, he is comfortable seeing contemporary events in terms of continuity, not revolution. As he told Zach Handlen in 2010, "We like to tell ourselves that we're changing the fundamental basis of everything right now, and this is a unique time, but maybe not, you know? That may just be hubris on our part, and we're just finding new ways to do the things we've always done." Regarding new technologies, Gibson told Noel Murray in 2007, "I'm often saddened and dismayed to see myself portrayed as either a Luddite, or as a raving technophile. I've always thought that my job was to be as anthropologically neutral about emerging technologies as possible." Gibson sees his political stance as middle-of-the-road, describing himself to Cory Doctorow in 1999 as "a lazy, apolitical sort of guy," and claiming in an October 21, 2004, blog entry, "I am, as far as I can tell, more or less a centrist, equally repelled by either extreme of the political spectrum."

Gibson's characters endure superficial uncertainties but otherwise lead curiously placid lives, disrupted but not disturbed by various vicissitudes. Indeed, revelations about the fates of Case in *Mona Lisa Overdrive* and Cayce in *Zero History* suggest that Gibson ultimately envisions for his restless characters the same destiny he himself achieved after a turbulent youth: a long, committed relationship, stable existence in one place, and a happily domestic lifestyle as "a really nice family guy," as the interviewer Donna McMahon described him in 2003. In a February 22, 2003, blog entry, he wishes that two of his characters will achieve such a life: "I can only hope that Rydell and Chevette, after the close of ALL TOMORROW'S PARTIES, make their way up the coast to Boonville. He, at least, would be very happy there." Also in that entry, Gibson seemingly acknowledged some truth in a reader's arch comment, paraphrased by Gibson, that *Pattern Recognition* involved "nice people doing nice things to one another," which is indeed the type of narrative that Gibson settled into.

Further, while Gibson once took drugs, like many members of his generation—he calls himself a "regular cannabis user" in *No Maps for These Territories*—"Dougal Discarnate" suggests that he is now opposed to drugs, a view also conveyed in the documentary, where he criticizes drug taking as a damaging matter of "tweaking the incoming data." When a young person in 2012 asked Gibson to "[g]ive my generation whatever you think is helpful for it to survive," he first responded, as reported by Mike Doherty, "[O]ne should distrust people on stages offering programs for how to build the future," but he later told Doherty that he "should have said, 'Never pass up a chance to use the toilet,' and 'It's a good idea to eat three reasonably sized meals a day. Take care of your gums' [laughs]"—suggesting, despite the laughter, that he is mostly a very conventional person, as also indicated by the comment in the interview below that he has "never been a nude beach kind of guy."

And despite the stylishly cynical attitude said to characterize cyberpunk, Gibson has shown himself to be unfashionably optimistic, as he repeatedly says in interviews. His futures seem dark and grim to many readers, but determined, resourceful individuals can always survive, and even prosper, in troubled circumstances. I repeatedly note Gibson's aversion to the science fiction tropes of space travel and alien life, but he even more assiduously avoids creating apocalyptic futures like *Alas, Babylon* and similar science fiction visions that terrified him as a child. He even told David Wallace-Wells in 2011 that he set *Neuromancer* in a functioning world following a brief nuclear war as "a conscious act of imaginative optimism," and added, "I've always been taken aback by the assumption that my vision is fundamentally dystopian." As early as 1987, he described himself to Lou Stathis as "wildly optimistic" (38); he told Andrew Leonard in 2007, "I find myself less pessimistic than I sometimes imagined I should be" (162); and he tweeted on July 26, 2012, that there is "nothing" he is "constantly gloomy about." Illuminatingly, as the title of his nonfiction collection, Gibson instructed readers to "distrust that particular flavor" of doomsday predictions epitomized by H. G. Wells and criticized in "Time Machine Cuba" (208), as if he regarded a pessimistic outlook as the worst possible sin. In contrast, he remains confident that humanity will always contrive to muddle through, whatever might lie ahead. As he said in his "Talk for Book Expo, New York," "The Future, capital-F, be it crystalline city on the hill or radioactive postnuclear wasteland, is gone. Ahead of us, there is merely . . . more stuff. Some tending toward the crystalline, some to the wasteland-y. Stuff; the mixed bag of the quotidian" (44).

Far from being characterized as the vanguard of everything new, Gibson may ultimately be seen as a writer who was a little behind his times, still committed to values and beliefs being abandoned by his contemporaries. In this respect, again, Gibson recalls Heinlein, who for the most part also held true to the beliefs he absorbed as a boy. Had I discovered "A Tale of the Badger Folk" at an earlier stage in my research, I might have alternatively developed an extended analogy between Gibson and Clifford D. Simak—for despite the stark contrast between Simak's celebration of rural America and Gibson's embrace of urban life, they share an optimistic viewpoint, strong traditional values, and a disinclination to moralize not observed in Heinlein. In *No Maps for These Territories,* discussing how nanotechnology might someday make humans "completely protean," he confesses to being uncomfortable with the idea, stating, "I really do belong to the old order," and later acknowledges that "most people, myself included, are most comfortable conceptually living about ten years back." Gibson admits, then, that he not a person who constantly stays on the cutting edge of scientific and social change.

Yet Gibson will never lose sleep worrying about what future generations might say about him; asked in a 2010 interview to assess how his works would likely be regarded in "twenty or thirty years," he simply answered, "As some sort of attempt to take the measure of the day I lived in" ("Prophet of the Real"). For Gibson, anyone thinking about the future is really thinking about the present, precluding genuine speculation about the future, so there is no reason to worry about the unknowable judgments of posterity. In any event, Gibson is never overly concerned about others' judgments, preferring to remain committed to his own beliefs. As he told David Mathew in 2000, "[Y]ou can't build a career on trying to please other people" (13). In this respect, he reveals a final similarity to Heinlein: an enormous strength of character and determination to follow his own course to the extent it is practically possible. In striking contrast to the people who attached themselves to his coattails, Gibson is the antithesis of a "coolhunter." He is keenly interested in certain things, and pursues those interests regardless of what others think, while making necessary concessions to marketplace demands. And if his writings come to seem less and less representative of an entire era, they nonetheless convey the essence of a remarkable individual whose works will always remain worth reading.

AN INTERVIEW WITH WILLIAM GIBSON

On February 22 and July 24, 2012, William Gibson kindly responded to various questions in five email messages. With Gibson's permission, I have edited the questions and his answers into the format of a single interview.

I noticed in No Maps for These Territories *that you are left-handed. As a child, did anyone ever force you to write with your right hand? More broadly, do you feel that being left-handed had any impact on your career?*

My mother was left-handed and had been forced by her parents to learn to use her right hand. She insisted that this had done her harm, and she was proud of not having done that to me. I think this may have been an important early example, for me, of the idea that the historical past was not necessarily a better place.

I want to ask about your contributions to fanzines, since no other scholar, it seems, has read or discussed them. What are your general feelings about these materials? Would you ever be willing to make them available to a wider audience?

Surely anything one produces at age fourteen should stay in the juvenilia file. (I can only imagine what this will be like for writers fifty years after the advent of Facebook and Twitter. And cringe.)

The '70s fanzine pieces were five-finger exercises of sorts, inclining shyly toward the fictive act. They may actually *be* fictive to whatever degree, which would unfortunately qualify them better as bullshit than juvenilia.

I'd love to hear the story of how you persuaded Fritz Leiber to contribute to your fanzine Votishal.

I had written him, I suppose, fan letters, and he replied via typewritten postcards. Perhaps three times. Whatever content of his I published would have been from those. He was an amiable and generous person, to judge from my recollection of our tiny interaction.

I wish I remembered more of my brief correspondence with Leiber. I know that I asked him about the shape/design of the Mouser's sword, and he responded with a sketch and a fencer's explanation of the shape. And of course I wish I hadn't lost it down the years. But nothing I asked him was any less fanboy fourteen-year-old than that.

If you feel like strolling down Memory Lane, the Eaton Collection at UC Riverside has copies of Wormfarm *Nos. 1 and 3,* Votishal *No. 1, and* Srith *No. 1, four of the five fanzines you published in the 1960s. Copies could be obtained, if you don't have them.*

Revisiting my own work has always been somehow powerfully antithetical to my process. (If my life depended on it, I would be unable, say, to produce a simple plot outline of *Count Zero*.) I need to recall it or not; for it to recede; for it to become a compost. Rereading it upsets some crucial creative ecology decades in the making.

Your early poem "A Tale of the Badger Folk" seems a homage to Clifford D. Simak's City, *an author I believe you have never mentioned. Did you read a lot of Simak? Do you think this very rural writer had any influence on you?*

I don't, today, recall reading any Simak. My guess is that I was inspired by reading about Simak's work. I read a lot about sf. Toward the end of my initial sf period, more about it than actually reading it. Mostly fan appreciation, which was really most of the critical writing available then.

In your fanzine Srith, *you describe yourself as a dedicated collector of science fiction memorabilia, mentioning a "collection of original drawings," a letter from Robert E. Howard to Farnsworth Wright, and autographed copies of Leiber's* Night's Black Agents *and Tolkien's* The Hobbit. *Do you have any idea about what happened to your collection?*

It was all lost, one way or another, after my mother's death. Though I've never actually regretted losing it. It wasn't at all in line with my later tastes. I doubt I would have hung on to it. Except for that copy of *The Hobbit*, which I'm sure I would have sold long before it had had a chance to acquire its current market value.

In the same fanzine, you reported you had been hired as a cartoonist for a local newspaper. Could you provide some details about this experience? Were any of your cartoons actually published?

I was definitely exaggerating about "hired," as I'm sure no pay would have been involved. I wasn't at all good on follow-through!

You've told interviewers that you wrote "The Gernsback Continuum" after a fanzine rejected your review of Donald J. Bush's The Streamlined Futuropolis, *and you decided to rewrite the review as a story. But that review appeared in* New Directions *in 1976; I've read it. Is this faulty memory, did you originally submit it elsewhere, or were you unaware that it was actually published?*

Perhaps the anger I recall was at having to do revisions I felt weakened the piece. If I did them, I might never have read it as published, while angrily writing "The Gernsback Continuum."

I'd like you to say something about the late Susan Wood, who describes you as a close friend in her "Susanzine." As an instructor, coeditor, and friend, how did she affect your life?

She was my age, an assistant professor of English at UBC in the last year of my B.A. I knew her first from the local sf scene. I took her sf course thinking it would be an easy mark, but she made me write a piece of fiction instead of a term paper. I turned in "Fragments of a Hologram Rose," and then she was as difficult as she needed to be in order to induce me to try to get it published. She was, in every best sense of the word as we use it today, a nerd.

Would you be willing to talk about the circumstances of her death, and your reaction to the news? Her other friends seemed reluctant to discuss this matter, at least in writing.

She was alcoholic, though that hadn't been at all apparent to me, earlier. Having since known a few people on the bipolar spectrum, some of them alcoholic, I've wondered if something like that might have been involved. I hadn't known anyone my age, in early adulthood, who'd died. Perhaps what struck me most, though I doubt I thought of it quite this way at the time, was that she had been destroyed by a disease process which I knew of theoretically, mainly from literature, but had never witnessed before in anyone I knew, and I could see that it wasn't anything she'd volunteered for, in any way.

It occurred to me that Wood's tragic fate might have informed your portrayal of Linda Lee in Neuromancer, *one of the few genuinely tragic figures in your stories. Would you agree?*

No. Linda Lee is very much a '70s zeitgeist figure, out of countless rock songs by way of the street itself. There is no nerd element whatever in Linda Lee. She's an abused sex worker, a bird with a wing down, and someone who's probably never read a book, if indeed she's even literate, which she gives no evidence of being. In my opinion, she's by far the most naturalistic major character in *Neuromancer*. I wrote "Hinterlands," though, shortly after Susan's death. I know the two are connected, but not in any way I could explain, nor could have explained then. More an atmosphere than symbolism.

Wood's "Susanzine" once discussed a trip to Wreck Beach, which she described as a popular destination for local science fiction fans. Did you ever visit this iconic Vancouver locale?

It's a nude beach. I have never been a nude beach kind of guy.

You've given seemingly contradictory accounts of how you obtained a contract from Terry Carr to write Neuromancer. *In a 1989 interview, you said that you ran into Carr, he spilled bourbon on your pants, and he offered you a contract to make up for damaging your pants. But in a 1994 afterword to the novel, you indicate that you initiated contact by writing Carr in the role of "the wanna-be novelist, fishing with desperate subtlety for the further professional attention of Mr. Carr, editor and anthologist." Can you clarify the exact chain of events that lead to that contract?*

The bourbon spilling probably had some approximate basis in fact, but I was engaging in a kind of joking fannish fabulism there, to judge by the tone. What passes for recollection, today, is that Terry brought it up at a convention, and I very nearly shat myself in terror, then immediately accepted, but only with the greatest misgiving. No idea which convention, though.

After examining your work for fanzines and later writings, I feel you have a natural affinity for art, poetry, and travel writing. Would you agree? Have you ever considered returning to artwork? Publishing a book of poems? Writing a book about your travels?

While those affinities are certainly there, I don't find them tempting in that way. I feel they serve me best as aspects of the novel.

Every book you've published begins with a different letter of the alphabet (if one regards The Difference Engine *as beginning with T). Is this a coincidence, or a deliberate pattern?*

I was unaware of this until your question, so the answer must be coincidence.

Believing that your family is the important thing in your life (as it is in mine), I'd appreciate any information you might choose to provide about your wife, your two adult children, and (perhaps) their own families.

I like to dedicate novels to my wife and children, but not to discuss them in the context of my writing.

You've been identified in a reference as one of Fifty Key Figures in Science Fiction, *and in my book, I compare your impact on the genre to that of Robert A. Heinlein. How would you characterize your overall impact on science fiction?*

I'm not sufficiently acquainted with enough of today's sf to judge that. I don't *feel* as though I've had that central an impact. It feels, rather, as though I've had a fairly big impact on what you might call "alternative science fiction." I don't seem to have done much damage to the central shaft. It remains its adamantine self. But when I see someone like Ned Beauman saying that he's always liked my books, I'm happy. Beauman, Nick Harkaway, Lev Grossman, Lauren Beukes, Dexter Palmer, Richard Kadrey's recent work: it's as though what I wanted to happen in the '80s is finally happening. I was never clear what I did want sf and fantasy to do, in the '80s, but they mostly never did.

My book argues that you rarely read academic critics and are not concerned about what they say, but you do perceive them as a key part of your audience and will sometimes include things in your books that are designed to either delight them or annoy them. Is that a fair statement?

I rarely read them, aren't particularly concerned about what they say, and don't consider them to be a key part of my audience. There aren't enough of them, for that, and I somehow don't imagine them to be that influential in the world at large. The Easter eggs, such as they are, are for clever readers, some of whom will naturally be literary academics, but I have never dogwhistled literary academics specifically. I wouldn't know how. I couldn't give you an example offhand, but literary academics have tended to miss the more esoteric Easter eggs that rock critics, for instance, have found, or so it's seemed to me. I am a generalist, and I plant Easter eggs, to whatever extent that I do, for clever generalists.

Regarding your later nonfiction, I was disappointed that Distrust That Particular Flavor *did not include three of my favorite items: "Alfred Bester, SF and Me" from the 1987 Worldcon program; your 1994 introduction to* Jeff de Boer: Articulation; *and "Paul Smith: A Most Benevolent Marvel" from his 2001 book. Any particular reason these items were excluded? Are they being saved for a volume 2 of your nonfiction?*

The Paul Smith piece struck me as too sucky. I think it reads like I was angling for a bespoke suit, which in fact I was, though I never got one. But writing it may have paved the way for the Bigend books, to some extent. The De Boer piece I'd forgotten until you mentioned it. The Bester felt as if I'd cannibalized it several times too often. No second volume in the works at present.

You've discussed your disinclination to address one of science fiction's central tropes, space travel and alien contact. Yet you've also avoided another common trope, time travel. Is this because you believe it to be impossible? Or is it simply something you're not interested in?

The novel I'm working on now involves a sort of virtual time travel. I write about memory a lot. Time travel in the physical sense doesn't sit so well with memory, for me.

Further, if one doesn't count your early poems, you've never engaged in any speculation about humanity's far future, one thousand or one million years from now. Is this solely a subject fit for fifteen-year-olds? Why or why not?

I've really never seen the point, as an adult. It just seems so witheringly abstract. And in the universe of Deep Time, the one we live in, our species might as well already be dust. To imagine otherwise seems to me to run counter to the Copernican revelation: that we are not the center.

You indicate to interviewers that you let your novels write themselves, then wait until they are published for interviewers and critics to tell you what they were about. But these comments are arguably disingenuous, a device to absolve you of any responsibility for what you have written; surely, some ideas in your novel are a result of conscious intent. Would you agree?

It's less disingenuous than you might think. In my view it's one of the more consistently honest aspects of my self-presentation as a novelist. I think about the factors that might determine the edges of what I'm going to write. I draw lines, create areas to be filled in with narrative, and then do my best to get out of the way of the process. I strongly suspect that more of us do that than admit to it, or know it. (It's not something publishers are fond of hearing, at all.) I don't believe in our cultural paradigm of creativity. I practice what Manny Farber called Termite Art. I don't have ready conscious access to the parts of myself capable of the higher reaches of creativity. I have to wait for them. I do what I hope might induce them to come. I'm like a cargo cultist, that way.

Your friend John Clute implies that you dislike giving interviews—yet my bibliography lists 175 transcribed interviews, not including video and podcast interviews that I didn't document. If you dislike them, why do you give so many interviews? Is there anything about them that you find rewarding or entertaining?

One cannot readily have a commercially successful literary career today without doing interviews. Well, one can, there are Pynchon and McCarthy, but it would be much more of a challenge. My publishers employ publicists to arrange and schedule interviews. I do the great majority of them as an aspect of the publicity surrounding the launch of a book, usually over about a month. I enjoy them more now than I did initially, but I'm still reluctant to do them between books. They are exactly the opposite of the place from which I write.

Also, on two occasions you have served as an interviewer—of Bono and the Edge and of Henry Rollins. Could you say something about how it felt to sit on the other side of the table?

It made me think that I actually wasn't that bad an interview subject myself.

Knowing that this interview will not be published until 2013, would you be willing to provide some details about the "spec script" that you tweeted about?

Given that it's a spec script, written without a contract, it's entirely possible that nothing will have happened to it by the time this is published. If there's no film interest, I may look at trying to make it a graphic novel. It involves time travel, and the elevator pitch is that it's *"Band of Brothers versus Blackwater."* It's set in Berlin 1945 and in an alternate 1997 USA.

Bearing the same fact in mind, could you also say something about the novel you're now working on?

As I said earlier, it involves a kind of virtual time travel, though I'm reluctant to say more.

Finally, my editor says I need your permission to quote passages of your poetry from early fanzines and later publications in my book. [I provided Gibson with copies of all quoted passages.]

Permission granted. But yikes, childhood poetry, how embarrassing.

A WILLIAM GIBSON BIBLIOGRAPHY

This bibliography attempts to list all Gibson publications, including film and television appearances but excluding video and podcast interviews. Works are listed in these categories: novels; film and television scripts; edited works; short fiction; collections (excluding foreign compilations); articles; forewords, introductions, and afterwords; reviews; poems and song lyrics; artwork; letters; interviews; film and television appearances; and adaptations of Gibson's works. Within categories, items are listed chronologically by year of publication, and in alphabetical order by title or author within years; unexamined items are marked "Unseen." A second bibliography covers secondary sources.

A more complete version of the bibliographies, including Web addresses, more data about certain items, and a comprehensive list of secondary resources, will be posted on my Web site: http://www.sfsite.com/gary/intro.htm.

NOVELS

1984   *Neuromancer*. New York: Ace, 1984.
1986   *Count Zero*. New York: Arbor House, 1986.
1988   *Mona Lisa Overdrive*. New York: Bantam, 1988.
1990   *The Difference Engine* (with Bruce Sterling). London: Gollancz, 1990.
1993   *Virtual Light*. New York: Bantam, 1993.
1996   *Idoru*. New York: Putnam's, 1996.
1999   *All Tomorrow's Parties*. New York: Putnam's, 1999.
2003   *Pattern Recognition: A Novel*. New York: Putnam's, 2003.
2007   *Spook Country*. New York: Putnam's, 2007.
2010   *Zero History*. New York: Putnam's, 2010.

FILM AND TELEVISION SCRIPTS

1989   *Alien 3*. [Story by David Giler and Walter Hill; never produced or published, but Gibson acknowledges a script posted on the internet as a shorter version of one script he wrote.]

1995   *Johnny Mnemonic*. TriStar, 1995. Screenplay published with "Johnny Mnemonic" as *Johnny Mnemonic: The Screenplay and the Story*. New York: Berkley, 1995.

1998   "The Kill Switch" (with Tom Maddox and Chris Carter, the latter uncredited). *The X-Files*. New York: Fox, February 15, 1998. Unpublished.

2000   "First Person Shooter" (with Tom Maddox and Chris Carter, the latter uncredited). *The X-Files*. New York: Fox, March 5, 2000. Unpublished.

EDITED WORKS

1963   *Votishal* No. 1 (1963).
        Wormfarm Nos. 1 and 2 (1963). No. 2. Unseen.

1964   *Srith* No. 1 (1964). Distributed as "rider" to *Wormfarm* No. 3.
        Wormfarm No. 3 (1964).

1977   *Genre Plat* (coedited with Allyn Cadogan, Susan Wood, and John Park). Nos. 1 and 2 (Spring and Summer 1977).

SHORT FICTION

1976   "Stoned" (with Lona Elrod, Daniel Say, and Others). *BCSFA Newsletter* No. 32 (February 1976): 6–9.

1977   "Fragments of a Hologram Rose." *Unearth* 1.3 (Summer 1977): 72–77. Republished in *Burning Chrome*, 41–48.

1981   "The Belonging Kind" (with John Shirley). In *Shadows 4*. Ed. Charles L. Grant. Garden City, N.Y.: Doubleday, 1981. 49–64. Republished in *Burning Chrome*, 43–57.
        "The Gernsback Continuum." In *Universe 11*. Ed. Terry Carr. Garden City, N.Y.: Doubleday, 1981. 81–90. Republished in *Burning Chrome*, 28–40.
        "Hinterlands." *Omni* 4.1 (October 1981): 104–19, 162–64. Republished in *Burning Chrome*, 65–86.
        "Johnny Mnemonic." *Omni* 3.8 (May 1981): 56–63, 98–99. Republished in *Burning Chrome*, 6–27.

1982   "Burning Chrome." *Omni* 4.10 (July 1982): 72–77, 102–7. Republished in *Burning Chrome*, 176–200.

1983   "Hippie Hat Brain Parasite." *Modern Stories* No. 1 (April 1983): 22–24. Republished in *Semiotext[e] SF*. Ed. Rudy Rucker, Peter Lamborn Wilson, and Robert Anton Wilson. New York: Semiotext[e], 1989. 109–12.
        "Red Star, Winter Orbit" (with Bruce Sterling). *Omni* 5.10 (July 1983): 84–90, 112–15. Republished in *Burning Chrome*, 87–109.

1984   "New Rose Hotel." *Omni* 6.10 (July 1984): 46–49, 92–94. Republished in *Burning Chrome*, 110–24.

1985   "Dogfight" (with Michael Swanwick). *Omni* 7.10 (July 1985): 44–46, 95–106. Republished in *Burning Chrome*, 150–75.
        "The Winter Market." *Vancouver Magazine* 18.11 (November 1985): 62–73, 108–14, 134–36. Republished in *Burning Chrome*, 125–49.

1987   "The Silver Walks" [Excerpt from *Mona Lisa Overdrive*]. *High Times* (November 1987). Unseen.

1988   "The Smoke" [Excerpt from *Mona Lisa Overdrive*]. *Mississippi Review* 47/48 (1988): 70–76.

1990   "The Angel of Gilead" (with Bruce Sterling) [Excerpt from *The Difference Engine*]. *Interzone* No. 40 (October 1990): 6–30.

"Doing Television." *The Face* (March 1990): 81–82. Simultaneously published in *Tesseracts³*. Ed. Candas Jane Dorsey and Gerry Truscott. Victoria, B.C.: Porcépic, 1990. 392–94. A slighter longer version was published as "Darwin," *Spin* 6.1 (April 1990): 60–61.

"Skinner's Room." *San Francisco Image*, June 10, 1990. Republished in *Visionary San Francisco*. Ed. Paolo Polledri. Munich: Prestal-Verlag, 1990. 153–65.

1991   "Academy Leader." In *Cyberspace: First Steps*. Ed. Michael Benedikt. Cambridge: Massachusetts Institute of Technology Press, 1991. 27–29.

"Cyber-Claus." In "'Twas the Night before Christmas. . . ." *Washington Post Book World*, December 1, 1991, 14–15.

1993   "Where the Holograms Go." In *The Wild Palms Reader*. Ed. Roger Trilling and Stuart Swezey. New York: St. Martin's, 1993. 122–23.

1996   "Lo Rez Skyline" [Excerpt from *Idoru*]. *Rolling Stone*, May 30, 1996, special section "Rolling Stone Technology '96," 1–2, 4, 6, 21.

1997   "Thirteen Views of a Cardboard City." In *New Worlds*. Ed. David Garnett. Consulting ed. Michael Moorcock. Clarkston, Ga.: White Wolf, 1997. 338–49.

2010   "Dougal Discarnate." In *Darwin's Bastards: Astounding Tales from Tomorrow*. Ed. Zsuzsi Gartner. Vancouver: Douglas and McIntyre, 2010. 231–42.

2012   "'Hawk' Ashtray." In *Significant Objects*. Ed. Joshua Glenn and Rob Walker. Seattle: Fantagraphics, 2012. [40–41.]

COLLECTIONS

1986   *Burning Chrome*. Preface by Bruce Sterling. New York: Arbor House, 1986. [Stories]

1992   *Neuromancer; Count Zero; Mona Lisa Overdrive*. Santa Monica, Calif.: Voyager, 1992. [Electronic book]

2012   *Distrust That Particular Flavor*. New York, Putnam, 2012. [Nonfiction, including new, untitled afterwords]

ARTICLES

1963   "The Screaming Crud: A Place to Hear the Crys [*sic*] of Editorial Rage." *Wormfarm* No. 1 (1963): 3. [Editorial]

Untitled editorial. *Votishal* No. 1 (1963): 1.

Untitled editorial comments. *Wormfarm* No. 1 (1963): 1.

1964   "Grunt and Groan: Happy Gibson Comments." *Wormfarm* No. 3 (1964): 1.

"Ohm Brew." *Wormfarm* No. 3 (1964): 5–6.

"A Short History of Coke Bottle Fandom." *Wormfarm* No. 3 (1964): 2.

Srith No. 1 (1964): 1–2. [Fanzine formatted as single article]

1975   "Imaginary Anthology of Imaginative Fiction: A Model Kit." *BCSFAzine/BCSFA Newsletter* No. 29 (October 1975): 6.

1977	"Dangerously Amateur . . . the Birth of *Genre Plat*" (with Allyn Cadogan). *Genre Plat* No. 1 (Spring 1977): 4–6. [Editorial]
1979	"Devo: A Carrier's Story." *Space Junk* No. 2 (1979): 14–16.
	"My Life under Fascism; or, Franco Killed My Dog." *Space Junk* No. 4 (1979): 15–18.
1980	"Anecdotal Evidence." *Genre Plat* No. 4 (Winter/Spring 1980): 23–26.
1981	"Lovecraft & Me." *Space Junk* No. 6 (1981): 21–22.
1982	"On the Surface." *Wing Window* No. 3 (July 8, 1982): 3–4. [Column]
	"On the Surface." *Wing Window* No. 4 (October 31, 1982): 8–9. [Column]
	" . . . With a Strange Device." *Wing Window* No. 2 (March 14, 1982): 5–6.
1983	"On the Surface." *Wing Window* No. 5 (January 30, 1983): 9–10. [Column]
	"On the Surface." *Wing Window* No. 6 (June 20, 1983): 12–13. [Column]
1984	"On the Surface." *Wing Window* No. 7 (February 13, 1984): 9–11. [Column]
1987	"Alfred Bester, SF and Me." *Frontier Crossings: A Souvenir of the 45th World Science Fiction Convention, Conspiracy '87*. Ed. Robert Jackson. London: Science Fiction Conventions, 1987. 28–30.
1988	"Tokyo Collage." *Science Fiction Eye* No. 4 (August 1988): 40–43.
	"Tokyo Suite." Trans. Hisashi Kuroma. *Penthouse*, Japanese ed. (1988). Unseen. [Probably the same item as "Tokyo Collage."]
1989	"Rocket Radio." *Rolling Stone*, June 15, 1989, 84–87. Republished in *Distrust That Particular Flavor*, 7–16.
1993	"Disneyland with the Death Penalty." *Wired* 1.4 (September–October 1993): 51–55, 114–15. Republished in *Distrust That Particular Flavor*, 69–88.
1994	"Jack's Acts." In "Vanities." *Vanity Fair* 57.9 (September 1994), 132. [Title on contents page: "William Gibson on Author Jack Womack"]
1996	"The Net Is a Waste of Time . . . and That's Exactly What's Right about It." *New York Times Magazine*, July 14, 1996, 30–31. Republished as "The Net Is a Waste of Time" in *Distrust That Particular Flavor*, 191–96.
	"Notes on a Process." *Wired* 3.6 (June 1995): 157–59, 207–8. Republished as "Johnny: Notes on a Process," in *Distrust That Particular Flavor*, 235–42.
	"'Virtual Lit': A Discussion" (with Pamela McCorduck). *Biblion* 5.1 (Fall 1996): 33–51. [Transcript of prepared remarks at May 11, 1995, presentation, followed by discussion and answers to audience questions.]
1997	"Jack Womack and the Horned Heart of Neuropa." *Science Fiction Eye* No. 15 (Fall 1997): 61.
1998	"Dead Man Sings." *Forbes* 162 (November 30, 1998), Supplement "Forbes ASAP's Big Issue III," 177. Republished in *Distrust That Particular Flavor*, 49–53.
1999	"My Obsession." *Wired* 7.1 (January 1999): 102–5, 156–58. Republished in *Distrust That Particular Flavor*, 131–51.
	"William Gibson's Filmless Festival." *Wired* 7.10 (October 1999): 227–29. Republished in *Distrust That Particular Flavor*, 219–32.
2000	"Will We Plug Chips into Our Brains?" *Time* 155.25 (June 19, 2000): 84–85. Republished as "Will We Have Computer Chips in Our Heads?" in *Distrust That Particular Flavor*, 211–16.
2001	"Blasted Dreams in Mr. Buk's Window." *National Post*, September 20, 2001. Republished as "Mr. Buk's Window" in *Distrust That Particular Flavor*, 91–95.

"The Future Perfect." *Time* Online (April 30, 2001).

"Modern Boys and Mobile Girls." *Observer Magazine,* April 1, 2001, 8–11. Republished in *Distrust That Particular Flavor,* 121–29.

"My Own Private Tokyo." *Wired* 9.9 (September 2001): 117–19. Republished in *Distrust That Particular Flavor,* 155–63.

"Paul Smith: A Most Benevolent Marvel." In *You Can Find Inspiration in Everything*: *And If You Can't, Look Again,* by Paul Smith. Ed. Robert Violette. London: Violette, 2001. 9–83. [Text in Japanese, 9–23; Italian, 25–39; French, 41–55; German, 57–71; English, 73–87]

2002　"The Baddest Dude on Earth." *Time International* (April 29, 2002). Republished in *Distrust That Particular Flavor,* 35–39.

"Shiny Balls of Mud." *Tate Magazine* No. 1 (September/October 2002). Unseen. Republished as "Shiny Balls of Mud: *Hiraku Dorodango* and Toyku Hands," in *Distrust That Particular Flavor,* 97–104.

"Since 1948." Posted on Gibson's blog, November 6, 2002. Republished, untitled, in *On the Other Side of the Lens: Images of Inspiration from 73 Cultural Icons.* London: Dazed, 2003. 8–15. Republished in *Distrust That Particular Flavor,* 19–25.

"William Gibson on *Burning Chrome.*" HarperCollins Publishers Web site (October 21, 2002).

2003　"My Talk about the Cyborg" [Speech, Vancouver Art Gallery, 2002]. Posted on Gibson's blog, January 28, 2003. Republished as "Googling the Cyborg" in *Distrust That Particular Flavor,* 243–54.

"The Road to Oceania." *New York Times,* June 25, 2003, A25. Republished in *Distrust That Particular Flavor,* 165–71.

"Skip Spence's Jeans." *Ugly Things* No. 21 (2003). Unseen. Republished in *Distrust That Particular Flavor,* 173–77.

"Up the Line" [Speech, Director's Guild of America, Los Angeles, May 17, 2003]. Posted on Gibson's blog, May 21, 2003. Republished in *Distrust That Particular Flavor,* 55–67.

William Gibson's blog. First entry January 6, 2003. Most recent entry September 5, 2010, suggesting abandonment. Contents include musings on various subjects, responses to questions, postings of Gibson's published or unpublished writings, links to articles, and photographs.

2005　"God's Little Toys: Confessions of a Cut & Paste Artist." *Wired* 13.7 (2005): 118–19.

"U2's City of Blinding Lights." *Wired* 13.8 (2005): 124–29.

2006　"Time Machine Cuba." *Infinite Matrix,* January 23, 2006. Republished in *Distrust That Particular Flavor,* 199–208.

"What Really Scares Us." In "10 Ways to Avoid the Next 9/11." *New York Times,* September 10, 2006, Section 4, 13.

2007　"Pining for Toronto's 'Gone World.'" *Toronto Globe and Mail,* May 31, 2007.

Untitled reminiscence beginning, "My pal Len Stoute." *c/o The Velvet Underground, New York, N.Y.: An Exhibit Celebrating Forty Years of the* Velvet Underground and Nico *Album.* Ed. Johan Kugelberg. Evanston, Ill.: Jeff Hirsch Books, JMC, and GHB Editions, 2007. [91].

2008　"William Gibson." In "Is Science Fiction Dying?" *New Scientist* 200 (November 15, 2008): 47.

2009   William Gibson's Twitter account (@greatdismal). First entries April 2009; continues to present. Contents include comments on current events, career developments, Vancouver life, and responses to questions.

2010   "Google's Earth." *New York Times,* September 1, 2010, A23.

2011   "Life in the Meta City." *Scientific American* 205.3 (September 2011): 88–89.

"25 Years of Digital Vandalism." *New York Times,* January 27, 2011, A31.

"Window." In *2:46: Aftershocks: Stories from the Japan Earthquake* [E-book]. Ed. "Our Man in Akibo." London: Enhanced Editions, 2011. Unseen.

2012   "1977." In *Punk: An Aesthetic.* Ed. Johan Kugelberg. New York: Rizzoli, 2012. 286. Unseen.

"Olds Rocket 88, 1950." *New Yorker* 88.16 (June 4 and 11, 2012): 104.

"Talk for Book Expo, New York" [Speech, Book Expo America, New York, May 27, 2010]. In *Distrust That Particular Flavor,* 41–48.

"Where I Like to Read." *Huffington Post* Books (February 8, 2012).

"William Gibson on *The Stars My Destination*: Appreciation." In *American Science Fiction: Classic Novels of the 1950s.* Ed. Gary K. Wolfe. New York: Library of America, 2012.

FOREWORDS, INTRODUCTIONS, AND AFTERWORDS

1986   "Lo Tek: An Introduction." In *Neuromancer.* West Bloomfield, Mich.: Phantasia, 1986. v–vi.

1989   Introduction to *Heatseeker,* by John Shirley. Ed. Stephen P. Brown. Los Angeles: Scream/Press, 1989. iii–v.

Introduction to *The Lost World and The Poison Belt: Professor Challenger Stories by Arthur Conan Doyle.* San Francisco: Chronicle, 1989. [vii–viii].

1990   "Foreword: Strange Attractors." In *Alien Sex: 19 Tales by the Masters of Science Fiction and Dark Fantasy.* Ed. Ellen Datlow. New York: Dutton, 1990. xv–xvi.

1992   Afterword to *Neuromanc* [*Neuromancer*]. Trans. Örkény Ajtay. Budapest: Valhalla Páholy, 1992 345–46.

1994   Afterword to *Neuromancer.* New York: Ace, 1994. 275–78.

Introduction to *Jeff de Boer: Articulation.* Calgary: Muttart Public Art Gallery, 1994. [4–5].

Introduction to *The Selected Letters of Philip K. Dick: 1974.* Ed. Paul Williams. Novato, Calif.: Underwood-Miller, 1994. [9–10].

1996   "The Recombinant City: A Foreword." In *Dhalgren,* by Samuel R. Delany. Hanover, N.H.: Wesleyan University Press, 1996. xi–xiii.

1997   Foreword to *The Artificial Kid,* by Bruce Sterling. San Francisco: Wired, 1997. 1–6.

Foreword to *Ray Gun: Out of Control.* Ed. Dean Kuipers and Chris Ashworth. New York: Simon and Shuster, 1997. 10–13.

"Introduction: Entering the Transit Lounge." In *Transit Lounge: An Interface Book from 21•C.* Ed. Ashley Crawford and Ray Edgar. North Ryde, New South Wales: Craftsman, 1997. 5.

1998   "The Absolute at Large." In *The Art of the X-Files.* Ed. Marvin Heiferman and Carole Kismaric. New York: HarperPrism, 1998. [8–11].

"'Naples': Introduction by William Gibson." In *The Avram Davidson Treasury*. Ed. Robert Silverberg and Grania Davis. New York: Tor, 1998. 344–45.

2000   Afterword to *The Art of the Matrix*. Ed. Spencer Lamm. New York: Newmarket, 2000. 451.

Foreword to *City Come a-Walkin'*, by John Shirley. New York: Four Walls Eight Windows, 2000. 1–4.

2001   Foreword to *The Matrix: The Shooting Script*, by Larry Wachowski and Andy Wachowski. New York: Newmarket, 2001. vii–viii.

"Foreword: Geeks and Artboys." In *Multimedia: From Wagner to Virtual Reality*. Ed. Randall Packer and Ken Jordan. New York: Norton, 2001. xi–xiv.

2004   Foreword to *American Whiskey Bar*, by Michael Turner. Vancouver: Arsenal Pulp, 2004. ix–x.

"Foreword: She's the Business." In *Stable Strategies and Others*, by Eileen Gunn. San Francisco: Tachyon, 2004. xi–xiv.

"Introduction: The Sky above the Port." In *Neuromancer*. New York: Ace, 2004. vii–xi.

2005   "Foreword: 'The Body.'" In *Stelarc: The Monograph*. Ed. Marquand Smith. Cambridge: Massachusetts Institute of Technology Press, 2005. vii–viii. Republished as "Introduction: 'The Body'" in *Distrust That Particular Flavor*, 185–89.

2007   Foreword to *Phantom Shanghai*, by Greg Girard. Toronto: Magenta Foundation, 2007. Republished as "Terminal City" in *Distrust That Particular Flavor*, 179–82.

"An Invitation." In *Labyrinths: Selected Stories and Other Writings*, by Jorge Luis Borges. New York: New Directions, 2007. ix–xii. Republished in *Distrust That Particular Flavor*, 105–11.

2010   "Sui Generis: A Testimony." In *The Ware Tetralogy*, by Rudy Rucker. Rockville, Md.: Prime, 2010. 7–9. Accessed online.

2012   "Introduction: African Thumb Piano." In *Distrust That Particular Flavor*, 1–6.

REVIEWS

1964   "Mailing Comments" [Rev. of the fanzines *Iscariot* No. 1; *Dol-Drum* No. 2; *STF* No. 4; *Warlock* No. 3; *The Invader* Nos. 1 and 2; *Nemesis* No. 1; and *Zaje Zaculo* No. 1]. *Wormfarm* No. 3 (1964): 3–5.

1975   "*Dhalgren*, an Unreview" [Rev. of *Dhalgren*, by Samuel R. Delany]. *New Directions* No. 23 (1975): 2–3.

"*The Investigation*: Stanislaw Lem's Fortean Novel" [Rev. of *The Investigation*, by Stanislaw Lem]. *New Directions* No. 22 (August 1975): 3–4. Republished as "Lem's Fortean Novel" in *Science Fiction Review* 4.4 [No. 15] (November 1975): 35–36.

1976   "In the Airflow Futoropolis" [Rev. of *The Streamlined Decade*, by Donald J. Bush]. *New Directions* No. 25 (1976): 1–2.

1977   "Them & Us; or, 'Toto, I Don't Think We're in Kansas Anymore'" [Rev. of *Nebula Award Stories Eleven*, ed. Ursula K. Le Guin]. *Genre Plat* No. 1 (Spring 1977). 11–13. [Formatted as a review, though Gibson announces that he will solely discuss two essays in the collection.]

1978   Rev. of *The Jewel-Hinged Jaw: Notes on the Language of Science Fiction*, by Samuel R. Delany. *Locus* 11.4 [No. 211] (May 1978): 8.

1979   Rev. of *Dracula in Love*, by John Shirley. *Science Fiction Review* 8.5 [No. 33] (November 1979): 49–50.

Rev. of *Gloriana*, by Michael Moorcock. *Science Fiction Review* 8.2 [No. 30] (March 1979): 51–52.

1980   Rev. of *City Come a-Walkin'*, by John Shirley. *Science Fiction Review* 9.3 [No. 36] (August 1980): 31.

Rev. of *Mockingbird*, by Walter Tevis. *Science Fiction Review* 9.2 [No. 35] (May 1980): 41.

1981   Rev. of *The Flute Player*, by D. M. Thomas. *Science Fiction Review* 10.1 [No. 38] (Spring 1981): 56.

Rev. of *Port of Saints*, by William S. Burroughs. *Science Fiction Review* 10.1 [No. 38] (Spring 1981): 56–57.

Rev. of *Ratner's Star*, by Don DeLillo. *Science Fiction Review* 10.1 [No. 38] (Spring 1981): 57.

1982   Rev. of *Cellars*, by John Shirley. *Science Fiction Review* 11.3 [No. 44] (Fall 1982): 52.

1996   Rev. of *The Acid House*, by Irvine Welsh. *Science Fiction Eye* No. 14 (Spring 1996): 77.

2000   "Steely Dan's Return" [Rev. of *Two against Nature* {CD}, by Steely Dan]. In *Addicted to Noise* 6.3 (March 1, 2000). Unseen. Republished as "Any 'Mount of World" in *Distrust That Particular Flavor*, 27–32.

2001   "Metrophagy: The Art and Science of Digesting Great Cities" [Rev. of *London: The Biography*, by Peter Ackroyd]. *Whole Earth* (Summer 2001). Unseen. Republished in *Distrust That Particular Flavor*, 113–18.

POEMS AND SONG LYRICS [All poems unless otherwise indicated]

1963   "The Last God." *Wormfarm* No. 1 (1963): 1.

"Observations on a Nightfear." *Wormfarm* No. 1 (1963): 1.

"A Tale of the Badger Folk." *Wormfarm* No. 1 (1963): 4.

1991   "The Beloved: Voices for Three Heads." In *Robert Longo: Art Random*. Ed. Dir. Kyoichi Tsuzuki. Kyoto: Kyoto Shoin, 1991. 26–31.

1992   *Agrippa: A Book of the Dead*. Etchings by Dennis Ashbaugh. New York: Kevin Bogos, 1992.

"Memory Palace" [Gibson script, evidently a prose poem, performed at the 1992 Art Futura performance event in Barcelona. Unpublished, but an excerpt is read in *No Maps for These Territories*].

1993   "Dog Star Girl" (with Deborah Harry and Chris Stein). *Debravation*. [CD] By Deborah Harry. London: Chrysalis, 1993. [Song lyrics]

"Floating Away." *Technodon*. [CD] By Yellow Magic Orchestra. London: EMI, 1993. [Spoken lyrics]

1997   "Our Brief Eternity" (with Christopher Halcrow). [Poetic passages to accompany 1997 performance by Holy Body Tattoo dance group, Vancouver. Unpublished, but excerpts are posted online]

2006   "Cold War Water." In *Polder: A Festschrift for John Clute and Judith Clute*. Ed. Farah Mendlesohn. Baltimore: Old Earth, 2006. 132.

ARTWORK [All interior cartoons unless otherwise described]

1963 "Arrrh!" *Wormfarm* No. 1 (1963): 3.

Cartoon, uncaptioned. *Votishal* No. 1 (1963): 1.

Cartoon, uncaptioned. *Votishal* No. 1 (1963): 1. [Different from above item]

Cartoon, uncaptioned. *Votishal* No. 1 (1963): 11.

Cartoon, uncaptioned. *Wormfarm* No. 1 (1963): 1.

Cartoon, uncaptioned. *Wormfarm* No. 1 (1963): 4.

"Gibson's View of Fandom: Three Fannish Cartoons by (Who Else?)." ["No, It's Not a War. The Neffers Are Fueding [sic]"; "Now! *You* Can Build a Real Psionic Space Ship! 1. Glue Tab *A* into Slot *B*. 2. Glue Tab *C* into Slot *D*. 3. Grab Tab *E* Firmly. Hold On. 4. Think Hard!"; "I Don't Know Who He Is, but He Keeps Muttering, 'Revenge, Revenge!'"] *Wormfarm* No. 1 (1963): 5.

"Hssst! Thy Fly Is Open!" *Fanac* No. 96 (October/November, 1963): 8.

"Let's Be Non-Conformists. Everybody Else Is Doing It." *Wormfarm* No. 1 (1963): 2.

"Let's Make Tracks to London in '65!" *Wormfarm* No. 1 (1963): 3.

"No, We Don't Have a Mr. Fafhrd Registered Here—Why Do You Ask?" *Fanac* No. 96 (October/November, 1963): 1.

"Now It's '64 'Frisco or Fight." *Wormfarm* No. 1 (1963): 2.

"Well, Then He Said Something about Putting a Dean Drive in His Propbeanie. . . . Then, Whooosh!!" *Wormfarm* No. 1 (1963). [Cover drawing]

1964 Cartoon, uncaptioned. *Wormfarm* No. 3 (1964): 6.

"There Is a Meeting Here Tonight . . . !" *Wormfarm* No. 3 (1964). [Cover drawing]

1975 Cartoon, uncaptioned. *New Directions* No. 23 (1975): 4.

"A Good Solid Genzine with Too Many Staples. . . ." *New Directions* No. 24 (1975). [Cover drawing]

"'Jeez . . . I Haven't Seen One of You Little Guys Around in Years . . . What're You Doing These Days?' 'We Make Porn Flicks.'" *New Directions* No. 23 (1975): 4.

"So I Stood There in the Rain, Feeling the Hot Metal of the Remington Pump-Gun through My Custom-Made Italian Driving Gloves, and Twitching My Vestigial Tail—I Knew That This Was It—The Long Goodbye." *New Directions* No. 22 (August 1975): 5.

"Traditional Folk Arts of Fandom: The Hand-Cut Illo. Next Month: Underwater Beanie-Weaving and How to Spot a Corflu Junkie." *BCSFA Newsletter* No. 29 (October 1975). [Cover drawing]

"Weird Tails/The General Refuses to Understand That the Sight of These Natives Consuming Ice-Cream Cones Will Have an Adverse Effect on the Morale of the Troops. . . ." *New Directions* No. 22 (August 1975). [Cover Drawing]

1976 "And Then Sex Reared Its Ugly Head." *BCSFAzine* No. 42 (December 1976): 1. Re-published in *Genre Plat* No. 5 (Fall 1983): 20.

"Can This Be the Onset of General Paranoia?" *BCSFAzine* No. 40 (October 1976): 3. Republished in *Genre Plat* No. 5 (Fall 1983): 21.

Cartoon, uncaptioned. *BCSFAzine* No. 40 (October 1976): 3.

Cartoon, uncaptioned. *BCSFAzine* No. 41 (November 1976): 6.

Cartoon, uncaptioned. *BCSFAzine* No. 42 (December 1976): 5. Republished in *Genre Plat* No. 5 (Fall 1983): 18.

"A Leading Thinker Seriously Considering New Directions." *New Directions* No. 25 (1976). [Cover drawing]

"Start Worrying." *BCSFAzine* No. 41 (November 1976): 9. Republished in *Genre Plat* No. 5 (Fall 1983): 22.

"Veez, What a . . . Planet of Slobs." *BCSFAzine* No. 35 (May 1976): 5.

"Whereas My Previous Work Often Dealt with Invasions of Earth by Ant-Like Creatures with Periscope Eyes and Garish Neck-Wear, I Now Feel Such Themes to Be Below My Serious Consideration as a Novelist. . . . . . ." *BCSFA Newsletter* No. 32 (February 1976). [Cover drawing, signed "J. Cornelius"]

1977   "Barbarian Comix." *BCSFAzine* No. 44 (February 1977): 5. Republished in *Genre Plat* No. 5 (Fall 1983): 38.

"Canadian Union of Opposites—on Strike." *Genre Plat* No. 2 (Summer 1977): 4.

Cartoon, uncaptioned. *BCSFAzine* No. 43 (January 1977): 7.

Cartoon, uncaptioned. *BCSFAzine* No. 44 (February 1977): 9.

Cartoon, uncaptioned [unsigned]. *Genre Plat* No. 1 (Spring 1977): 13.

Cartoon, uncaptioned [unsigned]. *Genre Plat* No. 1 (Spring 1977) 22. [Heading for Susan Wood column "Tidepool"] Republished in *Genre Plat* No. 2 (Summer 1977): 18; *Genre Plat* No. 3 (Winter/Spring 1978): 38.

Cartoon, uncaptioned [unsigned]. *Genre Plat* No. 2 (Summer 1977): 29. [Heading for letter column "Collation"] Republished in *Genre Plat* No. 3 (Winter/Spring 1978): 43; *Genre Plat* No. 4 (Winter/Spring 1980): 33; *Genre Plat* No. 5 (Fall 1983): 37.

"Cover Collage." *Genre Plat* No. 2 (Summer 1977). [Cover array of images, attributed to Gibson]

"Fine Points of Contemporary Fannish Cartooning (No. 1): How to Draw the Allyn Cadogan Smile." *Genre Plat* No. 1 (Spring 1977): 6.

"Hi, There. Bet You Didn't Know Giant Insects Wear Big Plastic Tits." *BCSFAzine* No. 43 (January 1977): 9.

"Is Mimeographer's Knee a Terminal Condition?" *Amor de Cosmos People's Memorial Quasirevolutionary Susanzine* No. 15 (October 31, 1977): 5.

"Some Day, Kid, All of This Will Be Yours—the Hugos, the Groupies, the Royalty Checks. . . ." *Genre Plat* No. 1 (Spring 1977): 21.

"There Ought to Be a Law about These Commie Bull-Dykes Polluting Science Fiction's Precious Bodily Fluids. And These New Wave British Faggots. . . ." *Genre Plat* No. 1 (Spring 1977): 27.

"A 2-Page Collaboration between Ken Fletcher and Wm. Gibson" (with Ken Fletcher). *Genre Plat* No. 1 (Spring 1977). [Sixteen-panel comic-book-style story, with Gibson and Fletcher drawing alternating panels, created as a public event]

"Walking a Lobster." *Genre Plat* No. 2 (Summer 1977): 5.

1978   Cartoon, uncaptioned. *Algol: A Magazine about Science Fiction* 15.3 [No. 32] (Summer/Fall 1978): 37.

1979   "And This Compulsion of Yours, to Shout 'Beam Me Up, Scotty' at the Moment of Orgasm—to What Do You Attribute That?" *Amor de Cosmos People's Memorial Exrevolutionary Susanzine* No. 17 (July 8, 1979): 11.

1980   "'Ard Day in th' 'Oles?' 'Bleeding 'Ard.'" *Genre Plat* No. 4 (Winter/Spring 1980): 22.

Cartoon, uncaptioned. *Genre Plat* No. 4 (Winter/Spring 1980): 14.

2003   "Detail of Pachinko Machine." In *On the Other Side of the Lens: Images of Inspiration
        from 73 Cultural Icons.* London: Dazed, 2003. 10–11. [Photograph]
        "Lights Abstract." In *On the Other Side of the Lens: Images of Inspiration from 73 Cultural
        Icons.* London: Dazed, 2003. 12–13. [Photograph]
        "Self-Portrait of Girl." In *On the Other Side of the Lens: Images of Inspiration from 73
        Cultural Icons.* London: Dazed, 2003. 14–15. [Photograph]
2011   "The Phoenix, Reborn!" *WCSFAzine* No. 22 (April 2011): 9. [Scan of drawing made
        by Gibson at 1996 Vancouver convention]

LETTERS

1976   Letter. *BCSFAzine* No. 34 (April 1976): 4.
        Letter. *Science Fiction Review* 5.3 [No. 19] (August 1976): 12–13.
1977   Letter. *Science Fiction Review* 6.1 [No. 20] (February 1977): 54.
        Letter. *Science Fiction Review* 6.4 [No. 23] (November 1977): 7.
1979   Letter. *Space Junk* No. 3 (1979): [20–21].
1984   Letter. *Ansible* No. 38 (Easter 1984): [10]. [Quoted in "Infinitely Improbable"]
1986   Letter. *Ansible* No. 45 (1986): [2].
1991   Letter. *Locus* 26.6 [No. 365] (June 1991): 61.
1993   Letter. *Science Fiction Eye* No. 12 (Summer 1993): 9.
        Letter. Quoted in *Then* No. 4 (August 1993). Unseen.

INTERVIEWS

1985   Nicholas, Joseph, and Judith Hanna. "William Gibson." *Interzone* No. 13 (Autumn
        1985): 17–18.
1986   Gilmore, Mikal. "The Rise of Cyberpunk: Science Fiction's Hottest New Author
        and His Depraved World." *Rolling Stone,* December 4, 1986, 77–78, 107–8.
        Greenland, Colin. "Nod to the Apocalypse." *Foundation* No. 36 (Summer 1986):
        5–10.
1987   Maddox, Tom. "Eye to Eye: Disclave 1986 Guest of Honor Interview with William
        Gibson." *Science Fiction Eye* No. 1 (Winter 1987): 18–26.
        McQuiddy, A. P. "William Gibson: Hallucinating on the Present." *Texas SF Inquirer*
        No. 22 (October/November 1987): 2–7.
        Stathis, Lou. "Cyberpunk." *High Times* (November 1987): 37–39, 72.
        Tatsumi, Takayuki. "Eye to Eye." *Science Fiction Eye* No. 1 (Winter 1987): 6–17.
1988   Greenfield, Adam. "New Romancer." *Spin* 4 (December 1988): 96–99, 119.
        Harper, Leanne C. "The Culture of Cyberspace." *Bloomsbury Review* 8.5 (September/
        October 1988): 16–17, 30.
        McCaffery, Larry. "An Interview with William Gibson." *Mississippi Review* 16.2–3
        (1988): 217–36. Republished in *Storming the Reality Studio: A Casebook of Cyber-
        punk and Postmodern Science Fiction.* Ed. Larry McCaffery. Durham, N.C.: Duke
        University Press, 1991. 263–85.
1989   Gross, Terry. "Terry Gross Interviews Author William Gibson." *Fresh Air.* National
        Public Radio, February 1989.

Hamburg, Victoria, and Aaron Rapaport. "The King of Cyberpunk." *Interview* 19.1 (January 1989): 84–86, 91.

Kelly, Kevin. "Cyberpunk Era." *Whole Earth Review* No. 63 (Summer 1989): 78–83. [Excerpts from interviews in *Bloomsbury Review, High Times, Impulse, Interview, Mississippi Review,* and *Science Fiction Eye*]

Leary, Timothy. "High Tech High Life—William Gibson and Timothy Leary in Conversation." *Mondo 2000* 7 (Fall 1989): 58–64. Republished as "Conversation with William Gibson." In *Chaos and Cyber Culture,* by Timothy Leary. Ed. Michael Horowitz. Berkeley, Calif.: Ronin, 1994. 22–27.

Tomlinson, Paul. "William Gibson Profile." *Starburst* No. 133 (September 1989): 34–35.

Walker, Douglas. "Doug Walker Interviews Science Fiction Author William Gibson." *Impulse* 15.1 (Winter 1989): 36–39.

Wershler-Henry, Darren. "Queen Victoria's Personal Spook, Psychic Legbreakers, Snakes and Catfood: An Interview with William Gibson and Tom Maddox" (with Tom Maddox). *Virus* 23 (Fall 1989): 28–36.

1990   Daurer, Gregory. "Interview with William Gibson." *Journal Wired* No. 3 (Summer/ Fall 1990): 314–32.

1991   "Gibson and Sterling: On the Virtual Chicken Circuit" (with Bruce Sterling). *Locus* 26 (May 1991): 5, 65–66. [Interviewer unidentified]

McVeigh, Kev. "Homo-Eroticism, Llamas, and (a Little Bit about) the C-Word: Bruce Sterling and William Gibson Interviewed" (with Bruce Sterling). *Vector* No. 159 (1991): 6–9.

"William Gibson: Cyber-Punk." *Cybervision* 2 (ca. 1991–92). [Interviewer unidentified]

William Gibson Interview. *Creem* (April–May 1991). Unseen. Accessed online. [Interviewer unknown]

Zuckerman, Edward. "William Gibson: Teen Geek Makes Good, Redefines Sci-Fi." *People* 35 (June 10, 1991): 103–8.

1992   Catchpole, Terry. "Cyberpunk." *Entertainment Weekly* 106 (February 21, 1992): 62–63. Unseen.

Fischlin, David, Veronica Hollinger, and Andrew Taylor. "The Charisma Leak: A Conversation with William Gibson and Bruce Sterling" (with Bruce Sterling). *Science Fiction Studies* 19 (March 1992): 1–16.

1993   Bolhafner, Stephen. "William Gibson: Making Light of Cyberspace Shtick." *St. Louis Post Dispatch,* August 29, 1993. [Another version of the interview published in the March 1994 issue of *Starlog*]

Denison, D. C. "William Gibson." *Boston Globe,* October 10, 1993, M8.

Killheffer, Robert K. J. "*PW* Interviews: William Gibson." *Publishers Weekly* 240.36 (September 6, 1993): 70–71.

Rogers, Mike. "Interview with William Gibson." Privately posted on interviewer's Web site. (October 1, 1993.)

Shepherd, Mark. "William Gibson's Reality." *Ottawa X-Press,* September 22, 1993.

Sims, Michael. "William Gibson: The Day after Tomorrow Meets Film Noir in the Imagination of This Writer." *BookPage* (August 1993): 3. Unseen.

1994   Bolhafner, Stephen. "Guide to Cyberspace: William Gibson Shines a 'Virtual Light' on His Own Cyberfuture." *Starlog* No. 200 (March 1994): 72–74, 87.

Gibson, William. "Turning Money into Light." *Details* 12.9 (February 1994): 64–69, 133. [Bono and the Edge interviewed by Gibson and Roger Trilling, with introduction by Gibson]

——. Interview of Henry Rollins. *huH* No. 2 (October 1994). Unseen.

Golini, Marisa. "Traveling the Cyber-Highway with William Gibson." *Cyberspace Vanguard* 2 (March 1994). Online.

Josefsson, Dan. "I Don't Even Have a Modem." Privately posted on interviewer's Web site. 1994.

Rosenberg, Scott. "The Man Who Named Cyberspace." *Digital Culture,* August 4, 1994. Unseen.

Salza, Giuseppe. "William Gibson Interview." Privately posted on interviewer's Web site. 1994.

Speller, Maurine. "Horribly Real." *Vector* No. 179 (June 1994): 12–17.

White, Tim. "William Gibson: Exploring the Newest Frontier." *Mindsparks* 2 (1994): 35–36. [Excerpts from interview on *TechnoPolitics,* October 29, 1993]

1995 Boreale, Aanta. "Cyberpunk." *E-Zone* (1995). Online.

Dargis, Manohla. "Cyber Johnny: SF Writer William Gibson Talks to Manohla Dargis." *Sight and Sound* 5.7 (July 1995): 6.

"The Father of Cyberpunk Discusses *Johnny Mnemonic*'s Complicated Birth and Other Adventures in the Screen Trade." *Cinescape* 1 (July 1995). Unseen. [Interviewer unknown]

Joisten, Bernard, and Ken Lum. "William Gibson Interview." *Purple Prose* (April 1995). Online.

Lynch, Stephen. "William Gibson Interview." *Orange County Register,* May 28, 1995.

Ryan, Mo. "Data Storm: Keanu Reeves and Director Robert Longo Explore the Dark Side of the Info-Age in *Johnny Mnemonic.*" *Cinescape* 1 (June 1995).

Van Bakel, Rogier. "Remembering Johnny: William Gibson on the Making of *Johnny Mnemonic*" (with Robert Longo). *Wired* 3.6 (June 1995): 154–57, 204–6.

1996 "Civilisation and the Edge of Popular Culture." *City* 1.5–6 (1996): 174–77. Unseen.

Ings, Simon. "Love on Line." *Dazed and Confused* No. 25 (1996). Unseen.

"It's Not Only Rock'n'Roll." *Wordpress.com,* 1996. [Originally published in *Alternative Press*; interviewer unidentified]

Interview. *Playboy.com* (August 1996). [Interviewer unidentified]

Neilson, Robert. "Exploring the Increasingly Unthinkable Present." *Albedo One* No. 12 (1996): 8–11.

O'Hara, Andrew. "Re:Mote Induction Interview: William Gibson." *Re:Mote Induction* (1996). Online.

Rosenberg, Scott. "The *Salon* Interview: William Gibson." *Salon* (October 14, 1996).

1997 Adams, Philip. "Accidental Guru: William Gibson." In *Transit Lounge: An Interface Book from 21C.* Ed. Ashley Crawford and Ray Edgar. North Ryde, Aus.: Craftsman House, 1997. 43–45.

Barker, Clive. "Gibson/Barker Interview." *Burning Chrome* (December 13, 1997). Online.

Diggle, Andy. "Interview with William Gibson." Privately posted on interviewer's Web site. 1997.

Ludovico, Alessandro. "William Gibson Interview." *Neural* (October 1997). Online.

McClelland, Stephen. "Coining Cyberspace: William Gibson." In *Future Histories: Award-Winning Science Fiction Writers Predict Twenty Tomorrows for Communications*. Ed. Stephen McClelland. London: Horizon, 1997. 119–23.

McIntyre, Tom. "William Gibson: Live and Unmediated." *Mondo 2000* 16 (Winter/Spring 1997): 49–55.

Womack, Jack. Interview with William Gibson. Excerpts "Interspersed" with Stephen P. Brown, "Jack Womack Interviewed by Stephen P. Brown." *Science Fiction Eye* No. 15 (Fall 1997): 46, 49, 50, 52, 53, 54, 56, 57, 58.

1998   Allemang, John. "William Gibson Neuromances *The X-Files*." *Toronto Globe and Mail*, February 13, 1998. Unseen.

Grimwood, Jon Courtenay. "An Interview with William Gibson." *Infinity Plus* (January 17, 1998). Online. [Originally published in *Manga Mania*, date unknown]

Lincoln, Ben. "Cyberpunk on Screen—William Gibson Speaks." *The Peak* 7.100 (October 19, 1998).

Van Belkom, Edo. "William Gibson." In *Northern Dreamers: Interviews with Famous Science Fiction, Fantasy, and Horror Writers*. Ed. Edo van Belkom. Kingston, Ont.: Quarry, 1998. 83–93.

"William Gibson on Cyberspace, Bohemia, Power, Aliens, and Burning Man." *Sandbox: Future Visions* No. 5 (Spring 1998). Unseen. [Interviewer unknown]

1999   Çakan, Myra. "William Gibson: Antiheld im Cyberspace." *Alien Contact* No. 34 (1999): 36–38.

Caplan, Paul. "Cyberpunk Rocks the Virtual Boat." *e-Volve* (November 11, 1999). Online. Unseen.

Doctorow, Cory. "William Gibson Interview Transcript." *Craphound.com* (November 23, 1999). Online.

Johnston, Antony. "William Gibson, *All Tomorrow's Parties*: Waiting for the Man." *Spike* (August 1, 1999). Online.

Martin, Robert Scott. "Cyberspace, Outer Space." *Space.com* (October 26, 1999). Online.

McClellan, Jim. "Cyber Punk 2000." *The Guardian*, October 9, 1999.

Moher, Frank. "Back to the Present." *National Post*, November 19, 1999. Unseen.

Sullivan, James. "Bridge to Tomorrow." *SF Gate* (October 19, 1999). Online.

"William Gibson Globe and Mail Story." *Toronto Globe and Mail*, November 30, 1999. [Interviewer unidentified]

2000   Daring, Peter. "Sandpapering the Conscious Mind with William Gibson." *Science Fiction Weekly* 146 (2000). Online.

Dowbenko, Uri. "William Gibson: Prophet of Cyber-Grunge." *Steamshovel Press* (2000). Online.

DuPont, Alexandra. "Alexandra DuPont Interviews William 'Freakin' Gibson!!!!" *Ain't It Cool News* (February 3, 2000). Online.

Mathew, David. "Feasts of Static: William Gibson." *The Third Alternative* No. 22 (2000): 12–15.

"William Gibson: The Online Transcript." *The Guardian*, March 24, 2000. [Various anonymous questioners]

2001   Harron, Mary. "William Gibson: Interview by Mary Harron." *Punk* No. 0 (25th Anniversary Ed.; 2001): 27–29.

"Q & A: William Gibson." *Popular Science* 259.4 (October 2001): 63. [Interviewer unidentified]

Dorsey, Candas Jane. "An Interview with William Gibson." *New York Review of Science Fiction* 15.9 [No. 177] (May 2003): 10–11.

Elkins, Eric S. "Gibson Confronts His Own Demons." *Denver Post,* February 9, 2003.

Epstein, Daniel Robert. "William Gibson." *Suicide Girls* (February 23, 2003). Online.

Flanagan, Mark. "William Gibson Interview." *About.com Contemporary Literature* (January 2003). Online.

Gill, Alexandra. "Back in the Here and Now." *Toronto Globe and Mail,* February 8, 2003, 1. Unseen.

Graham, Fiona. "Finding Faces in the Clouds." *The Telegraph,* April 30, 2003.

Kiausch, Usch. "Niemals Werde Ich Nur von Silbernen Stiefeln Reden!" In *Das Science Fiction Jahr 2003.* Ed. Wolfgang Jeschke and Sascha Mamczak. Munich: Heyne, 2003. 452–66. Unseen.

Leonard, Andrew. "Nodal Point: William Gibson Talks about How His New Present-Day Novel, 'Pattern Recognition,' Processes the Apocalyptic Mind-Set of a Post-911 World." *Salon,* February 13, 2003.

Lillington, Karlin. "Inventor of Cyberspace Steps Back to the Present." *Irish Times,* April 25, 2003.

Lim, Dennis. "Think Different." *Village Voice,* February 11, 2003.

Mackintosh, Hamish. "Talk Time: William Gibson." *The Guardian,* April 30, 2003.

Mallon, Matthew. "Which Bit of the Future Would William Gibson Get So Terribly Wrong?" *The Word* No. 5 (July 2003): 26–27.

McMahon, Donna. "Redefining William Gibson." *SF Site* (January 2003).

Means, Loren. "Interview with William Gibson." *YLEM Journal* 23.4 (March/April 2003): 11–14. Unseen.

Nippert, Matt. "William Gibson." *The Listener,* February 10, 2003. Unseen.

Poole, Steven. "Tomorrow's Man." *The Guardian,* May 2, 2003.

"Q & A: William Gibson." *Newsweek* 141.8 (February 24, 2003): 75. [Interviewer unidentified]

Ulin, David L. "Present Worries in Future Tense." *Los Angeles Times,* March 4, 2003, E1, E12–13.

Unruh, Wes. "William Gibson Interview." *Green Man Review* (February 2003). Online.

"William Gibson Answers Readers' Questions." *The Telegraph,* April 30, 2003. [Various anonymous questioners]

"William Gibson: Crossing Boundaries." *Locus* 50.5 [No. 508] (May 2003): 6–7, 63–64. [Interviewer unidentified]

2004 Anderson, Chris, and Jennifer Hillner. "Watch This Way: Extreme Advertising. TiVo Tribes. Googlevision. A Conversation about the Anytime, Anyware TV of Tomorrow" (with Rob Glaser, Yair Landau, and Ed Zuckerman). *Wired* 12 (May 2004): 156–57, 160.

Hiltbrand, David. "Squinting at the Present." *Philadelphia Inquirer,* February 17, 2004.

Murphy, Peter. "A Brief History of the Future." *New Review* (2004). Online.

Rapatzikou, Tatiani G. "Interview with William Gibson." In *Gothic Motifs in the Fiction of William Gibson,* by Tatiani G. Rapatzikou. Amsterdam: Rodopi, 2004. 217–30.

2005   De Vicente, José Luis. "El Padre del 'Ciberpunk' William Gibson." *El Mundo,* February 8, 2005.

2006   Shainblum, Mark, and Matthew Friedman. "Post-Modern Sublime: The William Gibson Interview (1993)." *Orion* No. 5 (February 2006): 37–47.

2007   Adams, Tim. "Space to Think." *The Guardian,* August 11, 2007.

Beers, David. "William Gibson Hates Futurists." *The Tyee,* October 18, 2007.

Bennie, Angela. "A Reality Stranger Than Fiction." *Sydney Morning Herald,* September 7, 2007.

Blume, Harvey. "Q & A with William Gibson." *Boston Globe,* August 19, 2007, E4.

Chang, Angela. "Q & A: William Gibson." *PC Magazine,* January 10, 2007. Online.

"Cognitive Weirdness." *Locus* 59.5 [No. 562] (November 2007): 8–9, 66. [Interviewer unidentified]

Cornea, Christine. "Interview: Writer William Gibson." In *Science Fiction Cinema: Between Fantasy and Reality,* by Christine Cornea. New Brunswick, N.J.: Rutgers University Press, 2007. 26–28.

Dueben, Alex. "William Gibson: The Father of Cyberpunk." *California Literary Review,* October 2, 2007.

Ellis, Warren. "Cracking the Gibson Code." *Wired* 15.8 (August 2007): 66.

Garreau, Joel. "Through the Looking Glass." *Washington Post,* September 6, 2007.

Goldsmith, Belinda. "Book Talk: William Gibson Says Reality Has Become Sci-Fi." *Reuters* (August 7, 2007). Online.

Gwinn, Mary Ann. "Futuristic Fantasy Lives Now for Author William Gibson." *Seattle Times,* August 6, 2007.

Hill, Logan. "Simcity '07." *New York* 40 (August 13, 2007): 72.

Leonard, Andrew. "William Gibson: Novelist." *Rolling Stone,* November 15, 2007, 162.

Lim, Dennis. "Now Romancer." *Salon,* August 11, 2007.

Linnemann, Mavis. "Days of Future Past: William Gibson Overdrive." *Phawker* (August 15, 2007). Online.

Long, Marion. "Q & A: William Gibson: Are You Spooked Yet?" *Discover* 28 (August 2007): 68–69.

Murray, Noel. "William Gibson." *A.V. Club* (August 22, 2007). Online.

Nissley, Tom. "Across the Border to *Spook Country.*" *Amazon.com* (2007).

Owens, Jill. "William Gibson Country." *Powell's Books* (August 21, 2007).

Parker, T. Virgil. "William Gibson: Sci-Fi Icon Becomes Prophet of the Present." *College Crier* 6.2 (2007). Online.

"Q & A William Gibson." *PC Magazine* 26 (February 6, 2007): 19. Unseen. [Interviewer unidentified]

Ranger, Steve. "William Gibson Heads for 'Spook Country.'" *CNET News* (August 6, 2007). Online.

Sharp, Rob. "William Gibson: He's Seen the Future." *The Independent,* September 5, 2007.

Solomon, Deborah. "Questions for William Gibson: Back From the Future." *New York Times Magazine,* August 19, 2007, 13.

"William Gibson." *Bat Segundo* 133 (2007). Online. [Interviewer unidentified]

2008   Gutmair, Ulrich. "William Gibson Interview." *Void Manufacturing* (October 1, 2008). Online.

Holstein, Eric, and Raoul Abdaloff. "Interview de William Gibson VO." *ActuSF* (March 2008). Online.

Newitz, Annalee. "William Gibson Interview." *io9,* June 10, 2008.

2010   Canavan, Gerry. "Our Full Interview with William Gibson." *IndyWeek* (September 16, 2010). Online.

Clarke, Maximus. "Maximus Clarke Talks with William Gibson about His 'Speculative Novels of Last Wednesday.'" *Maud Newton* (September 22, 2010). Online.

Gallagher, Aileen. "The Vulture Transcript." *New York,* September 27, 2010.

Gibson, Emma Alvarez. "William Gibson on Wa-Wa Pedals, Emotional Bandwidth, and Space Castles." *Jack Move* (September 2010). Online.

Gorney, Douglas. "William Gibson and the Future of the Future." *Atlantic Monthly,* September 14, 2010. Online.

Goss, Heather. "DCist Interview: William Gibson." *Dcist* (September 24, 2010). Online.

Handlen, Zack. "Interview: William Gibson." *A.V. Club* (September 7, 2010). Online.

Holman, Curt. "More with 'Neuromancer' Author William Gibson." *Creative Loafing Atlanta* (September 14, 2010). Online.

———. "Sci-Fi Author William Gibson Plants Himself in the Present with *Zero History.*" *Creative Loafing Atlanta* (September 14, 2010). Online.

Jackson, Tina. "*Zero History* Author William Gibson: Left to His Own Devices." *Metro* (August 31, 2010). Online.

McCool, Scott. "You Feelin' Cyber, Punk?" *Alibi.com* 19.36 (September 9–15, 2010). Online.

Metzger, Richard. "William Gibson: Devo World." *21•C* (September 13, 2010). Online.

Newitz, Annalee. "William Gibson Reveals a 'Secret Experiment' in His Bridge Trilogy, and Ponders A.I." *io9,* September 10, 2010.

O'Connor, Stuart. "William Gibson: 'I'm Agnostic about Technology. But I Want a Robotic Penguin.'" *The Guardian,* August 29, 2010.

Parsons, Michael. "Interview: *Wired* Meets William Gibson." *Wired.co.uk* (October 13, 2010). Online.

Pearson, Jesse. "Viceland Today: William Gibson." *Vice* (September 3, 2010). Online.

Perez, Hugo. "The Fascination of Old Denim." *Mother Board* (September 23, 2010). Online.

"Prophet of the Real." *Seattlest* (September 6, 2010). Online. [Interviewer unidentified]

Q, Shathley. "For Tomorrow: William Gibson, 'Zero History' and the Present." *PopMatters* (September 13, 2010). Online.

Rutherford, Ryan. "Cyberpunk Pioneer William Gibson Returns to Austin." *The Austinist* (September 15, 2010). Online.

Thill, Scott. "William Gibson Talks Zero History, Paranoia, and the Awesome Power of Twitter." *Wired.com* (September 13, 2010). Online.

Ward, Mark. "William Gibson Says the Future Is Right Here, Right Now." *BBC News* (October 12, 2010). Online.

Williams, Maxwell. "Exclusive Interview: William Gibson." *Flaunt* (2010). Online.

2011   Bourré, August C. "An Interview with William Gibson." *Canadian Notes and Queries,* August 17, 2011. Online.

Cavanaugh, Amy. "Interview: William Gibson." *A.V. Club* (October 14, 2011). Online.

DuChateau, Christian. "Sci-Fi Prophet Wraps High-Tech Trilogy." *CNN* (July 31, 2011). Online.

Frauenfelder, Mark. "William Gibson Interview." *Boing Boing* (September 1, 2011). Online.

Shattuck, Aaron, and Gary Stix. "Cities in Fact and Fiction." *Scientific American,* August 26, 2011. Online.

Wallace-Wells, David. "William Gibson, The Art of Fiction No. 211." *Paris Review* No. 197 (Summer 2011). Online.

"William Gibson, Novelist." *The Setup* (October 17, 2011). Online. [Interviewer unidentified]

2012   Adams, John Joseph, and David Barr Kirtley. "Why William Gibson Distrusts Aging Futurists' Nostalgia." *Wired.com* (February 8, 2012). Online. [Transcript of podcast interview]

Barber, John. "'You Can Never Know Your Own Culture': William Gibson." *Toronto Globe and Mail,* January 15, 2012.

Chai, Barbara. "Sci-Fi Writer William Gibson on His iPad." *Wall Street Journal,* January 15, 2012.

———. "William Gibson Calls SOPA 'Draconian.'" *Wall Street Journal,* January 17, 2012.

———. "William Gibson on Science Fiction and E-Reading." *Wall Street Journal,* January 25, 2012.

Dayal, Geeta. "William Gibson on Punk Rock, Internet Memes, and 'Gangnam' Style." *Wired.com* (September 15, 2012). Online.

———. "William Gibson on Twitter, Antique Watches, and Internet Obsessions." *Wired.com* (September 14, 2012). Online.

———. "William Gibson on Why Sci-Fi Writers Are (Thankfully) Almost Always Wrong." *Wired.com* (September 13, 2012). Online.

Doherty, Mike. "William Gibson: I Really Can't Predict the Future." *Salon,* January 22, 2012.

Hershkovits, David. "William Gibson Talks Facebook, the Kardashians, and His New Book, *Distrust That Particular Flavor.*" *Papermag* (January 3, 2012). Online.

Hicks, Jesse. "An Interview with William Gibson." *The Verge* (January 24, 2012). Online.

Kugelberg, Johan. "The Last Macro Tribe: Johan Kugelberg in Conversation with William Gibson and Jon Savage" (with Jon Savage). In *Punk: An Aesthetic.* Ed. Johan Kugelberg. New York: Rizzoli, 2012. 340–47.

Lackerbauer, Simone, and R. U. Sirius. "William Gibson on *Mondo 2000* and 90s Cyberculture (*Mondo 2000* History Project Entry No. 16)." *Acceler8tor* (May 20, 2012). Online.

Medley, Mark. "The Neuromantic: William Gibson's Latest Book is a Work of Science Non-Fiction." *National Post,* January 16, 2012.

Montgomery, Jesse. "Interview: William Gibson." *Full Stop* (January 31, 2012). Online.

Parish, Matt. "Trying to Find Now: William Gibson's Randomized Experience." *Boston Phoenix,* January 4, 2012.

"William Gibson: The Future Now." Nowness (January 1, 2012). Online. [Interviewer unidentified]

FILM AND TELEVISION APPEARANCES [All unseen except *No Maps for These Territories*]

1967   *Yorkville: Hippie Haven.* Toronto: CBC, September 4, 1967. [Documentary featuring Gibson as a purportedly representative Toronto "hippie," though he described its contents as largely fictional]

1989   *Decade: 1980–1989.* MTV, 1989. [Documentary]

1990   *Cyberpunk.* Intercon, 1990. [Documentary]
       Episode of *The Late Show.* London: BBC-TV, September 26, 1990.

1991   *Hyperdelic E-Mission.* Neoteny Video Label, 1991. [Documentary]

1993   *Brave New Worlds: The Science Fiction Phenomenon.* London: Arts Entertainment Network, 1993. [Documentary]
       "Everything Must Go." *Wild Palms.* New York: ABC-TV, May 16, 1993.
       Episode of *TechnoPolitics.* New York: PBS, October 29, 1993.

1994   *Visions of Heaven and Hell.* [Three-part documentary] Barraclough Carey, 1994.

1995   *The Making of Johnny Mnemonic.* TriStar, 1995. [Short documentary]

1998   *Rebels: A Journey Underground / Welcome to Cyberia.* Filmwest, 1998. [Documentary]
       The Sci-Fi Files, 4: Living in the Future. WinStar, 1998. [Documentary]
       The X-Files Movie Special. Twentieth-Century Fox, 1998. [Documentary]

2000   *No Maps for These Territories: On the Road with William Gibson.* Mark Neale Productions, 2000. [Documentary]

2001   *Mon Amour Mon Parapluie.* Little Wonder, 2001. [Short]

2002   *Cyberman.* Toronto: CBC, 2002. [Documentary]

2003   *Almost Real: Connecting in a Wired World.* National Film Board of Canada, 2003. [Documentary]
       "Bestseller Samtalen—William Gibson." *Bestseller.* Amsterdam: Danmarks Radio, February 27, 2003.
       Episode of *The Screen Savers.* G4 Media, February 5, 2003.

2007   Episode of *Webnation.* Toronto: City-TV, September 17, 2007.
       "Keanu Reeves." *Filmography.* Movie Central Network, 2007. [Exact date unknown]

2010   "William Gibson." *A Window Looking In.* Knowledge Network, October 2010. [Exact date unknown]

ADAPTATIONS OF GIBSON'S WORKS

1988   Miles, Troy A. *Neuromancer: A Cyberpunk Role-Playing Adventure.* Interplay, 1988. [Computer game]

1989   De Haven, Tom, writer. Bruce Jensen, artist. *William Gibson's Neuromancer.* New York: Berkley, 1999. [Graphic novel]

1993   *Tomorrow Calling.* London: Channel 4, 1993. Adaptation of "The Gernsback Continuum." [Short television film]

1994   *Neuromancer.* Los Angeles: Time Warner, 1994. [Audiobook] Abridged; read by author.

1995   Bisson, Terry. *Johnny Mnemonic: A Novel.* New York: Pocket, 1995. Based on story and film.

Johnny Mnemonic. Williams Electronic Games, 1995. [Pinball game]

Johnny Mnemonic: The Interactive Action Movie. Sony Electronic Publishing, 1995. [Computer game]

1998   *New Rose Hotel.* Pressman Films, 2006.

2005   Gloria Kondrup, instructor. *Binary Shift: Typographic Explorations of the Narratives of William Gibson.* Pasadena, Calif.: Archetype Press, 2005. [Gibson passages employed in creative graphic artworks]

This bibliography has two sections. The first is a bibliographical essay discussing selected secondary sources relevant to Gibson, including all secondary works cited in the text. The second section lists other works cited in the text. A more complete version of the bibliographies, including Web addresses, more data about certain items, and a comprehensive list of secondary resources, will be posted on my Web site: http://www.sfsite.com/gary/intro.htm.

A LOOK AT THE SECONDARY LITERATURE

The overall amount of material written *about* William Gibson surely equals, if not exceeds, the amount of material written *by* Gibson, making any survey of this secondary literature a formidable task. True, some materials—like newspaper articles and book reviews—are unlikely to offer worthwhile insights and can be dismissed unseen; but scholarly books, articles, and reference entries command more attention.

For an examination of Gibson's entire ouevre, Tom Henthorne's *William Gibson: A Literary Companion* (Jefferson, N.C.: McFarland, 2011) provides intelligent discussions of all his novels and stories, emphasizing major issues addressed by critics. Briefer but substantive overviews include: Douglas Barbour, "William Gibson," in *Science Fiction Writers,* 2d ed., ed. Richard Bleiler (New York: Scribner's, 1999), 309–22; Neil Easterbrook, "William [Ford] Gibson (1948–)," in *Fifty Key Figures in Science Fiction,* ed. Mark Bould, Andrew M. Butler, Adam Roberts, and Sherryl Vint (New York: Routledge, 2010), 86–91; Douglas Ivison, "William Gibson," in *Canadian Fantasy and Science-Fiction Writers,* ed. Douglas Ivison (Detroit: Gale, 2002), 96–107; and Brian Stableford, "William Gibson," in *Critical Survey of Long Fiction,* 3 vols., ed. Carl Rollyson

(Pasadena, Calif.: Salem, 2010), 1776–80. Thematic studies that exclusively or frequently discuss Gibson include: Scott Bukatman, *Terminal Identity: The Virtual Subject in Postmodern Science Fiction* (Durham, N.C.: Duke University Press, 1993); Dani Cavallaro, *Cyberpunk and Cyberculture: Science Fiction and the Work of William Gibson* (London: Athlone, 2000); William S. Haney II, *Cyberculture, Cyborgs, and Science Fiction: Consciousness and the Posthuman* (New York: Rodopi, 2006); Sabine Heuser, *Virtual Geographies: Cyberpunk at the Intersection of the Postmodern and Science Fiction* (New York: Rodopi, 2003); Matthew G. Kirschenbaum, *Mechanisms: New Media and the Forensic Imagination* (Cambridge: Massachusetts Institute of Technology Press, 2008); Tatiani G. Rapatzikou, *Gothic Motifs in the Fiction of William Gibson* (Amsterdam: Rodopi, 2004); and Lisa Yaszek, *The Self Wired: Technology and Subjectivity in Contemporary Narrative* (New York: Routledge, 2002).

Gibson's work in the 1980s has long been a major focus of criticism, particularly *Neuromancer,* though its sequels and preceding short stories have also been studied at length. One book—Lance Olsen's *William Gibson* (Mercer Island, Wash.: Starmont, 1993)—usefully surveys his work during this decade. Two collections of essays ostensibly about cyberpunk fiction in general, but usually most attentive to Gibson, are Larry McCaffrey's *Storming the Reality Studio: A Casebook of Cyberpunk and Postmodern Science Fiction* (Durham, N.C.: Duke University Press, 1991), which also includes fiction, and George Slusser and Tom Shippey's *Fiction 2000: Cyberpunk and the Future of Narrative* (Athens: University of Georgia Press, 1992). Essays in a later collection, Carl B. Yoke and Carol L. Robinson's *The Cultural Influences of William Gibson, the Father of Cyberpunk Science Fiction: Critical and Interpretive Essays* (Lewiston, N.Y.: Mellen, 2007), also deal mostly with the 1980s, with scattered attention to later works. Articles addressing all of Gibson's fiction in the 1980s, usually with an emphasis on novels, include: David Mead, "Technological Transfiguration in William Gibson's Sprawl Novels: *Neuromancer, Count Zero,* and *Mona Lisa Overdrive,*" *Extrapolation* 32.4 (Winter 1991), 350–60; Tom Moylan, "Global Economy, Local Texts: Utopian/Dystopian Tension in William Gibson's Cyberpunk Trilogy," *Minnesota Review* No. 43/44 (1995): 182–97; Nicola Nixon, "Cyberpunk: Preparing the Ground for Revolution or Keeping the Boys Satisfied?" *Science Fiction Studies* 19.2 (July 1992), 219–35; Andrew Ross, "Getting Out of the Gernsback Continuum," *Critical Inquiry* 17.2 (Winter 1991): 411–33;

Timo Siivonen, "Cyborgs and Generic Oxymorons: The Body and Technology in William Gibson's Cyberspace Trilogy," *Science Fiction Studies* 23.2 (July 1996): 227–44; Claire Sponsler, "Cyberpunk and the Dilemmas of Postmodern Narrative: The Example of William Gibson," *Contemporary Literature* 33.4 (December 1992): 625–44; Angela Vistarchi, "Cyperpunk in Gibson's Sprawl Trilogy," in *Technology and the American Imagination: An Ongoing Challenge,* ed. Francesca B. De Riz and Rosella M. Zorzi (Venice: Supernova, 1994), 509–15; and Darko Suvin, "On Gibson and Cyberpunk SF," *Foundation: The Review of Science Fiction* No. 46 (Autumn 1989): 40–51.

Studies solely devoted to Gibson's short fiction are rare, but they include: Thomas A. Bredehoft, "The Gibson Continuum: Cyberspace and Gibson's Mervyn Kihn Stories," *Science Fiction Studies* 22.2 (July 1995): 252–63; Paul Delany, "'Hardly the Center of the World': Vancouver in William Gibson's 'The Winter Market,'" in *Vancouver: Representing the Postmodern City,* ed. Paul Delany (Vancouver: Arsenal Pulp, 1994), 179–92; Heather J. Hicks, "Whatever It Is That She's Become: Writing Bodies of Text and Bodies of Women in James Tiptree Jr.'s 'The Girl Who Was Plugged In' and William Gibson's 'The Winter Market,'" *Contemporary Literature* 37.1 (Spring 1996): 62–93; and Jeffrey Yule, "The Marginalized Short Stories of William Gibson: 'Hinterlands' and 'The Winter Market,'" *Foundation: The Review of Science Fiction* No. 58 (Summer 1993): 76–84. Apparently the only article about Gibson's poetry is Paul Schwenger, "*Agrippa*: Or, the Apocalyptic Book," *South Atlantic Quarterly* 92.4 (Fall 1993): 617–26.

There are literally dozens of articles about *Neuromancer,* but ones worth looking for include: Andrew M. Butler, "William Gibson: *Neuromancer,*" in *A Companion to Science Fiction,* ed. David Seed (Malden, Mass.: Blackwell, 2005), 534–43; Eva Cherniavsky, "(En)gendering Cyberspace in *Neuromancer*: Postmodern Subjectivity and Virtual Motherhood," *Genders* No. 18 (Winter 1993): 32–46; Kevin Concannon, "The Contemporary Space of the Border: Gloria Anzaldua's *Borderlands* and William Gibson's *Neuromancer,*" *Textual Practice* 12.3 (Winter 1998): 429–42; Istvan Csicsery-Ronay Jr., "The Sentimental Futurist: Cybernetics and Art in William Gibson's *Neuromancer,*" *Critique* 33.3 (Spring 1992): 221–40; Cynthia Davidson, "Riviera's Golem, Haraway's Cyborg: Reading *Neuromancer* as Baudrillard's Simulation of Crisis," *Science Fiction Studies* 23.2 (July 1996), 188–98; Benjamin Fair, "Stepping Razor in Orbit: Postmodern

Identity and Political Alternatives in William Gibson's *Neuromancer*," *Critique* 46.2 (Winter 2005): 92–103; Glenn Grant, "Transcendence through Detournement in William Gibson's *Neuromancer*," *Science Fiction Studies* 17.1 (March 1990): 41–49; Haney, "William Gibson's *Neuromancer*: Cyberpunk and the End of Humanity," *Interactions* 18.1 (2009), 73–87; Doreen Hartmann, "Space Construction as Cultural Practice: Reading William Gibson's *Neuromancer* with Respect to Postmodern Concepts of Space," in *Futurescapes: Space in Utopian and Science Fiction Discourses,* ed. Ralph Pordzik (New York: Rodopi, 2009), 275–300; Veronica Hollinger, "Notes on the Contemporary Apocalyptic Imagination: William Gibson's *Neuromancer* and Douglas Coupland's *Girlfriend in a Coma*," in *Worlds of Wonder: Readings in Canadian Science Fiction and Fantasy Literature,* ed. Jean-Francois Leroux and Camille R. La Bossiere (Ottawa: University of Ottawa Press, 2004), 47–56; John Johnston, "Mediality in *Vineland* and *Neuromancer*," in *Reading Matters: Narratives in the New Media Ecology,* ed. Joseph Tabbi and Michael Wutz (Ithaca, N.Y.: Cornell University Press, 1997), 173–92; Ian Lancashire, "Ninsei Street, Chiba City, in Gibson's *Neuromancer*," *Science Fiction Studies* 30.2 (July 2003): 341–46; Chia-Yi Lee, "Beyond the Body: Kafka's *The Metamorphosis* and Gibson's *Neuromancer*," *Concentric: Literary and Cultural Studies* 30.2 (July 2004): 201–22; Tony Myers, "The Postmodern Imaginary in William Gibson's *Neuromancer*," *Modern Fiction Studies* 47.4 (Winter 2001): 887–909; Adam Roberts, "Case Study: William Gibson, *Neuromancer* (1984)," in *Science Fiction,* by Adam Roberts (London: Routledge, 2000), 169–80; Nicholas Ruddick, "Putting the Bits Together: Information Theory, *Neuromancer,* and Science Fiction," *Journal of the Fantastic in the Arts* 3.4 (1994): 84–92; Herbert Shu-Shun Chan, "Interrogation from Hyperspace: Visions of Culture in *Neuromancer* and 'War without End,'" in *Simulacrum America: The USA and the Popular Media,* ed. Elizabeth Kraus and Carolin Auer (Rochester, N.Y.: Camden House, 2000), 136–45; Tyler Stevens, "'Sinister Fruitiness': *Neuromancer,* Internet Sexuality, and the Turing Test," *Studies in the Novel* 28.3 (Fall 1996): 414–33; Andrew Strombeck, "The Network and the Archive: The Specter of Imperial Management in William Gibson's *Neuromancer*," *Science Fiction Studies* 37.2 (July 2010): 275–95; Lisa Swanstrom, "Landscape and Locodescription in William Gibson's *Neuromancer*," *Foundation: The International Review of Science Fiction* 98 (Autumn 2006): 16–27; and Timothy Yu, "Oriental Cities, Postmodern Futures: *Naked Lunch, Blade Runner,* and *Neuromancer*," *Melus* 33.4 (Winter 2008): 45–71.

The relatively few articles that focus on *Count Zero* and *Mona Lisa Overdrive* include: Joseph Childers, Townsend Carr, and Regna Meek, "White Men Can't . . . : Decentering Authority and Jacking into Phallic Economies in William Gibson's *Count Zero*," in *Science Fiction, Canonization, Marginalization, and the Academy*, ed. Gary Westfahl and George Slusser (Westport, Conn.: Greenwood, 2002), 151–60; Istvan Csicsery-Ronay, "Antimancere: Cybernetics and Art in Gibson's *Count Zero*," *Science Fiction Studies* 22.1 (March 1995): 63–86; Paul C. Grimstad, "Algorithm—Genre—'Linguisterie': 'Creative Distortion' in *Count Zero* and *Nova Express*," *Journal of Modern Literature* 27.4 (Summer 2004): 82–92; and Christopher Palmer, "*Mona Lisa Overdrive* and the Prosthetic," *Science Fiction Studies* 31.2 (July 2004): 227–42.

Gibson and Sterling's *The Difference Engine* has received a surprising amount of scholarly attention. Relevant articles include: Jay Clayton, "Hacking the Nineteenth Century," in *Victorian Afterlife: Postmodern Culture Rewrites the Nineteenth Century*, ed. John Kucich and Dianne F. Sadoff (Minneapolis: University of Minnesota Press, 2000), 186–210; Joseph Conte, "The Virtual Reader: Cybernetics and Technocracy in William Gibson and Bruce Sterling's *The Difference Engine*," in *The Holodeck in the Garden: Science and Technology in Contemporary American Literature*, ed. Peter Freese and Charles B. Harris (Normal, Ill.: Dalkey Archive Press, 2004), 28–52; Patrick Jagoda, "Clacking Control Societies: Steampunk, History, and the Difference Engine of Escape," *Neo-Victorian Studies* 3.1 (2010): 46–71; Nicholas Spencer, "Rethinking Ambivalence: Technopolitics and the Luddites in William Gibson and Bruce Sterling's *The Difference Engine*," *Contemporary Literature* 40.3 (Fall 1999): 403–29; Herbert Sussman, "Cyberpunk Meets Charles Babbage: *The Difference Engine* as Alternative Victorian History," *Victorian Studies* 38.1 (Autumn 1994), 1–23; and Phillip E. Wegner, "The Last Bomb: Historicizing History in Terry Bisson's *Fire on the Mountain* and Gibson and Sterling's *The Difference Engine*," *Comparatist: Journal of the Southern Comparative Literature Association* 23 (May 1999): 141–51. The novel is also discussed in Karen Hellekson's *The Alternate History: Refiguring Historical Time* (Kent, Ohio: Kent State University Press, 2001).

Gibson's Bridge novels are studied less often than the Sprawl novels, but articles to consult include: Michael Beehler, "Architecture and the Virtual West in William Gibson's San Francisco," in *Postwestern Cultures: Literature, Theory, Space*, ed. Susan Kollin (Lincoln: University of Nebraska Press, 2007),

82–94; Hanjo Berressem, "Of Metal Ducks, Embodied Iduros, and Autopoietic Bridges—Tales of an Intelligent Materialism in the Age of Artificial Life," in *The Holodeck in the Garden: Science and Technology in Contemporary American Literature*, ed. Peter Freese and Charles B. Harris (Normal, Ill.: Dalkey Archive Press, 2004), 72–99; Ross Farnell, "Posthuman Topologies: William Gibson's 'Architexture' in *Virtual Light* and *Idoru*," *Science Fiction Studies* 25.3 (November 1998): 459–80; Dominic Grace, "Disease, Virtual Life, and *Virtual Light*," *Foundation: The International Review of Science Fiction* No. 81 (Spring 2001): 75–83; Grace, "From *Videodrome* to *Virtual Light*: David Cronenberg and William Gibson," *Extrapolation* 44.3 (Fall 2003): 344–55; Tama Leaver, "Interstitial Spaces and Multiple Histories in William Gibson's *Virtual Light*, *Idoru*, and *All Tomorrow's Parties*," *Limina* 9 (2003): 118–30; Graham J. Murphy, "Post/Humanity and the Interstitial: A Glorification of Possibility in Gibson's Bridge Sequence," *Science Fiction Studies* 30.1 (March 2003): 72–90; Leonard Sanders, "Virtual Ephemeralities: *Idoru* and *Evangelion*, Popular Visual Cultures in Japan," in *On Verbal/Visual Representation*, ed. Martin Heusser, Michèle Hannoosh, Eric Haskell, Leo Hoek, David Scott, and Peter De Voogd (Amsterdam: Rodopi, 2005), 137–49; Takayuki Tatsumi, "Junk Art City: Or, William Gibson Meets Thomasson in *Virtual Light*," *Paradoxa* 2.1 (1996): 61–72; and James H. Thrall, "Love, Loss, and Utopian Community on William Gibson's Bridge," *Foundation: The International Review of Science Fiction* No. 91 (Summer 2004): 97–115.

Finally, *Pattern Recognition* has been addressed in a number of recent articles, though *Spook Country* and *Zero History*, at the time of writing, have not yet received much attention; relevant articles include: Lauren Berlant, "Intuitionists: History and the Affective Event," *American Literary History* 20.4 (Winter 2008): 845–60; Neil Easterbrook, "Alternate Presents: The Ambivalent Historicism of *Pattern Recognition*," *Science Fiction Studies* 33.3 (November 2006): 483–504; Neil Easterbrook, "Recognizing Patterns: Gibson's Hermeneutics from the Bridge Trilogy to *Pattern Recognition*," in *Beyond Cyberpunk: New Critical Perspectives*, ed. Graham J. Murphy and Sherryl Vint (New York: Routledge, 2010), 46–64; Jason Haslam, "Memory's Guilted Cage: Delany's *Dhalgren* and Gibson's *Pattern Recognition*," *English Studies in Canada* 32.1 (March 2006): 77–104; Veronica Hollinger, "Stories about the Future: From Patterns of Expectation to *Pattern Recognition*," *Science Fiction Studies* 33.3 (November

2006): 452–72; John Johnston, "The Intuitionist and *Pattern Recognition*: A Response to Lauren Berlant," *American Literary History* 20.4 (Winter 2008): 861–69; James Kneale, "Plots: Space, Conspiracy, and Contingency in William Gibson's *Pattern Recognition* and *Spook Country*," *Environment and Planning: Society and Space* 29.1 (February 2011): 169–86; Lee Konstantinou, "The Brand as Cognitive Map in William Gibson's *Pattern Recognition*," *Boundary 2* 36.2 (Summer 2009): 67–97; Alex Link, "Global War, Global Capital, and the Work of Art in William Gibson's *Pattern Recognition*," *Contemporary Literature* 49.2 (Summer 2008): 209–31; Em McAvan, "Paranoia in *Spook Country*: William Gibson and the Technological Sublime of the War on Terror," *Journal of Postcolonial Writing* 46.3/4 (2010): 405–13; Donald E. Morse, "Advertising and Calculators in William Gibson's *Pattern Recognition*," *Science Fiction Studies* 31.2 (July 2004): 330–32; Christopher Palmer, "*Pattern Recognition*: 'None of What We Do Here Is Ever Really Private,'" *Science Fiction Studies* 33.3 (November 2006): 473–82; and Alex Wetmore, "The Poetics of *Pattern Recognition*: William Gibson's Shifting Technological Subject," *Bulletin of Science, Technology, and Society* 27.1 (2007): 71–80.

OTHER WORKS CITED

Berg, David, story and pictures. "Little League." *Mad* No. 47 (June 1959): 16–19.

Berry, John D. Untitled comments. *Wing Window* No. 9 (March 20, 1986): 7.

Cameron, Richard Graeme. Canadian Fancyclopedia: V (June 2009). Online.

Dick, Philip K. *Do Androids Dream of Electric Sheep?* 1968; reprint, New York: Del Rey/
  Ballantine Books, [1982].

Duncan, David D. "The Push Within: The Extrapolative Ability of Theodore Sturgeon."
  Available online. [Originally published in *Phoenix* in 1979]

Gunn, Eileen. "The Secret of Writing." In *Stable Strategies and Others*. San Francisco:
  Tachyon, 2004. xv–xvi.

Kaufman, Jerry. Letter. *Space Junk* No. 5 (1980): 31.

Langford, David. "Infinitely Improbable." *Ansible* No. 50 (August/September 1987).
  Online.

———. "Mimsy Were the Borogoves." *Ansible* No. 82 (May 1994). Online.

Leiber, Fritz. "Mouser Mythos." *Votishal* No. 1 (1963): 11.

Lynch, Richard. "Preliminary Outline for a Proposed Fan History Book of the 1960s."
  Available online.

Montgomery, Larry J. "1997 Southern Fandom Confederation Handbook & History, Part
  II: DSCs, Rebels, Rubbles, & Phoenixes." Online.

"Retro Fanzines: AMOR No. 10 by Susan Wood, Aug. 5th, 1976." *WCSFAzine* 1.4
  (December 2007): 7–8. [No author given]

Shapiro, Fred, ed. *The Yale Book of Quotations.* New Haven, Conn.: Yale University Press, 2006.

Skene, Fran. "News." *The BCSFA Newsletter* No. 32 (February 1976): 3.

Sterling, Bruce, ed. *Mirrorshades: The Cyberpunk Anthology.* 1986; reprint, New York: Ace, 1988.

"A Weird Story." *BCSFA Newsletter* No. 33 (March 1976): 3. [No authors given]

Westfahl, Gary. "Greyer Lensmen, or Looking Backward in Anger." *Interzone* No. 129 (March 1998): 40–43.

Wood, Susan. Untitled comments. *The Amor de Cosmos Peoples' Memorial Quasi-Revolutionary Susanzine* No. 12 (December 19, 1976).

———. Untitled comments. *Amor* No. 13 (February 11, 1977).

———. Untitled comments. *Amor* No. 16 (December 9, 1977).

GARY WESTFAHL is an adjunct professor teaching in the Writing Program at the University of La Verne. His many publications on science fiction include the three-volume *Greenwood Encyclopedia of Science Fiction and Fantasy* and the Hugo Award–nominated *Science Fiction Quotations: From the Inner Mind to the Outer Limits*.

MODERN MASTERS OF SCIENCE FICTION

John Brunner *Jad Smith*

William Gibson *Gary Westfahl*

THE UNIVERSITY OF ILLINOIS PRESS

is a founding member of the

Association of American University Presses.

———————————————————

Designed by Kelly Gray

Composed in 10.75/14.5 Dante

with Univers display

by Lisa Connery

at the University of Illinois Press

Manufactured by Sheridan Books, Inc.

University of Illinois Press

1325 South Oak Street

Champaign, IL 61820-6903

www.press.uillinois.edu